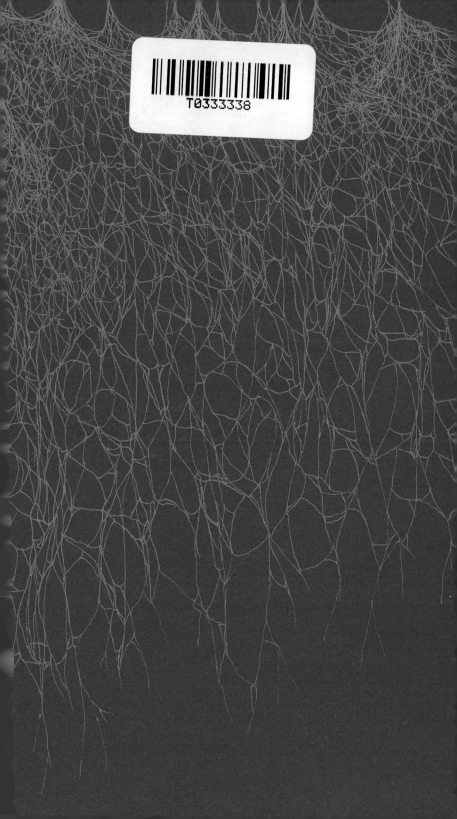

A stunning international collaboration that reveals how trees make our world, change our minds and rewild our lives – from root to branch to seed.

In this beautifully illustrated collection, artist Katie Holten gifts readers her visual Tree Alphabet and uses it to masterfully translate and illuminate pieces from some of the world's most exciting writers and artists, activists and ecologists.

Holten guides us on a journey from prehistoric cave paintings and creation myths to the death of a 3,500-year-old cypress tree, from Tree Clocks in Mongolia and forest fragments in the Amazon to the language of fossil poetry. In doing so, she unearths a new way of seeing the natural beauty that surrounds us and creates an urgent reminder of what could happen if we allow it to slip away.

KATIE HOLTEN is an artist and activist, born in Ireland and living in New York City and Ardee, Ireland. In 2003, she represented Ireland at the Venice Biennale. She has had solo exhibitions at the Bronx Museum of the Arts, the New Orleans Museum of Art, the Contemporary Art Museum St. Louis, and Dublin City Gallery: The Hugh Lane. Her drawings investigate the entangled relationships between humans and the natural world. She has created Tree Alphabets, a Stone Alphabet, and a Wildflower Alphabet to share the joy she finds in her love of the more-than-human world. Her work has appeared in the *Irish Times, New York Times, Artforum*, and *frieze*. She is a visiting lecturer at the New School of the Anthropocene. If she could be a tree, she would be an Oak.

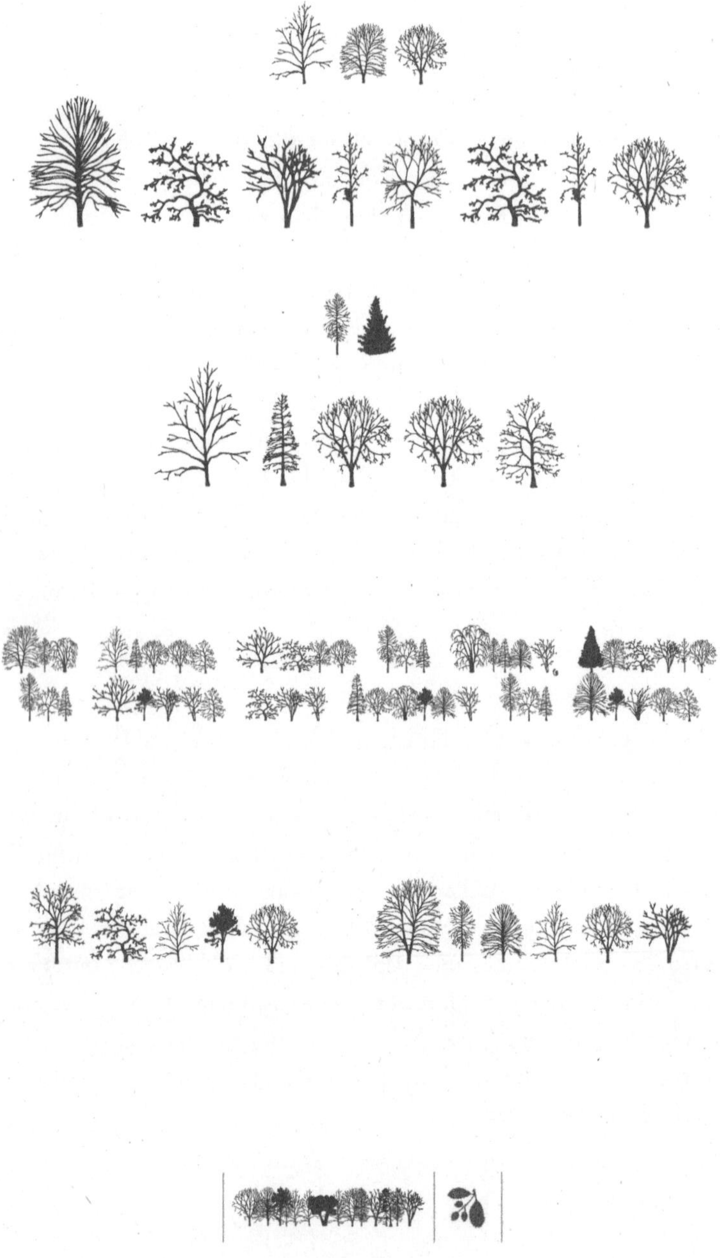

The
Language
of
Trees

How Trees Make Our World, Change
Our Minds and Rewild Our Lives

KATIE HOLTEN

Elliott&Thompson

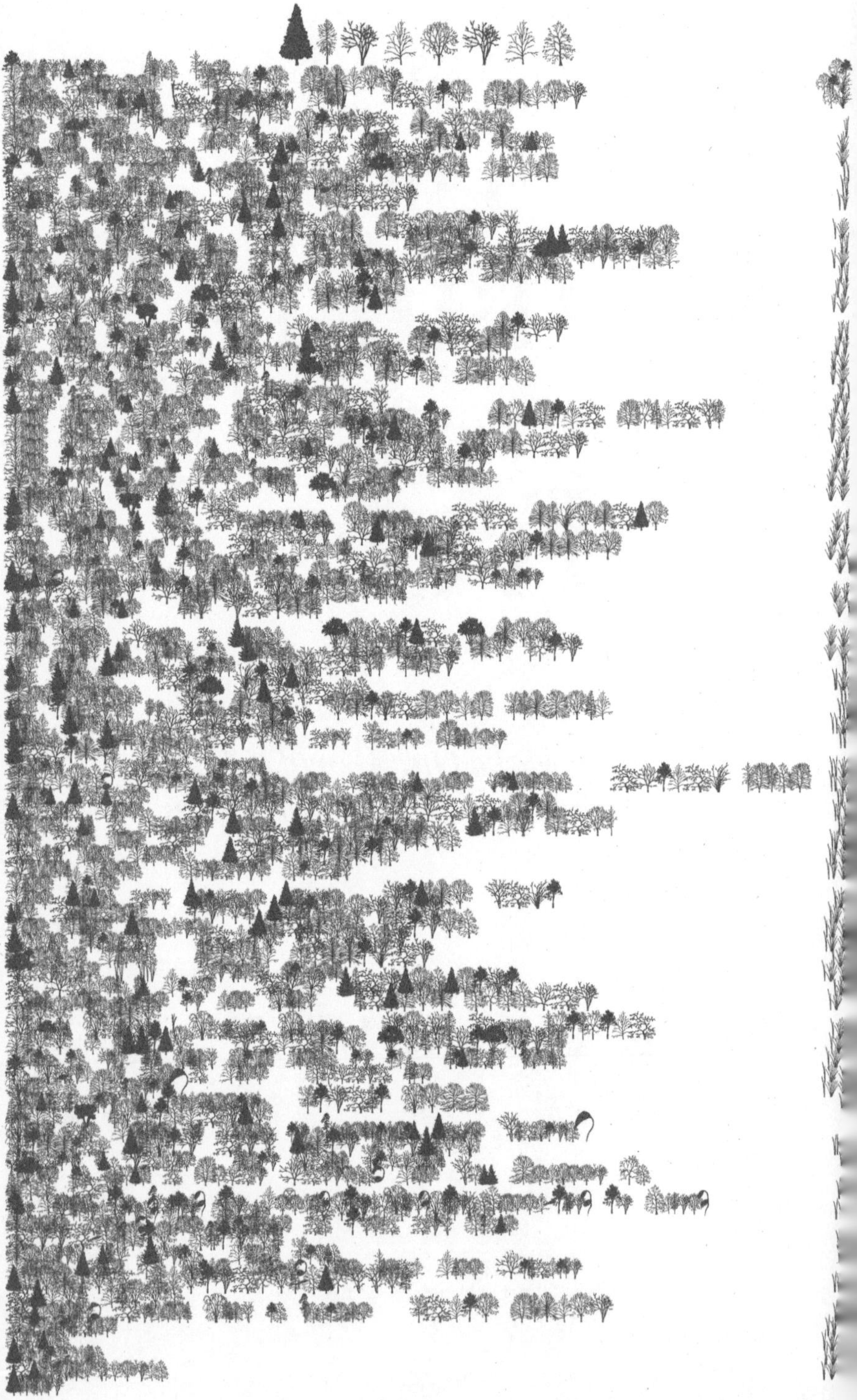

Contents

Introduction | ROSS GAY   xi

Tree Alphabet | KATIE HOLTEN   xiv

Trees Typeface (A Rewilding Tool) | KATIE HOLTEN   xv

SEEDS, SOIL, SAPLINGS

The Ojibwe New Year | WINONA LADUKE   3

He who plants a tree Plants a hope | LUCY LARCOM   7

Michael Hamburger | TACITA DEAN   9

I am the seed of the free | SOJOURNER TRUTH   11

Palas por Pistolas | PEDRO REYES   13

Acorn Bread Recipe | LUCY O'HAGAN   15

BUDS, BARK, BRANCHES

Oak Gall Ink Recipe | RACHAEL HAWKWIND   19

Branches, Leaves, Roots and Trunks
ROBERT MACFARLANE   23

Tree Theory, Biogeography and Branching
BRIAN J. ENQUIST   29

Cultivating the Courage to Sin | ANDREA BOWERS   33

The Wrong Trees | ZADIE SMITH   35

Fractal Vision | JAMES GLEICK   37

LEAVES & TRUNKS

It's the Season I Often Mistake | ADA LIMÓN   43

from Why Information Grows | CÉSAR A. HIDALGO   45

Tree University | FUTUREFARMERS   47

from *Funes, the Memorious* | JORGE LUIS BORGES   49

Under a Plane Tree | PLATO   51

Fake Plastic Trees | RADIOHEAD   55

The Trees Breathe Out, We Breathe In | LUCHITA HURTADO   57

The Elm Stand | THOMAS PRINCEN   59

The Exact Opposite of Distance | IRENE KOPELMAN   63

Their Own Stories | KERRI NÍ DOCHARTAIGH   65

Medicine of the Tree People | VALERIE SEGREST   67

Blad 2 / Leaf 2 | ÅSE EG JØRGENSEN   69

FLOWERS & FRUITS

from *Sketch of the Analytical Engine* | ADA LOVELACE   73

An Droighneán Donn | SUSAN MCKEOWN   75

The Tree with the Apple Tattoo | NICOLA TWILLEY   77

Millenniums of Intervention | AMY HARMON   81

Cacao: The World Tree and Her Planetary Mission
JONATHON MILLER WEISBERGER   85

Tree of Life | ROZ NAYLOR   91

FORESTS

Two Trees Make a Forest | JESSICA J. LEE   97

The Word for World is Forest | URSULA K. LE GUIN   99

from *How Forests Think* | EDUARDO KOHN   101

from *Forests* | GAIA VINCE   107

Bewilderness | E.J. MCADAMS   111

from *Islands on Dry Land* | ELIZABETH KOLBERT   113

Ghost Forest | MAYA LIN   117

Forest | FORREST GANDER *and* KATIE HOLTEN   121

FAMILY TREES

Being | TANAYA WINDER   127

Brutes: Meditations on the myth of the voiceless
AMITAV GHOSH   129

Trophic Cascade | CAMILLE T. DUNGY   132

Catalpa Tree | AIMEE NEZHUKUMATATHIL   135

Notes for a Salmon Creek Farm Revival | FRITZ HAEG   141

We Are the ARK | MARY REYNOLDS   145

Among the Trees | CARL PHILLIPS   149

Mother Trees | SUZANNE SIMARD   157

TREE TIME

Tree Clocks and Climate Change | NICOLE DAVI   161

from *Alphabet* | INGER CHRISTENSEN   165

The Horse Chestnut | CHARLES GAINES   167

Future Library | KATIE PATERSON   169

Liberty Trees | ROBERT SULLIVAN   171

January 23, 2015 | ANDREA ZITTEL   179

A Matter of Time | AMY FRANCESCHINI   181

All the Time in the World | RACHEL SUSSMAN   185

TREE PEOPLE

Mujer Waorani / Waorani Women | NEMO ANDY GUIQUITA 191

TREE X OFFICE | NATALIE JEREMIJENKO   193

This is not our world with trees in it | RICHARD POWERS 195

I Want to Be a Tree | SUMANA ROY   197

What's Happening? | ⊗   199

Declaration of Interbeing | KINARI WEBB   203

ROOTS & RESISTANCE

Why Are There No Trees in Paleolithic Cave Drawings?
WILLIAM CORWIN AND COLIN RENFREW   207

Speaking of Nature | ROBIN WALL KIMMERER   211

"Joy Is Such a Human Madness": The Duff Between Us
ROSS GAY   223

*Of Trees in Paint; in Teeth; in Wood; in Sheet-Iron; in Stone;
in Mountains; in Stars* | AENGUS WOODS   225

Legere and βιβλιοϑήκη: The Library as Idea and Space
ANNA-SOPHIE SPRINGER   233

Lessons from Fungi | TOBY KIERS   241

They Carry Us With Them: The Great Tree Migration
CHELSEA STEINAUER-SCUDDER   245

AFTER TREES

Afterword: Another World is Possible | KATIE HOLTEN   253

Bibliography   259

Sources   279

Contributors   287

Acknowledgments   299

Colophon   304

Introduction

ROSS GAY

I SOMETIMES THINK OF MAKING A BOOK OF ALL THE TREES I HAVE really loved. Here's a very incomplete list: the mulberry tree in the tiny woods between the school and the apartments where I grew up outside of Philadelphia, into which every June we'd squirrel to harvest; the chokecherry tree in Verndale, Minnesota, where my grandpa parked his hospital-green '68 Chevy pickup, atop which I'd scoot to pull some fruit for the both of us; the redbud tree on Third Street my partner Stephanie showed me, whose leaves, backlit late in the day, became a canopy of luminescent, blood red hearts; the pear tree at the end of the block, a sale tree from a box store that is the sweetest, most reliable fruit in town and a local oasis for human, deer, possum, yellowjackets, and more; the giant sycamore with the fleshy, oceanic bark towering in the southeast corner of the graveyard, in the shade of which on hot days is about ten degrees cooler and so is a no-brainer gathering spot; the fig tree on Christian Street in Philadelphia, between 9th and 10th; and there's that beech tree in Vermont I met on a night hike two summers back, against whose smooth trunk I leaned my head, and though prayed isn't quite the word, it was something like that. The beech's breathing seemed to sync up with mine, or mine with the beech's, and though I can't exactly say what I was hearing, or feeling, I know it was a language coursing between us.

The word beech, I was delighted to learn a few years back, is the proto-Germanic antecedent for the English word book. The words for book in some other languages too derive from or overlap with words for trees. And though I suspect part of that common root has to do with trees providing the material for books, it's also the case that being in a library—I mean, the best libraries—can sometimes feel like being in a forest: a wild variety of plants from the canopy to the ground; all manner of life, some of it visible, most of it not; patches of dense shade, swaths of deckled light, clearings where a huge tree just fell and you can almost hear the turning beneath, toward the light. Just as being in the forest can sometimes feel like being in a library—I mean, the best libraries—where what maybe begins as an illegible and almost foreboding place (see every fairy tale; see half of all horror movies), becomes, with time, and maybe with guidance, and patience, and wonder, all these voices, all these stories. Oh, with wonder we say, the trees have a language. There's a language of trees.

We watch the light flickering across their leaves, or the wind blowing them into song. We see the squirrel peeking out from the porthole in the oak thirty feet up, or the yellowjackets entering and departing the withering branch which until today you would have called dead. And the bloom of fungus underneath. We enter the canopy and soften our eyes or hear or feel the thousand pollinators perusing the blooms. We reach down to pick up one in the constellation of persimmons glowing at our feet. The woodpecker and the chipmunk, the beetle and the worm. We notice the branches and all their reaching. We learn the root systems sometimes scribble through the earth far beyond their massive canopies, some of them for miles and miles and miles, entangling with other roots and life, knitted to all this other life with all this other life. Made possible by being knitted, the trees seem to be trying to tell us, to all this other life. Except the trees never say other.

What the trees say, and how they say it—the language of trees—has never been as interesting to me as it is right now. Not only because, as you now know, I have a book of beloved trees (On the first page of which is a map! Let's figure out how to get seeds in there too! And birdsong!), not only because I have been lucky enough to work with the community orchard in my town, not only because of that beech tree whispering to me in Vermont. The language of trees is so interesting to me because whether or not we learn to understand it, or at least try to, seems so obviously, well, life or death. Our capacity and willingness to learn the language of trees, to study the language of trees, it's so obvious to me now, might incline us to be less brutal, less extractive. It might incline us to share, to collaborate. It might incline us to give shelter and make room. The language of trees might incline us to patience. To love. It might incline us to gratitude.

Which is precisely what I would call *The Language of Trees: How Trees Make Our World, Change Our Minds and Rewild Our Lives*—a gratitude. A gratitude immense. Redwood gratitude. Sycamore gratitude. Aspen gratitude. Pawpaw gratitude. Not only for the gathering of wonderers and lovers of the arboreal that it brings together. But for the literal language of trees—a script made of different trees—by which it is conveyed to us. Can I tell you how batshit beautiful I find this? Can I tell you how each piece, translated into this language of trees, each essay or poem or song becoming a forest or orchard, rattles me, flummoxes me really, with how beautiful? Yes, I mean they are graphically beautiful; they are beautiful to look at as pictures, or arboreal maps or something. Like, astonishingly so. But what moves me so deeply, by which I mean into the loam, my own roots reaching out to yours, is the listening and care, the devotion and curiosity by which this script of trees comes into being. The gratitude, I mean to say, by which the language of people becomes the language of trees. The gratitude by which this book turns us into trees.

For which gratitude, I am thankful.

—*Ross Gay, 2023*

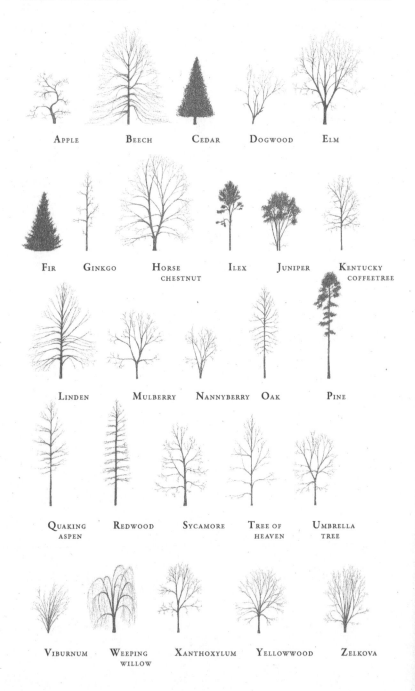

APPLE   BEECH   CEDAR   DOGWOOD   ELM

FIR   GINKGO   HORSE CHESTNUT   ILEX   JUNIPER   KENTUCKY COFFEETREE

LINDEN   MULBERRY   NANNYBERRY   OAK   PINE

QUAKING ASPEN   REDWOOD   SYCAMORE   TREE OF HEAVEN   UMBRELLA TREE

VIBURNUM   WEEPING WILLOW   XANTHOXYLUM   YELLOWWOOD   ZELKOVA

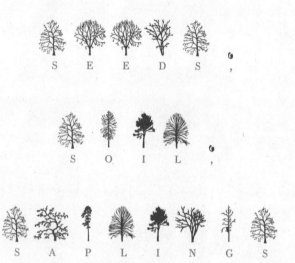

S E E D S ,

S O I L ,

S A P L I N G S

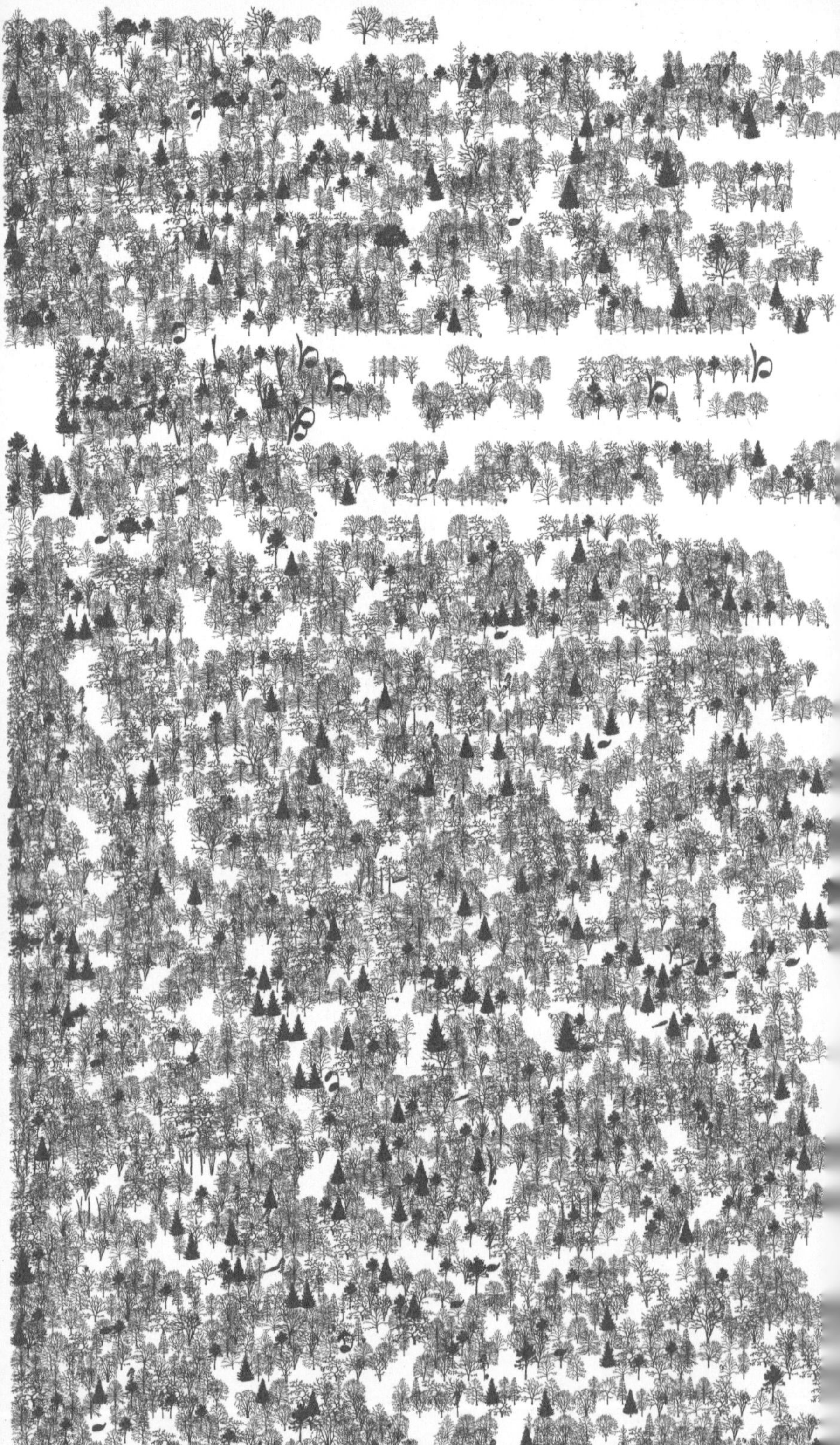

The Ojibwe New Year

WINONA LADUKE

APRIL 16, 2022

Land determines time. Giiwedinong, or up north, we have six seasons, including a couple shorter seasons: "freeze up" and "thaw." The Cree and Ojibwe people are the northern people here; to the west the Dene, Gwichin and Inuit have different descriptions of the seasons.

What's for sure is that the freeze up, Gashkaadino Giizis or November in Anishinaabemowin, is called the Freezing Over Moon. March is referred to as Onaabaanigiizis, or the Hard Crusted Snow Moon.

In the Anishinaabe world, and the calendar of our people, there's nothing about Roman emperors like Julius or Augustus. Those are not months to most of us. In an Indigenous calendar time belongs to Mother Earth, not to humans.

Bradley Robinson, from Timiskaming, Quebec, writes these seasons, not only in Cree and Ojibwe, but in syllabics, the orthography of the north:

- **Ziigwan (spring): ᓰ ᑲᐧᐣ**
- **Minookamin (the good Earth awakening): ᒥ ᓅ ᑲ ᒥᐣ**
- **Niibin (summer): ᓃ ᐱᐣ**
- **Tagwaagin (falling leaves time): ᑕ gᐚ ᑭᐣ**
- **Piiji-Piboon (on the way to winter, the freezing time): ᐲ ᒋ ᐱ ᐴᐣ**
- **Piboon (winter): ᐱ ᐴᐣ**

If language frames your understanding of the world, those who live on the land have a different understanding than those who live in the memories of emperors. There's no empire in creator's time.

The Ojibwe new year has arrived.

That's what I know. Gregorian calendars are based on commemorative times, while the Anishinaabe view the new year to begin as the world awakens after winter. Indigenous spiritual and religious practices are often said to be reaffirmation religions, reaffirming the relationship with Mother Earth.

The maple sugarbush, that's really when the year begins, when the trees awaken. We are told that long ago, the maples ran all year, and the trees produced a sweet syrup. Our own folly changed that equation, and today the maple sap runs only in the spring, and it takes 40 gallons of sap to make a gallon of syrup.

We learned to be respectful of the gifts provided by Mother Earth. That's a good lesson for all of us. We go to the sugarbush now, and we are grateful for the sugar which comes from a tree. This sugar is medicine.

As spring approaches, we prepare our seeds of hope, and we think about the future plants, foods and warm ahead—aabawaa, it's getting warm out. Minookamin, the land, is warming up and with that, the geese and swans return in numbers to our lakes, thankful to be home. After that 5,000-mile flight, it seems that we could make sure their homes are in good shape, their waters clean.

I've been worrying about that Roundup stuff and the unpronounceable chemicals big agriculture is about to levy on these lands. I've always maintained that if you put stuff on your land that ends in "-cide," whether herbicide, fungicide or pesticide, it's going to be a problem. After all, that's the same suffix as homicide, genocide and suicide.

Don't eat stuff that ends with -cide. So, heading into a local Fleet Farm, or Ace Hardware, there's going to be a lot of that in the aisles. Take Monsanto's Roundup, that's the stuff we are going to see all over these stores; there are thousands of lawsuits about the non-Hodgkin's lymphoma. Or maybe paraquat, associated with Parkinson's disease. An estimated 6.1 billion kilos of glyphosate-based weed killers were sprayed across gardens and fields worldwide between 2005 and 2014 (the most recent point at which data has been collected). That is more than any other herbicide, so understanding the true impact on human health is vital.

A 2016 study found a 1,000% rise in the levels of glyphosate in our urine in the past two decades—suggesting that increasing amounts of glyphosate is passing through our diet.

From the micro-plastics in our blood to the weedkiller in our urine, I'd like a little less weird stuff in my body, and maybe we move toward organic— the geese and bees like that better. That's one of my prayers for this New Year. Along with my New Year's resolutions: to listen better, to not lose my mittens, be with my family, and to grow more food and hemp. It's time to make those plans.

As climate change transforms our world, I am still hoping we can keep a few constants, like our six seasons.

This is what I know, the geese return, and that's a time. When the crows gather, the maple trees flow with sap and the world is being born again.

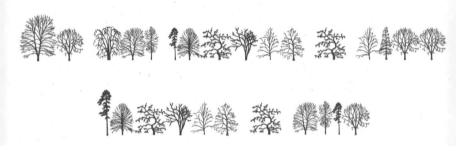

He who plants a tree

Plants a hope

LUCY LARCOM

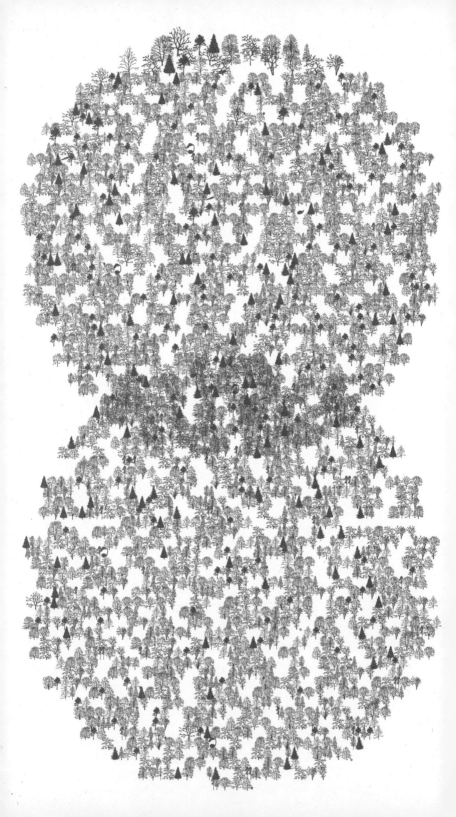

Michael Hamburger

TACITA DEAN

MICHAEL COULDN'T BE DRAWN INTO TALKING ABOUT HIS LIFE OR HIS poetry, but was content to talk about his friend, the writer W. G. Sebald, whom Michael knew as Max. I realize now that I had quite strong feelings about how I imagined the person Sebald to be from reading his books: the German academic in self-imposed exile, plodding his rueful way down the country lanes of East Anglia, meeting, encountering, watching and remembering in the strangest of rural places, before returning home to a beautiful but run-down Norfolk home to write some of the most moving prose to come out of the twentieth century. I feel that's what Sebald wanted us to believe he was like, especially in his book, *The Rings of Saturn,* because he wrote it that way. The truth is inevitably different. Max, according to Michael, was quite the opposite: a less romantic figure, anxious and obsessively tidy, courting no chaos around him as he worked, and with a restlessness of spirit that made him continue correcting his books long after they had been published. Evidently, something of the same driving dissatisfaction manifested in his work, impelling him to inexhaustible research, and to write such emotionally immense and mysteriously unquenchable books. Very clearly in *The Rings of Saturn,* Sebald visits the one person he would have us believe he was most like: the poet in his library in a much-loved house surrounded by piles of manila envelopes and looking out upon an English wildflower wilderness, and that person was Michael Hamburger.

Michael's Suffolk garden was so fecund that one only had to throw an apple core out of the window and it sprung up as a tree. His orchard was cultivated in the most part from seeds, as he eschewed grafting as a method and preferred to extract the pips and plant them himself. He spent his days preserving and cultivating many varieties of apple, some long out of favor or wilfully forgotten by the commercial world. His orchard was an encyclopaedia of apples, a resource for both horticulturalist and poet.

His house had been a row of farmhand cottages, so was oddly stretched out and one room deep: you could sit looking out front and back from the same chair. The outside was unusually present inside, but of late, it had begun transgressing further, as creepers crept in under doors and around windows.

Michael seemed at home with this, content to surrender to his wasteland and almost bidding it enter. He realized, he said, that he could no longer stem the tide of entropy and had begun acquiescing to old age. He had stopped planting trees, he said, because they took twelve years to bear fruit and he would no longer be around to witness it. He worried what would happen to his orchard after he died, whether it would be understood or not, and whether it would be preserved. He worried in the same way about his poetry. Michael was in spirit a harvester: a harvester of fruit as well as of words, and he has left a legacy of apples and poems.

I AM

THE SEED

OF THE FREE.

I INTEND TO

BEAR GREAT

FRUIT.

SOJOURNER TRUTH

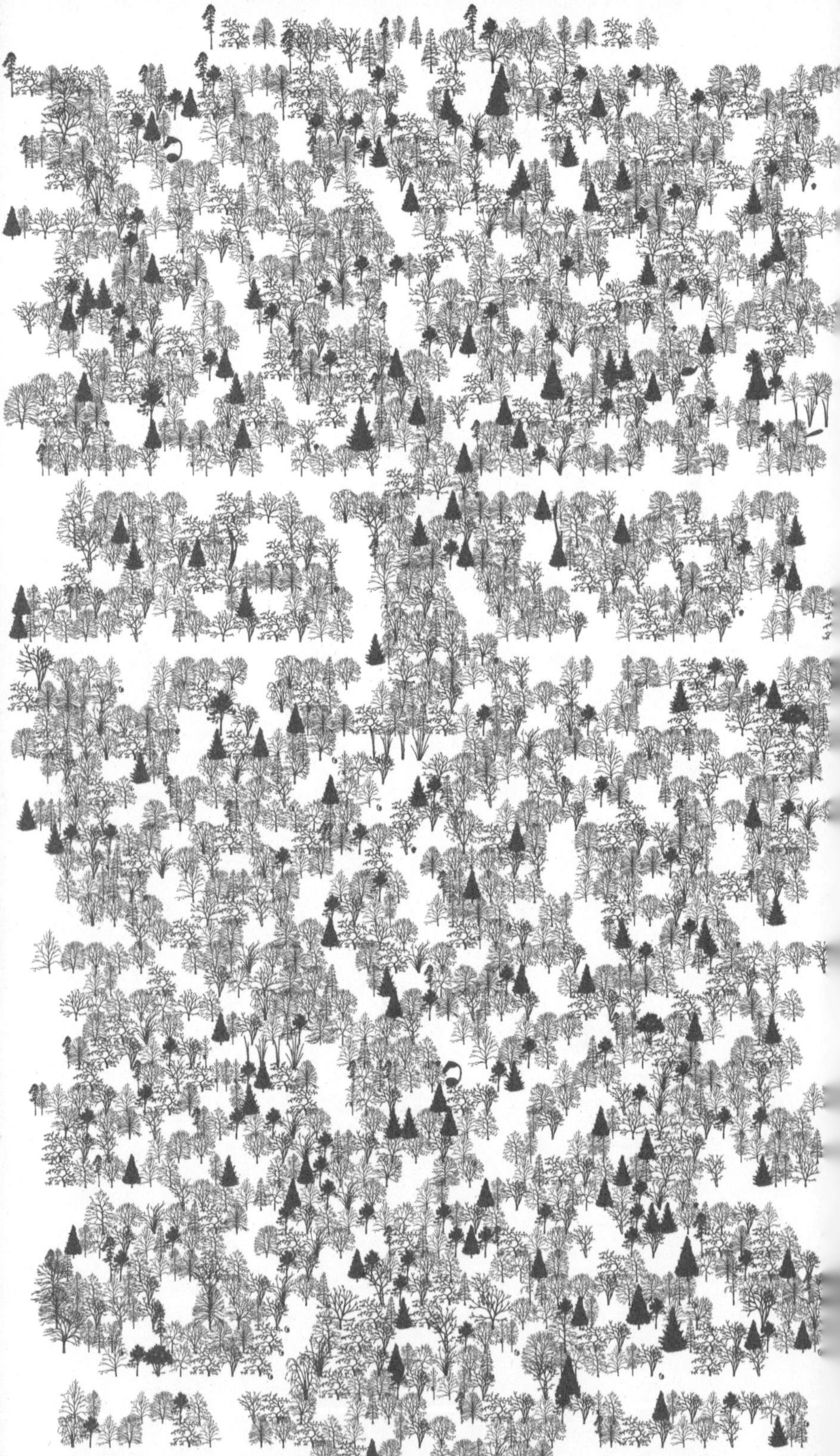

Palas por Pistolas

PEDRO REYES

PALAS POR PISTOLAS IS A COMMISSION BY THE BOTANICAL GARDEN OF Culiacán, Sinaloa, Mexico. The initiative addresses two problems: the proliferation of small arms and the urgent need for reforestation.

We started a campaign calling for community members to voluntarily donate their guns. Three ads were made for a local television station, featuring different family members making the decision to give up their weapons. Thanks to private sponsors, incentives such as domestic appliances were offered in exchange for weapons at Culiacán's City Hall. It was a record campaign with 1,527 guns collected. Forty percent were high-powered guns used exclusively by the army.

These arms were collected by the Secretaría de Defensa (Secretary of Defence) and publicly crushed with a steamroller. The wood and plastic components of the guns were removed. The crushed remnants were then taken to a foundry.

Next, they were melted to obtain the alloy that was then used to fabricate shovels. In collaboration with a major hardware factory, 1,527 shovels were made, one for every gun melted. The metal was pressed, cut, fired until red hot, forged by pressure, and then a protective finish was applied. Each handle was engraved with a legend telling the story. Through this process the weapons were made into tools, so agents of death became agents of life.

These shovels have been distributed to a number of public schools and museums where children and adults have contributed to the project of planting 1,527 trees. This ritual has a pedagogical purpose: if the violent potential of a gun can be diverted to yield positive effects on communities and the environment, so too can other aspects of society be transformed from destructive to constructive.

Several institutions in different countries have participated in *Palas por Pistolas* in cities such as Culiacán, Boston, Denver, Dinard, Greensboro, Guelph, London, Lyon, Marfa, Mexico City, New York, Puebla, San Diego, San Francisco, Tijuana, Vancouver, Houston, and Washington D.C.

To this day tree plantings continue, with at least one tree planted for each shovel.

Acorn Bread Recipe

LUCY O'HAGAN

FIND AN OAK TREE IN LATE AUTUMN. TOUCH THE RIDGES OF THEIR wrinkled bark and say hello. Look on the ground to see if they have dropped their seed—the deliciously smooth and chocolate brown acorn. Within each one lies the potential wisdom of a new oak tree.

Gather them in your basket, skirt or arms, and watch as the squirrels do the same. Bring them home and lay them out somewhere warm to dry completely—careful they don't touch one another, lest the fungi take hold and consume the bunch!

Once dry, you can rattle them and hear the seed's movement within the shell. Crack open the shell with a mortar and pestle, revealing the not-yet-ready-to-eat seed. This will be covered by a bitter papery membrane which needs to be removed. Rub them between a tea towel to loosen the membrane and then either peel it off with your hands or put them in a bucket of water where the membrane can float to the surface.

Now time to leach! Acorns are full of tannins—clever compounds which make them too bitter to eat straight off the tree. Grind the acorns to increase the surface area and put your grinds into a mesh bag. Now immerse this bag into flowing water which will carry off the tannins, leaving you with deliciously nutty acorn mush. Alternatively, you can boil them in a pot of water for ten minutes, strain and boil again in fresh water. Repeat this process until the water runs clear.

Dry, then toast on a pan to enhance that delicious nutty flavor and grind it into a fine flour. Hey presto, you're now able to make your acorn bread!

Combine your acorn flour with water and salt or add honey. Form small balls with the mixture and press flat. Bake on a hot stone, roof tile or pan over the fire. Serve with blackberry jam, birch syrup or tree nuts and honey.

The wisdom of the oak now resides in your body!

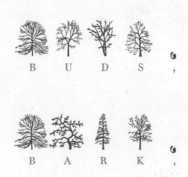

B U D S ,

B A R K ,

B R A N C H E S

Oak Gall Ink Recipe

RACHAEL HAWKWIND

OAK GALLS ARE ABNORMAL PLANT GROWTHS FOUND ON TWIGS ON many species of oak trees, similar to benign tumors or warts in animals. They can be caused by various parasites including insects and midges. Oak galls have traditionally been used in inks and dyes because of their ability to produce rich dark blacks. This recipe can be altered to make wood stain, dye for natural fibers such as wool, silk and cashmere, and of course ink, which was in very common use for centuries. Oak gall ink was used to write the United States Declaration of Independence, U.S. Constitution, and the Bill of Rights. The tannic quality of the oak galls, which are created by insect larvae, give it its rich dark color.

INGREDIENTS
For the mordant
Rusty nails
Vinegar
Time

For the ink
20–30 oak galls
Paper bag
Water
Colander
Cheesecloth

FOR THE MORDANT
Soak rusty nails in vinegar for at least two weeks. This will create an iron mordant. A mordant, or dye fixative, is a substance used to bind dyes on fabrics.

FOR THE INK

Crush 20–30 oak galls in a paper bag.

In a large pot cover them with water and boil for at least one hour.

Strain out oak galls with a colander and then again with a cheese-cloth to remove the fine particles. Add a splash of the vinegar mixture, our iron mordant.

The iron mordant is what makes the dye black and colorfast, so the longer you soak the rusty bits and the more of the solution you add, the darker your ink will be.

Return the pot to the stove and reduce further until you achieve desired consistency and color.

I have used this recipe to dye wool and most recently as a wood stain on a little cabin that I just built!

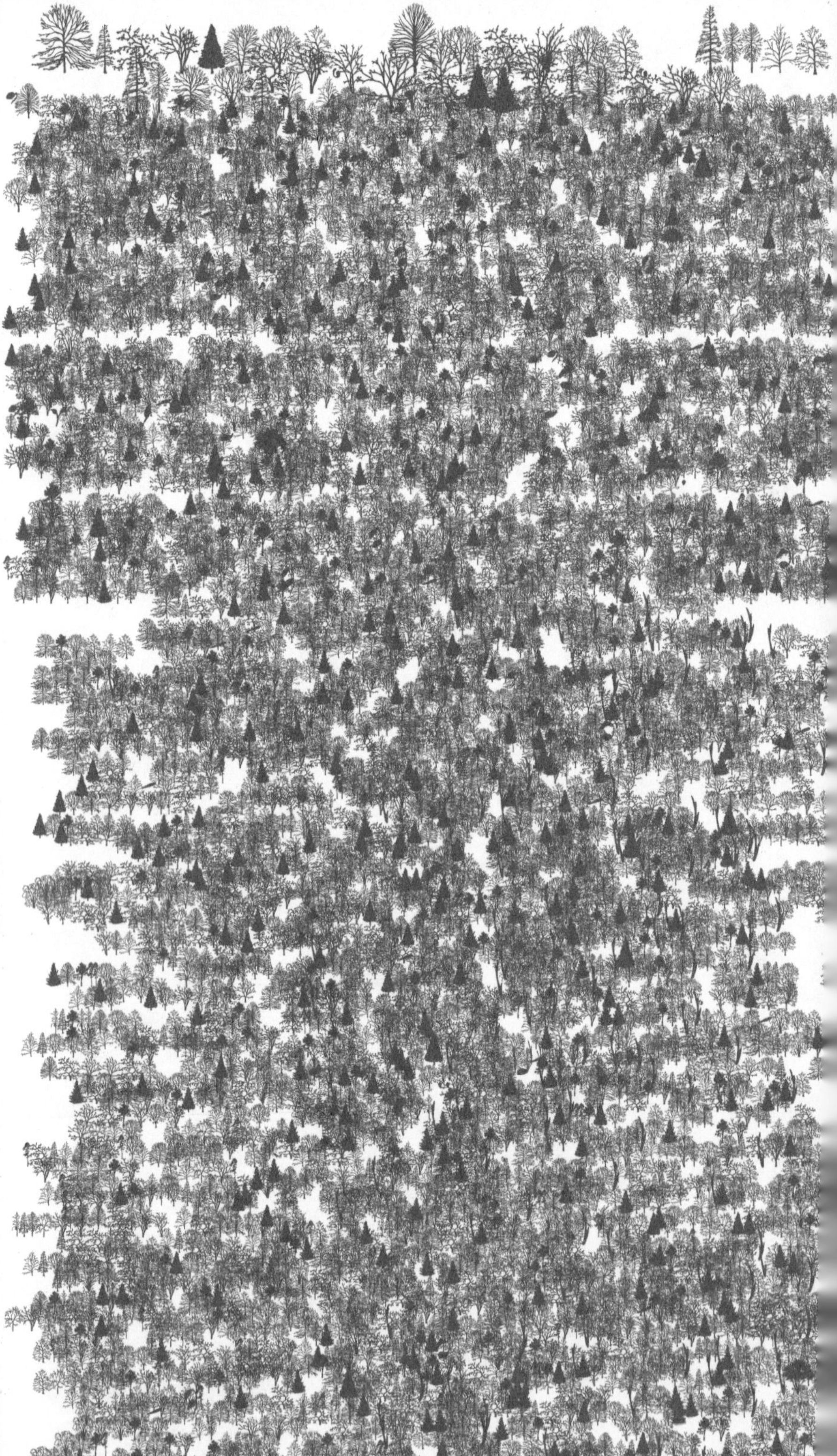

Branches, Leaves, Roots and Trunks

ROBERT MACFARLANE

THE WORD-HOARD

'Language is fossil poetry,' wrote Ralph Waldo Emerson in 1844, '[a]s the limestone of the continent consists of infinite masses of the shells of animalcules, so language is made up of images, or tropes, which now, in their secondary use, have long ceased to remind us of their poetic origin.' Emerson, as essayist, sought to reverse this petrification and restore the 'poetic origin' of words, thereby revealing the originary role of 'nature' in language. Considering the verb *to consider*, he reminds us that it comes from the Latin *considerare*, and thus carries a meaning of 'to study or see with the stars'. Etymology illuminates—a mundane verb is suddenly starlit. Many of the terms in the glossaries of landscape-language that I have collected over the last decade seem, at least to me, as yet unpetrified and still vivid with poetry. They function as topograms—tiny poems that conjure scenes.

There is no single mountain language, but a range of mountain languages; no one coastal language, but a fractal of coastal languages; no lone tree language, but a forest of tree languages. To celebrate the lexis of landscape is not nostalgic, but urgent. 'People *exploit* what they have merely concluded to be of value, but they *defend* what they love,' writes the American essayist and farmer Wendell Berry, 'and to defend what we love we need a particularising language, for we love what we particularly know.'

We are and always have been name-callers, christeners. Words are grained into our landscapes, and landscapes grained into our words. 'Every language is an old-growth forest of the mind,' in Wade Davis's memorable phrase. We see in words: in webs of words, wefts of words, woods of words. The roots of individual words reach out and intermesh, their stems lean and criss-cross, and their outgrowths branch and clasp.

'I want my writing to bring people not just to think of "trees" as they mostly do now,' wrote Roger Deakin in a notebook that was discovered after his early death, 'but of each individual tree, and each kind of tree.' John Muir, spending his first summer working as a shepherd among the pines of the Sierra Nevada in California, reflected in his journal that 'Every tree calls for special admiration. I have been making many sketches and regret that I cannot draw every needle.'

'I have come to understand that although place-words are being lost, they are also being created. Nature is dynamic, and so is language. Loanwords from Chinese, Urdu, Korean, Portugese and Yiddish are right now being used to describe the landscapes of Britain and Ireland; portmanteaus and neologisms are constantly in manufacture. As I travelled I met new words as well as salvaging old ones: a painter in the Hebrides who used *landskein* to refer to the braid of blue horizon lines in hill country on a hazy day; a five-year-old girl who concocted *honeyfur* to describe the soft seeds of grasses held in the fingers.

BRANCHES, LEAVES, ROOTS AND TRUNKS

atchorn	acorn *(Herefordshire)*
balkcut	tree *(Kent)*
bannut-tree	walnut tree *(Herefordshire)*
beilleag	bark of a birch tree *(Gaelic)*
biests	wen-like protuberances on growing trees *(East Anglia)*
bole	main part of the trunk of a tree before it separates into branches *(forestry)*
bolling	permanent trunk left behind after pollarding (pronounced to rhyme with 'rolling') *(forestry)*

brattling	sloppings from felled trees *(Northamptonshire)*
breakneck, brokeneck	tree whose main stem has been snapped by the wind *(forestry)*
browse line	level above which large herbivores cannot browse woodland foliage *(forestry)*
burr	excrescence on base of tree: some broad-leaved trees with a burr, especially walnut, can be very valuable, the burr being prized for its internal patterning *(forestry)*
butt	lower part of the trunk of a tree *(forestry)*
cag	stump of a branch protruding from the tree *(Herefordshire)*
cant-mark	stub pollarded tree used to mark a land boundary *(forestry)*
celynnoga	bounding in holly (place-name element) *(Welsh)*
chats	dead sticks *(Herefordshire)*
chissom	first shoots of a newly cut coppice *(Cotswolds)*
cramble	boughs or branches of crooked and angular growth, used for craft or firewood *(Yorkshire)*
crank	dead branch of a tree *(Cotswolds)*
crìonach	rotten tree; brushwood *(Gaelic)*
daddock	dead wood *(Herefordshire)*
damage cycle	narrower rings in the stump of the tree, indicating the accidental loss of branches which are gradually replaced. Useful in helping to work out when and at what intervals a tree has been pollarded/coppiced *(forestry)*
deadfall	dead branch that falls from a tree as a result of wind or its own weight *(forestry)*
dodderold	pollard *(Bedfordshire)*
dosraich	abundance of branches *(Gaelic)*
dotard	decaying oak or sizeable single tree *(Northamptonshire)*
eirytall	clean-grown sapling *(Cotswolds)*
eller	nelder tree *(Herefordshire)*
flippety	young twig or branch that bends before a hook or clippers *(Exmoor)*

foxed	term applied to an old oak tree, when the centre becomes red and indicates decay *(Northamptonshire)*
frail	leaf skeleton *(Banffshire)*
griggles	small apples left on the tree *(south-west England)*
interarboration	intermixture of the branches of trees on opposite sides (used by Sir Thomas Browne in *The Garden of Cyrus*, 1658) *(arboreal)*
kosh	branch *(Anglo-Romani)*
lammas	second flush of growth in late summer by some species, e.g. oak *(forestry)*
leafmeal	tree's 'cast self,' disintegrating as fallen leaves (Gerard Manley Hopkins) *(poetic)*
lenticels	small pore in bark or a leaf for breathing *(forestry)*
maiden	tree which is not a coppice stool nor a pollard *(forestry)*
mute	stumps of trees and bushes left in the ground after felling *(Exmoor)*
nape	when laying a hedge, to cut the branch partly through so that it can be bent down *(East Anglia)*
nubbin	stump of a tree after the trunk has been felled *(Northamptonshire)*
palmate	leaves that have lobes arranged like the fingers of a hand, e.g. horse chestnut *(forestry)*
pankto	knock or shake down apples from the tree *(Herefordshire)*
pollard	tree cut at eight or twelve feet above ground and allowed to grow again to produce successive crops of wood *(forestry)*
raaga tree	tree that has been torn up by the roots and drifted by the sea *(Shetland)*
rammel	small branches or twigs, especially from trees which have been felled and trimmed *(Scots)*
rootplate	shallow layer of radially arranged roots revealed when a tree has blown over *(forestry)*
rundle	hollow pollard tree *(Herefordshire)*

scocker	rift in an oak tree caused either by lightning blast or the expansive freezing of water that has soaked down into the heart-wood from an unsound part in the head of the tree *(East Anglia)*
scrog	stunted bush *(northern England, Scotland)*
slive	rough edge of a tree stump *(northern England, Warwickshire)*
spronky	of a plant or tree: having many roots *(Kent)*
staghead	dead crown of a veteran tree *(forestry)*
starveling	ailing tree *(forestry)*
stool	permanent base of a coppiced tree *(forestry)*
suthering	noise of the wind through the trees (John Clare) *(poetic)*
tod	stump of a tree sawn off and left in the ground; the top of a pollard tree *(Suffollk)*
wash-boughs	straggling lower branches of a tree *(Suffolk)*
wewire	to move about as foliage does in wind *(Essex)*
whip	thin tree with a very small crown reaching into the upper canopy *(forestry)*
wolf	bigger than average tree which is dominant in the crop, often removed at first thinning *(forestry)*

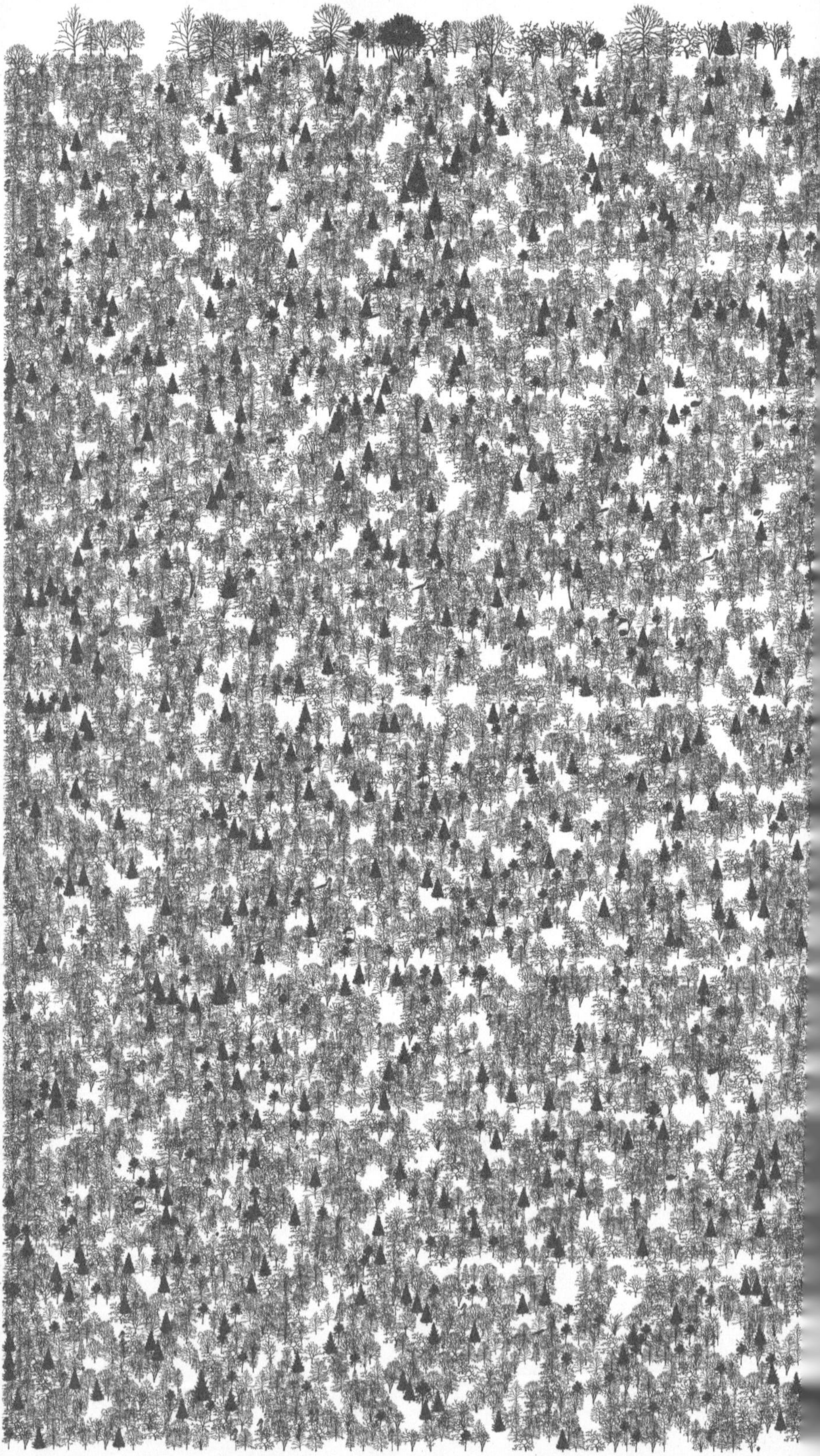

Tree Theory, Biogeography and Branching

BRIAN J. ENQUIST

EVERYONE KNOWS MORE OR LESS WHAT A TREE LOOKS LIKE. Although the architecture of any two trees across the world may at first look very diverse, analysis of the mathematics of branching shows a different story. We now know that the diversity of tree architecture can be generated by very simple and common rules across all plants—if not all of life, including animals. These rules basically govern not only how trees branch and when they branch but also the sizes and shapes of those branches, as well as the structure and functioning of forests across the globe.

Understanding these branching rules has allowed us, as scientists, to make accurate predictions about how plants and even whole forests work—in particular how they flux carbon dioxide. If you know something about the branching network, you can make predictions about the entire plant's functioning. Then you can extend that to understand the ecology of the forest.

The rules appear both in the external branching architecture, or how the branches are arranged, and in the internal structure of the tissues that transport nutrients throughout the tree.

The study of plant architecture has revealed two important yet disparate viewpoints about the evolutionary origin of plant branching patterns. On the one hand, plant architecture often reflects differences in specific growth environments and taxon-specific selection on allocation and life history. Indeed, diverse architectural branching designs that exist in nature as well as specific genes that regulate growth and development often match differences in architecture. On the other hand, categorizing the diversity of plants has sometimes focused on similarities in the patterns of branching and the scaling of branch dimensions, such as number, radius, and length.

Perhaps the most significant insight about the math of real trees comes from Leonardo da Vinci's original observation of tree construction. He noted that 'all the branches of a tree at every stage of its height, when put together, are equal in thickness to the trunk below them'. We call this branching rule 'area-preserving'. Take any mother branch and its daughter branches—the cross sectional area of the mother branch will equal the total cross sectional area of the daughter branches. This was an amazing insight—the total cross-sectional area of the twigs of a tree will be approximately equal to the cross-sectional area of the main trunk. We have used Leonardo's 'area-preserving' as a basis for understanding the structural and functional design of trees. We have come to know that area preserving reflects evolution by natural selection for optimal branching networks. Area-preserving ensures that a tree is biomechanically stable (it will resist gravity better and be less prone to being knocked down). Further, area-preserving networks are more efficient at transporting resources (water and sugar) within their vascular systems.

We can break down tree architecture into a handful of rules. For a branch of a given size: 'Grow so much and then branch, and then grow so much and then branch.' This rule governs what the dimensions of the branches have to be. That is, 'grow until your branch is such and so much length, or so much in width'. Repeating this rule as a plant grows results in a tremendously complicated but beautiful form such as a tree and ultimately it stems down to a very efficient code.

This rule or code can be described mathematically and can be seen to reoccur as the tree grows, creating a fractal—a repeating pattern—like a spiral of daughter branches emanating from the mother branch or tree trunk. These branching rules hold true across species, so the ratios of lengths and radii of a mother branch to daughter branches are similar for almost all trees. But palm trees don't count: That's basically one big branch with a bunch of leaves at the end.

There are additional branching rules that can also kick in. You can still follow these basic branching rules of radii and lengths, but if you change the angles at which they branch this will result in a tremendously different looking tree.

So why do these rules exist in the first place? We have proposed that all tree architectures are the result of natural selection acting on the scaling of resource uptake and resource distribution. Our theory predicts that whole-plant carbon and water fluxes, net primary production, and population density should also be characterized by similar scaling functions. Natural selection would select for shapes of trees that, as they grow from seedling to adult plant, solve two important problems: taking in as much resources such as light, water and nutrients as possible, while transporting resources within the plant with as little work as possible.

There are these two conflicting evolutionary pressures on the architectures of trees. In biology we call this a trade-off. For plants the question is how to get food, or resources, with as little work as possible. Work is transporting nutrients and water through internal tissues called xylem and phloem, and the less energy they have to expend to transport nutrients, the more they have for growth and reproduction. Ultimately, natural selection has fine-tuned the rules that govern plants' internal and external frameworks to a simple repeating pattern coded for by their DNA. The external branching network governs a plant's shape, which determines the number of leaves on a tree, which then also influences how much carbon is fluxed within the tree.

Biology is basically all about trees. It turns out that the organization and design of biological networks are all around us. We have cardiovascular systems, we have neural systems, we have plant vascular networks. Biological trees are built around common themes in the geometry of vascular networks. Vascular networks flux resources, and resources are basically what maintain us. The speed at which you're able to flux resources will then influence the speed of your physiology: How fast you grow, how long it will take you to reach reproductive maturity, how long ultimately organisms live. In the case of trees, how much carbon dioxide they are able to absorb from the atmosphere. If you understand the organization of vascular networks you can actually predict an enormous amount about the functioning of organisms.

Because nearly all plants grow by the same network rules, we can scale up these rules to make accurate predictions about the functioning of an entire forest. In a forest, where resources such as sunlight and water are limited, trees compete with each other to get as much of what they need to live and grow as possible. The result is a fractal-like filling of the forest space, with a few large trees taking up most of the resources and many small trees filling in the cracks. The ratio of big trees to little trees in a forest turns out to be the same as the ratio of big branches to little branches on a single tree from that forest. From this we can determine many aspects of how entire forests work. If we know something about these branching rules we can start saying something about what may happen in the future. These branching patterns are so prevalent that they will govern and influence how plants respond in a changing world.

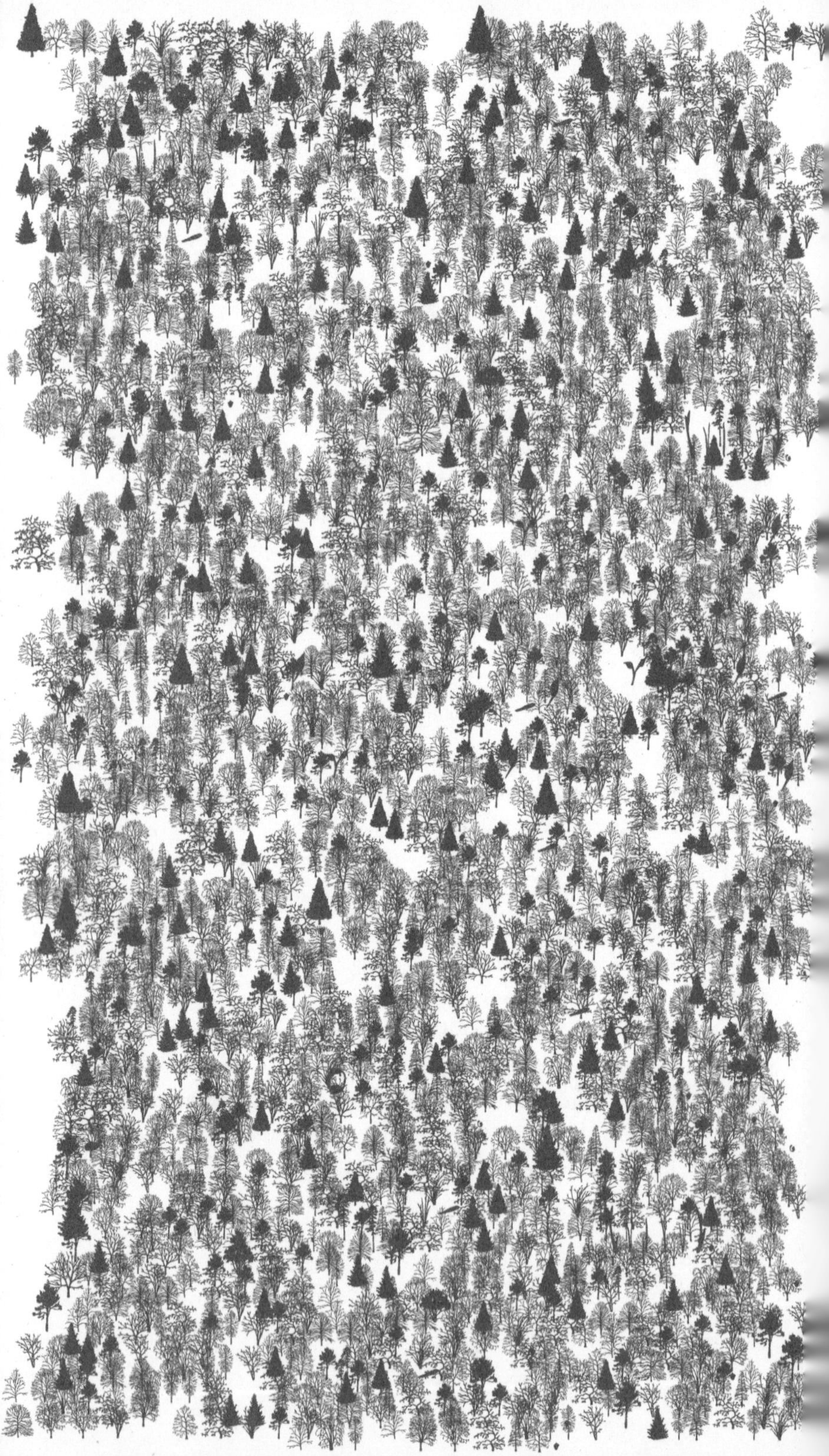

Cultivating the Courage to Sin

ANDREA BOWERS

CULTIVATING THE COURAGE TO SIN FOCUSES ON CLIMATE JUSTICE AND feminist subjectivity in art and activism. Particularly it focuses on a non-violent act of civil disobedience in which I was involved. In 2011 I was arrested, with three other activists, for climbing into the trees of a native oak woodland habitat in Arcadia, California and trying to save a pristine forest of 250 trees from being clear-cut by the county of Los Angeles. One of the horrible and unanticipated outcomes of this action was that all of the trees were ripped out of the forest around us as we were tied to the canopies of two oaks. All of the destroyed trees were then put in woodchippers. Ultimately I was arrested on three misdemeanour charges and placed in jail for two days. I videotaped the entire experience until the sheriffs took my camera into evidence. The video, *I Plan to Stay a Believer* (2013), includes my footage, local news footage and sheriff department recordings.

The exhibition title comes from a quote by the controversial pioneering feminist Mary Daly from an essay about her personal history, called "Sin Big." Although I do not agree with some of her positions, this particular text, published originally in *The New Yorker*, has been very influential. She explains that, "Ever since childhood, I have been honing my skills for living the life of a Radical Feminist Pirate and Cultivating the Courage to Sin." The word "sin" is derived from the Indo-European root "es-," meaning "to be." When I discovered this etymology, I intuitively understood that for a woman trapped in patriarchy, which is the religion of the entire planet, "to be" in the fullest sense is "to sin." *Cultivating the Courage to Sin* has become my battle cry.

One of the activists from the Arcadia tree-sit is a veteran tree sitter at the age of 29. He has spent the last six years living in old growth redwoods throughout Humboldt County in Northern California. Tree sitting is a form of environmentalist civil disobedience in which a protester sits in a tree, usually on a small platform built for the purpose, to protect it from being cut down. I asked him what his fantasy tree-sitting platform would be. All of my frustration, insecurities and inequalities of living in a patriarchal culture flooded over me with his two words: Pirate Ship. I was immediately annoyed and unamused, of course. A typical man, I thought. Somehow it was so obvious, yet I would never have thought of that. For years I've been negotiating the gender imbalances in both art and activism. Together the Humboldt activist and I built a 25-foot *Radical Feminist Pirate Ship Tree Sitting Platform* (2013).

Immediately upon release from jail I returned to the site of the clear cut. Mountains of woodchips were all that remained from the once majestic trees. It was intellectually and emotionally devastating for me to witness this. I decided to save as many of the woodchips as possible. I filled a pick-up truck with the wood before I was served with a restraining order to stay off the land. I have been saving the wood for over two years.

BIRDS SINGING

THE WRONG TUNES

IN THE WRONG TREES

TOO EARLY

IN THE YEAR

ZADIE SMITH

Fractal Vision

Benoît Mandelbrot Changed How We View the World

JAMES GLEICK

HERE IS A MATHEMATICIAN'S NIGHTMARE I HEARD IN THE 1980S when that irritating, unconforming, self-regarding provocateur Benoît Mandelbrot was suddenly famous—fractals, fractals everywhere. The mathematician dreamed that Mandelbrot died, and God spoke: "You know, there really was something to that Mandelbrot."

Sure enough. Mandelbrot created nothing less than a new geometry, to stand side by side with Euclid's—a geometry to mirror not the ideal forms of thought but the real complexity of nature. He was a mathematician who was never welcomed into the fraternity ("Fortress Mathematics," he said, where "the highest ambition is to wall off the windows and preserve only one door"), and he pretended that was fine with him. When Yale first hired him to teach, it was in engineering and applied science; for most of his career he was supported at IBM's Westchester research lab. He called himself a "nomad by choice". He considered himself an experienced refugee: born to a Jewish family in Warsaw in 1924, he immigrated to Paris ahead of the Nazis, then fled farther and farther into the French countryside.

In various incarnations he taught physiology and economics. He was a non-physicist who won the Wolf Prize in physics. The labels didn't matter. He turns out to have belonged to the select handful of twentieth century scientists who upended, as if by flipping a switch, the way we see the world we live in.

He was the one who let us appreciate chaos in all its glory, the noisy, the wayward and the freakish, from the very small to the very large. He gave the new field of study he invented a fittingly recondite name: "fractal geometry." But he wanted me to understand it as ordinary.

"The questions the field attacks are questions people ask themselves," he told me. "They are questions children ask: What shape is a mountain? Why is a cloud the way it is?" Only his answers were not ordinary.

Clouds are not spheres—the most famous sentence he ever wrote—
*mountains are not cones, coastlines are not circles and bark is not
smooth, nor does lightning travel in a straight line.*

If you closely examine the florets of a cauliflower (or the bronchioles of a
lung; or the fractures in oil-bearing shale), zooming in with your magnify-
ing glass or microscope, you see the same fundamental patterns, repeating.
It is no accident. They are all fractal. Clouds, mountains, coastlines, bark
and lightning are all jagged and discontinuous, but self-similar when viewed
at different scales, thus concealing order within their irregularity. They are
shapes that branch or fold in upon themselves recursively.

I was following him from place to place, reporting a book on chaos,
while he evangelized his newly popular ideas to scientists of all sorts. Wisps of
white hair atop his outsize brow, he lectured at Woods Hole to a crowd
of oceanographers, who had heard that fractals were relevant to cyclone
tracks and eddy cascades. Mandelbrot told them he had seen the same
channels, flows and back flows in dry statistics of rising and falling cotton
prices. At Lamont-Doherty Geological Observatory, as it was then known,
the geologists already spoke fractally about earthquakes. Mandelbrot laid
out a mathematical framework for such phenomena: they exist in fractional
dimensions, lying in between the familiar one-dimensional lines, two-
dimensional planes and three-dimensional spaces. He revived some old and
freakish ideas—"monsters," as he said, "mathematical pathologies" that had
been relegated to the fringes.

"I started looking in the trash cans of science for such phenomena," he
said, and he meant this literally: one scrap he grabbed from a Paris mathematician's wastebasket inspired an important 1965 paper combining two
more fields to which he did not belong, "Information Theory and Psycho-
linguistics." Information theory connected to fractals when he focused on
the problem of noise—static, errors—in phone lines. It was always there;
on average it seemed manageable, but analysis revealed that normal bell-curve
averages didn't apply. There were too many surprises—outliers. Clusters and
quirks always defied expectations.

It's the same with brainwaves, fluid turbulence, seismic tremors and—oh,
yes—finance.

From his first paper studying fluctuations in the rise and fall of cotton
prices in 1962 until the end of his life, he maintained a simple and constant

message about extraordinary economic events. The professionals plan for "mild randomness" and misunderstand "wild randomness." They learn from the averages and overlook the outliers. Thus they consistently, predictably, underestimate catastrophic risk. "The financiers and investors of the world are, at the moment, like mariners who heed no weather warnings," he wrote near the peak of the bubble, in 2004, in *The (Mis)behavior of Markets*, his last book.

Fractals have made their way into the economics mainstream, as into so many fields, though Mandelbrot was not really an economist; nor a physiologist, physicist, engineer. . . .

"Very often when I listen to the list of my previous jobs, I wonder if I exist," he said once. "The intersection of such sets is surely empty."

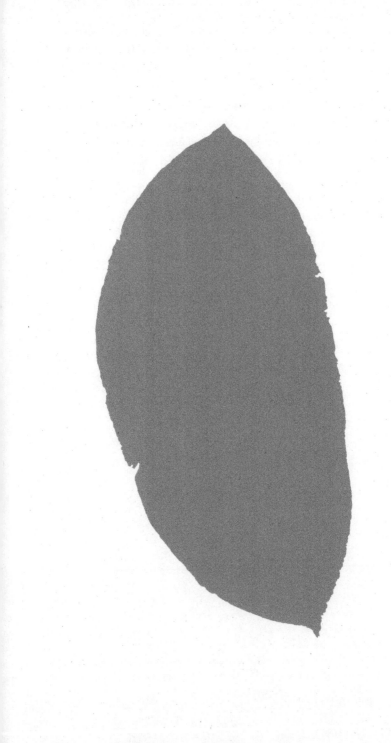

L E A V E S

&

T R U N K S

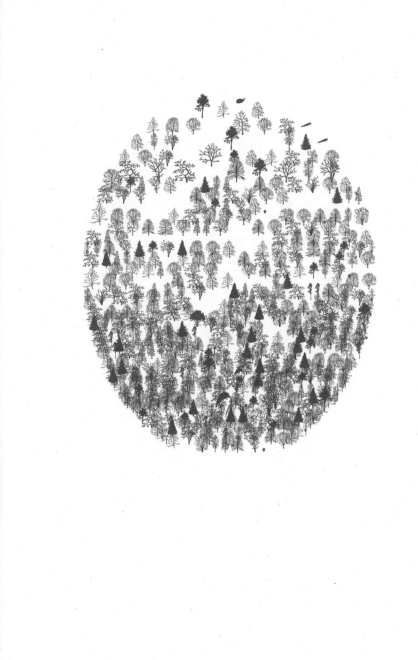

It's the Season I Often Mistake

ADA LIMÓN

Birds for leaves, and leaves for birds.
The tawny yellow mulberry leaves
are always goldfinches tumbling
across the lawn like extreme elation.
The last of the maroon crabapple
ovates are song sparrows that tremble
all at once. And today, just when I
could not stand myself any longer,
a group of field sparrows, that were
actually field sparrows, flew up into
the bare branches of the hackberry
and I almost collapsed: leaves
reattaching themselves to the tree
like a strong spell for reversal. What
else did I expect? What good
is accuracy amidst the perpetual
scattering that unspools the world.

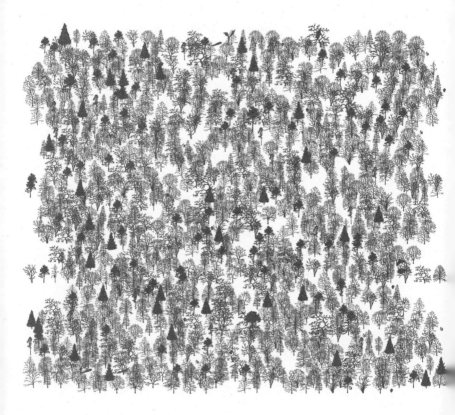

from

Why Information Grows

CÉSAR A. HIDÁLGO

CONSIDER A TREE. A TREE, IN ITS SEMI-"FROZEN" STATE, IS A COM-
puter powered by sunlight. A tree in New England reacts to the length of the
day, running a different program in the summer than in the winter. It figures
out when to shed its leaves and when to sprout new ones. A tree processes
the information that is available in its environment. Its proteins, organized in
signaling pathways, help the tree figure out how to grow its roots toward the
water it needs, how to activate an immune response when it is threatened by
disease, and how to push its leaves toward the sun it craves. A tree does not
have the consciousness or language that we have, but it shares with us a general
ability to process information. A tree has knowledge, even though the way in
which it processes information is unlike our mental abilities and more similar
to the processes our own bodies do without knowing how: digestion, immu-
nity, hormonal regulation, and so on.

While a tree is technically a computer, its power source is not an
electrical outlet but the sun. A tree is a computer that, just like us, cannot
run MATLAB, but unlike computers and us, it has the knowhow to run
photosynthesis. Trees process information, and they are able to do so
because they are steady states of out-of-equilibrium systems. Trees embody
knowhow, which they use to survive.

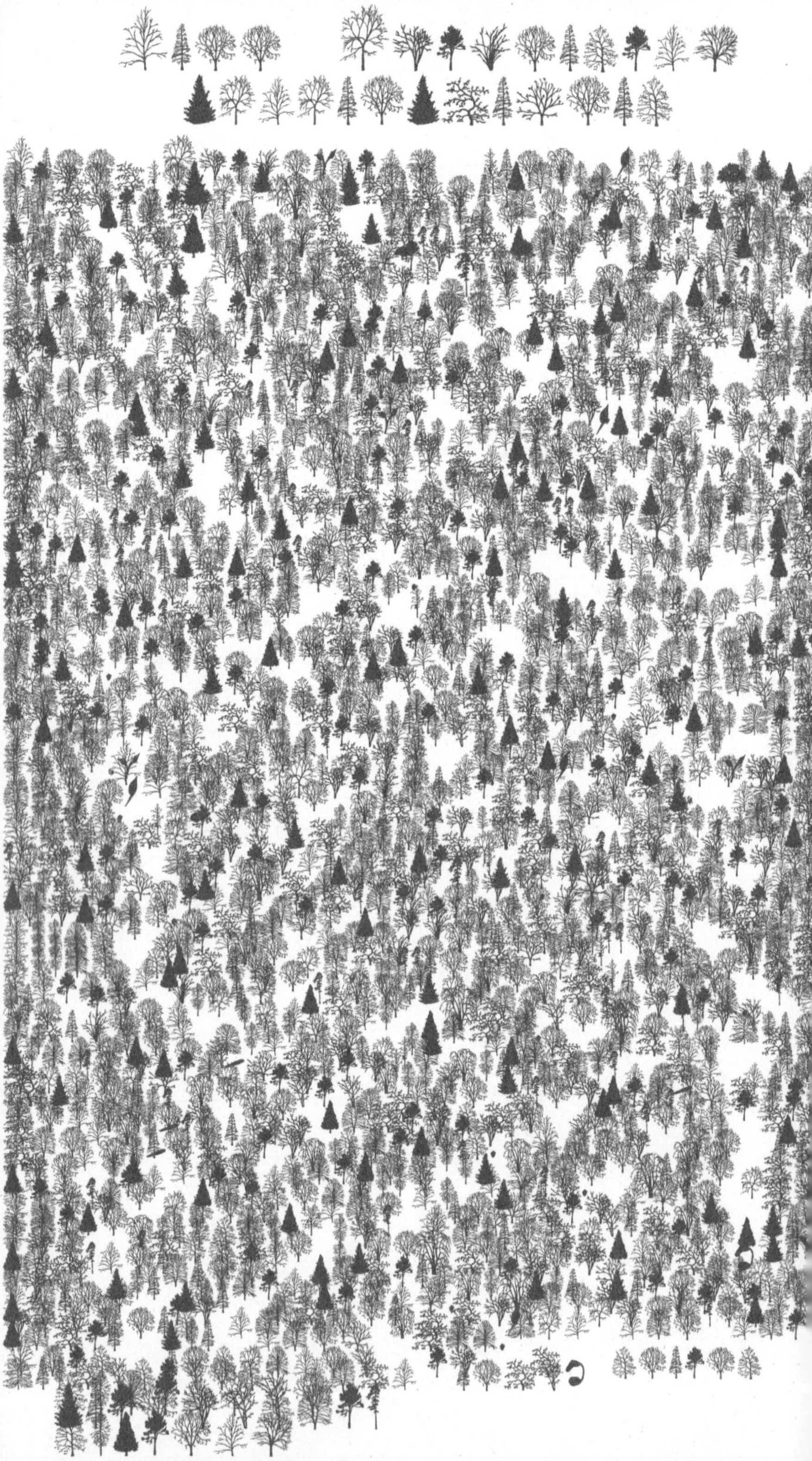

Tree University

FUTUREFARMERS

TREE UNIVERSITY GREW OUT OF A LINEAGE OF "FREE SCHOOL" PROJ-
ects that Futurefarmers had been organizing. We had been wanting to create a
whole "curriculum" from a tree for a while. When the deCordova approached
us for a show, a reexamination of Henry David Thoreau's work and the site of
Walden Pond, we proposed to do it there, but the cost of bringing in a tree or
felling a tree was prohibitive. A few months after our first conversations with
the museum, we got a call. Dina Deitsch, the curator, told us that Hurricane
Sandy had felled a Norwegian spruce tree on their property. So we opened up
the conversation again.

We feel that the continuous model of the "prototype" is quite liberating
when creating work that is site/situation responsive. Most of our work happens on or in a site for a specific duration. We set up parameters beforehand,
but the production happens within a spirit of readiness. You can figure out
many things through quick prototypes—there is not time for perfecting,
which often can cause paralysis.

As we got to know the tree, working with a group of people who participated in workshops at the site with us, we linked what we were learning with
specific histories connected to Thoreau's life. One such history turned out to
fit wonderfully with our shared desire to write down what we were learning.
We had invited an arborist and microbial ecologist to introduce us to the
tree—to help us listen to the tree, taste and touch it.

One Thoreau quote that influenced the "Tree University" was, "Men
have become the tools of their tools." This was a meta line that guided
our inquiry throughout. Thoreau's father was a pencil maker and Thoreau
improved the pencil by introducing a clay binder made with clay found
at the bottom of Walden Pond. Mixing this clay with graphite revolution-
ized pencils. This vignette related to our early conversations about tools
with the workshoppers—what tools do we have among us, what tools scare
us, oppress us, liberate us, etc. One tool we agreed was still very powerful
was the pen, or in our case the pencil. So we set out to Walden Pond to
harvest some clay. We bored to the bottom of the lake and collected enough

clay to run a pencil-making workshop at the museum using wood from the tree.

After we did the pencil-making workshop, we had a competition between a chainsaw expert and a two-person sawing duo to cut the tree in slices. Then we ran a two-day workshop where we took one of the slices of the tree and cut it into wood type. We used simple chisels to form type and then used the remains of the slice to lock up texts drawn from the workshop on Thoreau directly. One passage we extracted from chapter six of Walden was: "I had three chairs in my house; one for solitude, two for friendship, three for society. When visitors came in larger and unexpected numbers there was but the third chair for them all."

This resulted in a series of broadsides that read:

SOLITUDE
FRIENDSHIP
SOCIETY

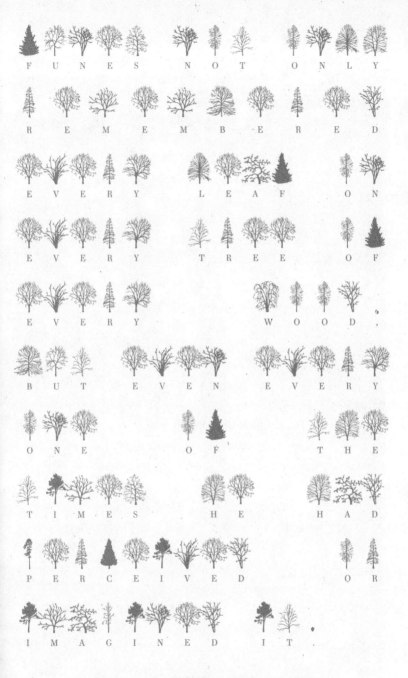

FUNES NOT ONLY

REMEMBERED

EVERY LEAF ON

EVERY TREE OF

EVERY WOOD,

BUT EVEN EVERY

ONE OF THE

TIMES HE HAD

PERCEIVED OR

IMAGINED IT.

JORGE LUIS BORGES

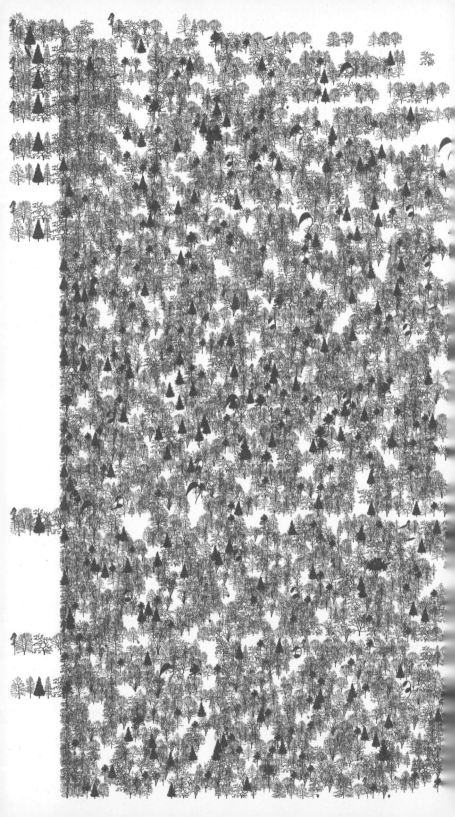

Under a Plane Tree

PLATO

SCENE   Under a plane tree, by the banks of the Illissus.

SOCRATES   Lead on, and look out for a place in which we can sit down.

PHAEDRUS   Do you see the tallest plane-tree in the distance?

SOCRATES   Yes.

PHAEDRUS   There are shade and gentle breezes, and grass on which we may either sit or lie down.

SOCRATES   Move forward.

PHAEDRUS   I should like to know, Socrates, whether the place is not somewhere here at which Boreas is said to have carried off Orithyia from the banks of the Illissus?

SOCRATES   Such is the tradition.

PHAEDRUS   And is this the exact spot? The little stream is delightfully clear and bright; I can fancy that there might be maidens playing near.

SOCRATES   I believe that the spot is not exactly here, but about a quarter of a mile lower down, where you cross to the temple of Artemis, and there is, I think, some sort of an altar of Boreas at the place.

PHAEDRUS   I have never noticed it; but I beseech you to tell me, Socrates, do you believe this tale?

SOCRATES   The wise are doubtful, and I should not be singular if, like them, I too doubted. I might have a rational explanation that Orithyia was playing with Pharmacia, when a northern gust carried her over the neighboring rocks; and this being the manner of her death, she was said to have been carried away by Boreas. There is a discrepancy, however, about the locality; according to another version of the story she was taken from Areopagus, and not from this place. Now I quite acknowledge that these allegories are very nice, but he is not to be envied who has to invent them; much labor and ingenuity will be required of him; and when he has once begun, he must go on and rehabilitate Hippocentaurs and chimeras dire. Gorgons and winged steeds flow in apace, and numberless other inconceivable and portentous natures. And if he is sceptical about them, and would fain reduce them one after another to the rules of probability, this sort of crude philosophy will take up a great deal of time. Now I have no leisure for such enquiries; shall I tell you why? I must first know myself, as the Delphian inscription says; to be curious about that which is not my concern, while I am still in ignorance of my own self, would be ridiculous. And therefore I bid farewell to all this; the common opinion is enough for me. For, as I was saying, I want to know not about this, but about myself: am I a monster more complicated and swollen with passion than the serpent Typho, or a creature of a gentler and simpler sort, to whom Nature has given a diviner and lowlier destiny? But let me ask you, friend: have we not reached the plane tree to which you were conducting us?

PHAEDRUS   Yes, this is the tree.

SOCRATES   By Hera, a fair resting-place, full of summer sounds and scents. Here is this lofty and spreading plane tree, and the agnus castus high and clustering, in the fullest blossom and the greatest fragrance; and the stream which flows beneath the plane tree is deliciously cold to the feet. Judging from the ornaments and images, this must be a spot sacred to Achelous and the Nymphs. How delightful is the breeze: so very sweet; and there is a sound in the air shrill and summerlike which makes answer to the chorus of the cicadae. But the greatest charm of all is the grass, like a pillow gently sloping to the head. My dear Phaedrus, you have been an admirable guide.

PHAEDRUS What an incomprehensible being you are, Socrates: when you are in the country, as you say, you really are like some stranger who is led about by a guide. Do you ever cross the border? I rather think that you never venture even outside the gates.

SOCRATES Very true, my good friend; and I hope that you will excuse me when you hear the reason, which is, that I am a lover of knowledge, and the men who dwell in the city are my teachers, and not the trees or the country. Though I do indeed believe that you have found a spell with which to draw me out of the city into the country, like a hungry cow before whom a bough or a bunch of fruit is waved. For only hold up before me in like manner a book, and you may lead me all round Attica, and over the wide world. And now having arrived, I intend to lie down, and do you choose any posture in which you can read best. Begin.

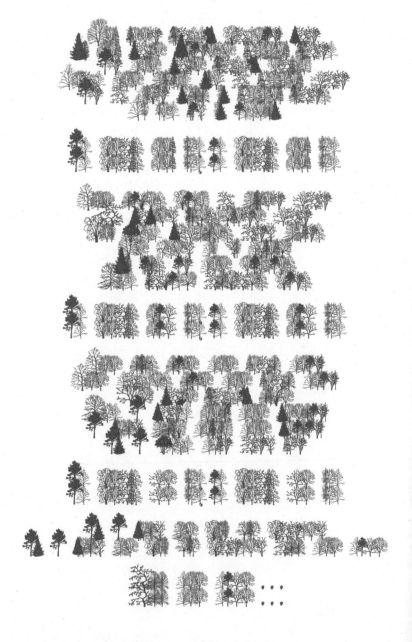

Fake Plastic Trees

RADIOHEAD

Her green plastic watering can
For her fake Chinese rubber plant
In the fake plastic earth
That she bought from a rubber man
In a town full of rubber plans
To get rid of itself

It wears her out, it wears her out
It wears her out, it wears her out

She lives with a broken man
A cracked polystyrene man
Who just crumbles and burns
He used to do surgery
For girls in the eighties
But gravity always wins

It wears him out, it wears him out
It wears him out, it wears him out

She looks like the real thing
She tastes like the real thing
My fake plastic love
But I can't help the feeling
I could blow through the ceiling
If I just turn and run

It wears me out, it wears me out
It wears me out, it wears me out

If I could be who you wanted
If I could be who you wanted all the time

All the time . . .
All the time . . .

THE TREES

BREATHE OUT,

WE BREATHE IN.

LUCHITA HURTADO

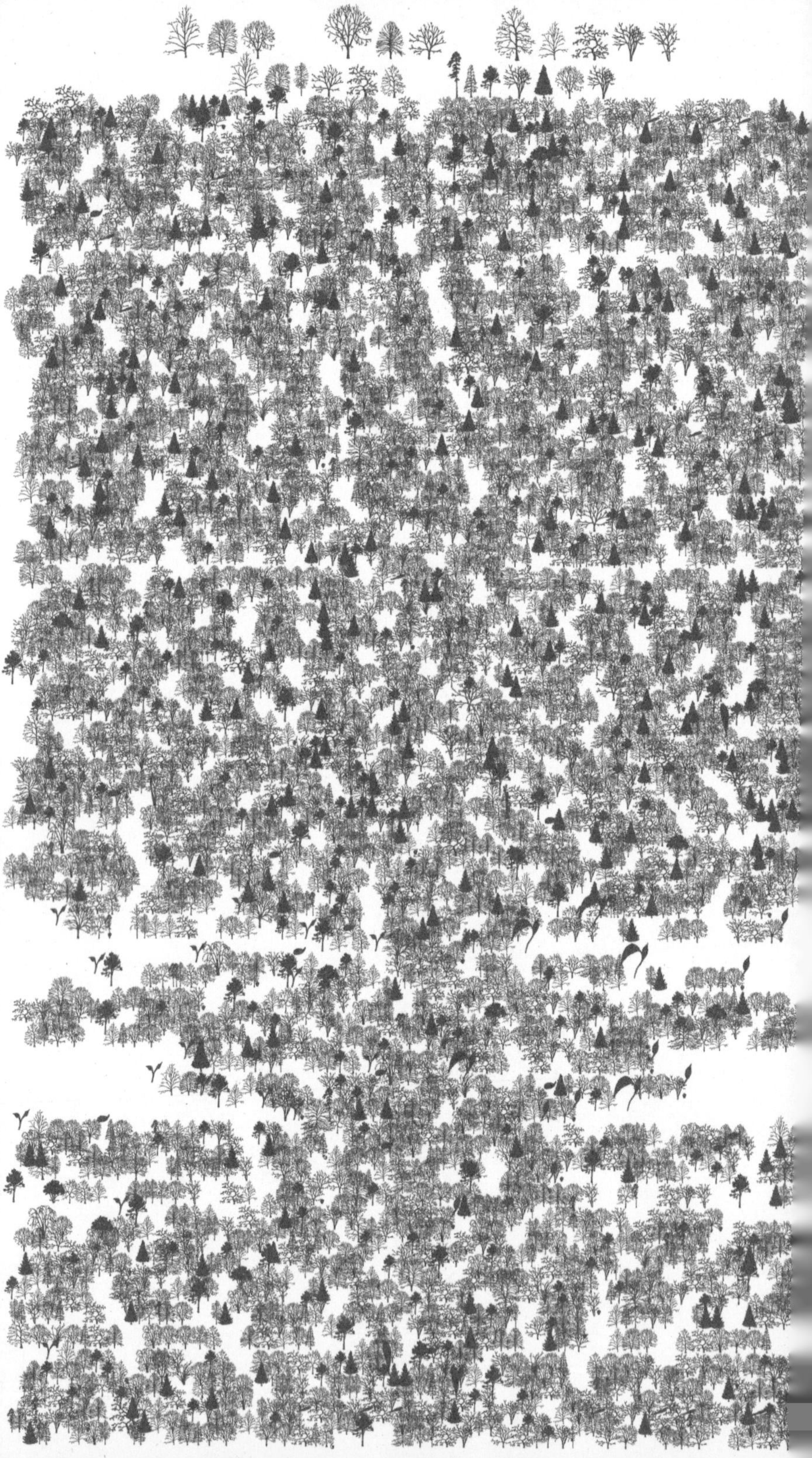

The Elm Stand

THOMAS PRINCEN

AT MY OFFICE I HAVE A KEYBOARD STAND MADE OF AMERICAN ELM. I made it myself, from one-and-a-half-inch planks I dried, planed, edged, rip-sawed, crosscut, routed, scraped, and sanded. Its four pieces fit together without nails or screws, only with dovetail joints and glue. Once the stand was assembled, I finished the wood with tung oil, hand-rubbing it and allowing each coat to dry for several days before sanding. Repeating the process a half dozen times brought out the full richness of the grain and at the same time added a patina to the wood's surface. Finally, I applied three coats of wax, hand-rubbing and polishing each coat till the surface fairly gleamed.

It would never win a prize or a spot in a woodworker's magazine. But I see it as quite a piece of work because it is my work, and work that, I only realized some time later, connects my everyday practice—writing—to a once-living thing. It turns out that it is also the work of many others, some going back, I surmise, a century or more. Some university landscaper probably planted the sapling knowing that over the years it would take the classic vase shape of the American elm. No doubt he also knew that he would never see it in such magnificence, but he planted it anyway. It was his work, and through that work he created value. In fact, all of us involved with this tree created value. For me, though, the story goes back some fifteen years.

One bright spring day I was walking my five-year-old son across campus after day care when we came upon a yellow caution ribbon. Behind the ribbon, a university tree-cutting crew was preparing to take down a giant elm. Quite a crowd had gathered. We stopped to watch.

The crew had secured ropes high up on the trunk to keep it from falling on a nearby building—my own office building, actually, the University of Michigan's School of Natural Resources and Environment. The crew told everyone to stand back as the chainsaw operator, a burly man with a confident swagger, approached the base of the tree.

He wore a sleeveless T-shirt, probably to show off his ample biceps. His chest puffed out and his muscles became taut as he revved up the chain saw. He exuded power. I detected a sense of anticipation, of a major event, on his face.

Having cut down a few trees myself, I knew the feeling. Whatever one thinks about trees and logging, felling a tree, especially one this big, is a thrill. And this guy had an audience to boot.

In no time he cut a wedge out of the base, the others tugged on the ropes, and down it came. My son's jaw dropped, his eyes opened wide. My heart raced. I could imagine, in fact, I could feel the rush the chainsaw operator must have felt. What a spectacle!

So that was that. Another elm tree bites the dust, no doubt another victim of Dutch elm disease, which has ravaged American elms across North America for decades and nearly driven them to extinction. My son went home with my wife, and I entered the Dana Building (named after Samuel Trask Dana, one of the country's early scientific foresters). I sat in my office trying to work while listening to the chainsaw and chipper make short work of the elm's carcass.

What a shame, I thought. All that wood just cut up and ground up, destined most likely for a landfill somewhere. I couldn't sit still, so I went back out. Only the trunk was left, some ten feet long and two and a half to three feet in diameter. The chainsaw operator was about to chop it into blocks. I approached him.

"You going to cut this up?"

"Yup. Gotta get it out before the end of the day."

"It's elm, right?"

"Yeah."

"Wouldn't it make good lumber?"

"I suppose so. I just gotta get it out of here."

"Kind of a waste."

He shrugged. I turned to go, not wanting to interfere anymore with this guy, who was just doing his job and who, I guessed, did not appreciate being questioned by some tree hugger from the environment school. But then he cleared his throat and spoke.

"Cutting this tree was a waste."

"What?"

"This tree didn't have to come down."

"It was diseased, wasn't it?"

"No. Perfectly healthy."

"But why would—"

"They're putting in a sidewalk with a short wall. The wall requires a footer, below the frost line, they'd cut off almost half the tree's roots. Eventually it'd fall. So they ordered me to take it down. I fought it all summer, but I lost."

I just looked at him. His eyes welled up and I could see he was choking up.

"I lost a friend today." He turned away.

We just stood there. Somehow we got to talking about elm wood and how rare it is and how, with proper milling and curing, it can be made into some very nice furniture. Before I knew it, I was asking to take the trunk and do just that. He agreed, as long as I got it out by the end of the day. Having ridden my bike that day, I was in a bit of a bind. But in short order a couple of loggers were hauling the trunk off campus and to a nearby mill.

Several weeks later I got a call from the sawyer at the mill.

"This wood is beautiful! I've never seen anything like it. Every cut is different—brown, blonde, red. You got yourself some good wood here!" I was proud. He called again in a few days and said it was ready to pick up, all cut into one-and-a-half and two-and-a-half-inch planks. After letting the wood dry in the campus woodshop for two or three years, I began making my elm stand.

The Exact Opposite of Distance

IRENE KOPELMAN

MAY 9, 2012

Amsterdam. The jungle—the Amazonian forest, or Amazonia—has always been a fantasy.

MAY 22, 2012

In Lima. People tell stories about Amazonia—here, in relative proximity to the jungle, stories are another way for this place to establish ground and gain territory in my imagination.

MAY 24, 2012

The Manu Learning Centre. I am here.

MAY 25, 2012

Every corner of my sight, and further beyond in all possible directions, the world is green and never ending. A forest continuum, taking in the complex situation—never quite seeing where plants begin or end, the forest a web or giant root of all its elements, interwoven and entangled—I realize that it's my habit to frame and to translate the view into compositional fragments. I also realize that it's impossible here to see the fragment, the parts that constitute the whole. The forest is a dense and disorderly mass of various green tones, and I have the feeling I'm not yet able to see the depths of its full color range. Right now, I only see blotches of undefined green.

MAY 29, 2012

Last night I dreamt in different shades of green. Lights and shadows were entering the dream, offering bright tints, dark or dull shades, endless varieties of the endless green.

MAY 31, 2012

Today, my first moment here that I could call truly sublime, while watching the rain fall down through the canopy: Areas begin to define themselves in terms of glimmer and shine. Some trees move, shiver. Others stand erect, motionless, and indifferent to the life that awakens by the touch of the raindrops. The forest also seems to define itself in terms of flexibility and rigidity.

JUNE 4, 2012

For the third consecutive day, I returned to the same spot. Forms are becoming familiar to me—a small victory. Here's a patch in this endless forest that, perhaps, I can master. Maybe tomorrow I'll move two meters, and maybe a few more in a couple of days.

JUNE 13, 2012

I see a leaf behind the first cluster of trees, popping out from the third or fourth layer of depth. The leaf is moving, rocking, folding as if dancing in the wind. There is no breeze, neither inside nor outside the canopy. Who knows why the leaf moves—there is no clear cause. It no longer makes me paranoid, just curious.

JUNE 18, 2012

400 steps are not the same as 400 steps back home, these steps are made in mud, uneven ground that is covered in roots. The forest changes quite a bit over such a relatively small distance. There are many epiphytes where I am right now. It also feels more humid here. Tree trunks appear to have been burst open by the force of moldy plants. There's a group of noisy birds up and above the canopy; I just saw one with a bright yellow tail.

JUNE 20, 2012

Last morning in the forest. I leave, knowing that there are a few spots in this landscape of unknowing that I have managed to know.

Their Own Stories

KERRI NÍ DOCHARTAIGH

The Irish language views there as being no real difference between what many folk might view as "the otherworld" and this one—of blood and bone. Language matters. The way we speak of something creates ripples. If we trust and believe that things are named based on past occurrences; that the seasons, creatures, and wilderness around us hold their own stories in their core—then it is not too huge of a leap to see a hawthorn tree as a portal. There is wisdom in the things with which we share this earth; in the language we use to speak of them; in the ways we choose to honour both.

Medicine of the Tree People

VALERIE SEGREST

IN OUR MODERN WORLD, CONIFERS AND EVERGREENS ARE USED FOR a spectrum of staples ranging from homesteads to holiday decor, though we rarely stop to recognize the Tree People who provide us these essentials. We can deepen our relationship with them in whatever ways resonate: Sit with them, draw them, pray with them, sing to them, clean up garbage nearby, make an offering, or harvest some boughs and hang them inside your home.

Evergreen trees are brilliantly engineered, manufacturing exactly what they need to be able to live an entire life standing in one place. In spring we see fresh fluorescent green growth emerge from the ends of the evergreen trees. Those tips are full of vitamin C and electrolytes. Simply pinch off the new growth and consider that you are pruning the tree, careful not to take too much. You can eat them fresh or as a woodsy trailside snack. These tips can also be used to prepare a sun tea, or an infused water, making a refreshing, hydrating beverage.

TO MAKE THE SUN TEA:

What deepens a connection to the forest more than tasting it? Enjoy the evergreen's piney, zingy terpenes that bear anti-inflammatory, immune-building, and astringent qualities for our human bodies.

Add 1 cup of fresh evergreen tree tips to a quart jar of room temperature water. Add lemon or lime as an optional ingredient. Place in a warm or sunny spot for 2 to 8 hours. Strain out the water and drink straight or add a splash of maple syrup as a sweetener.

CONIFER SEASONING SALT

½ cup evergreen tree needles (preferably Douglas Fir or Western Hemlock)
1 cup sea salt
Optional: 1 tbsp. pink peppercorns or dried juniper berries
Optional: 1 tsp. lemon or orange peel

Combine all ingredients in a spice grinder. Blend until the salt turns a hint of green and the needles are completely pulverized. Store in a glass jar. Sprinkle on eggs, potatoes, steamed vegetables, fish, chicken.

WARNING: *Properly identify the tree you are harvesting or consult a tree identification expert. Poisonous evergreens are not common, but they do exist. Avoid yew tree species and commercially grown Christmas trees. Edible species include Firs* (Abies spp.), *Hemlocks* (Tsuga spp.), *Spruces* (Picea spp.), *and Douglas Firs* (Pseudotsuga menziesii).

Blad 2 / Leaf 2

ÅSE EG JØRGENSEN

Man blader i bogen, mens at blade i naturen er noget en hjort gør, dens lyd.

Bogen kan have et friblad. Planternes blade bliver frie, når de visner. Så falder bladene af, mens bogens friblad sidder fast.

Et nodeblad kan man synge fra, det hedder sang fra bladet. Det er ikke almindeligt at synge fra andre blade.

Flyveblade er vel nok den selvstændigste form for trykt blad. De kastes nogle gange ned fra luften og bliver båret med vinden, før de lander. Træet slipper bladene om efteråret, og vinden blæser dem andre steder hen.

I dette kompendium ses silhouetter af blade fra følgende planter, nævnt i den rækkefølge de forekommer: pærekvæde, sveskeblomme, hindbær, valnød, vindrue, æble, morel, hassel, brombær, blåbær, figen, stikkelsbær, morbær, ribs, solbær, jordbær.

You can leaf through a book while to peruse leaves in nature is something animals do.

A flyleaf is a blank leaf at the beginning or end of a book. A plant leaf may fly freely in autumn. A leaf in a book is stuck there, unless someone removes it on purpose.

Flyers are probably the most autonomous variety of printed leaf. Sometimes dropped from above and carried by the wind until they land.

As dry leaves hop, skip, and are blown along, they may flitter and flutter like hands leafing through pages of a book; the sound it makes. Leaves of paper and leaves from plants might even get caught up in the same whirling breeze.

This compendium presents a selection of leaf silhouettes in the following order: quince, plum, walnut, grape, apple, morello, hazelnut, fig, gooseberry, mulberry.

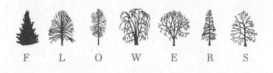

F L O W E R S

&

F R U I T S

Sketch of the Analytical Engine

ADA LOVELACE

WE MAY SAY MOST APTLY, THAT THE ANALYTICAL ENGINE *WEAVES algebraical patterns* just as the Jacquard-loom weaves flowers and leaves.

An Droighneán Donn

The Blackthorn Tree

SUSAN MCKEOWN

Of late I've been captivated by a handsome young man
I am daily complaining for my own darling John
Confuse them consume them who will say I'm not true
Through green groves and lofty mountains I will roam love with you

O down by the river the wild birds sing
O'er mountains and valleys the dewy leaves spring
The wild flowers are shining gazed on by the sun
And fairest of all shines the droighneán donn

If I had a small boat on the ocean to float
I would follow my darling wherever he would go
I would rather my darling to roll, sport and play
Than all the golden treasures by land or by sea

I am constantly waiting for my true love's return
And for his long absence I will never cease to mourn
I will join with the sweet birds till the summer comes on
And I'll be shaded by the green leaves of the droighneán donn

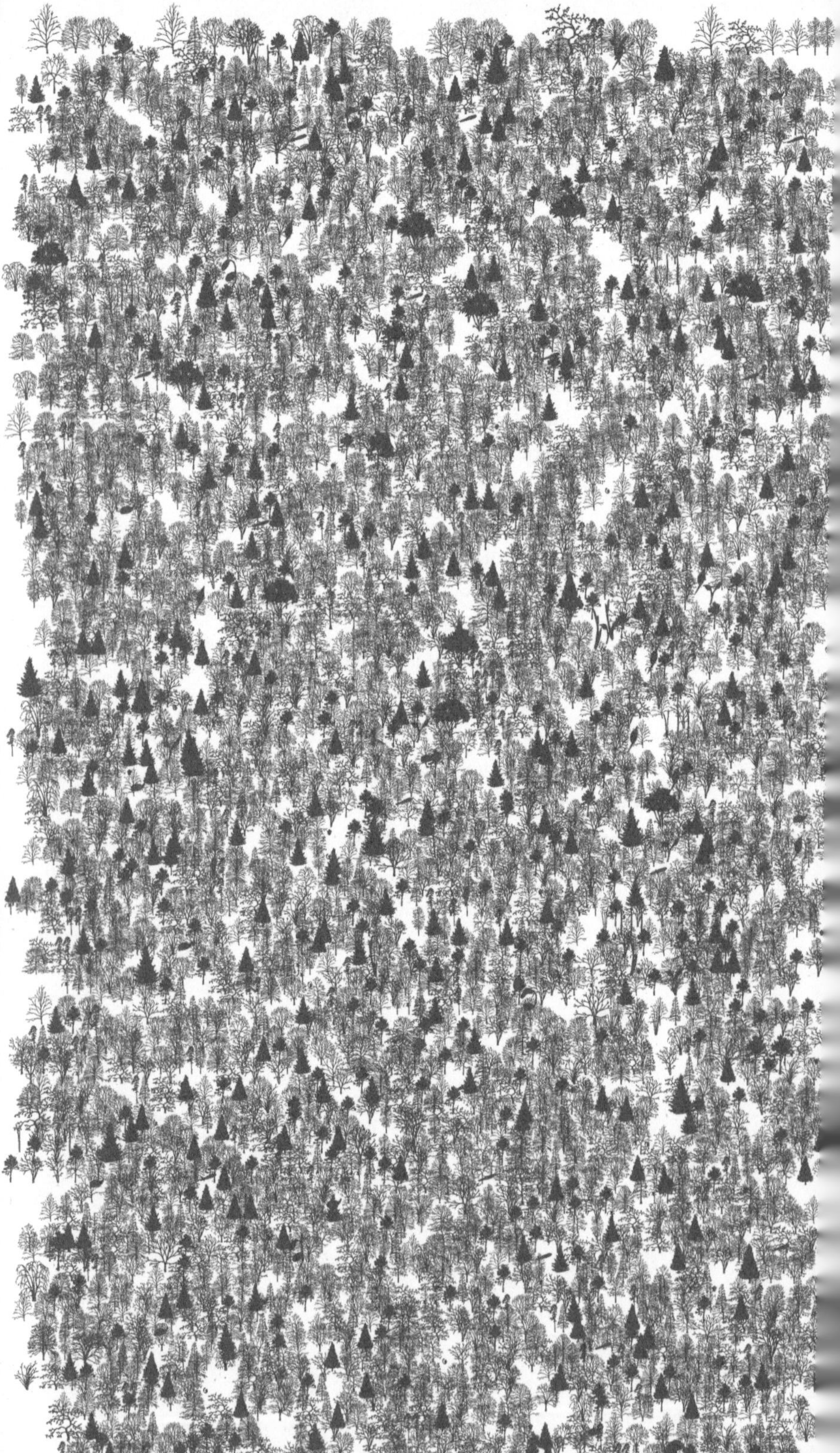

The Tree with the Apple Tattoo

NICOLA TWILLEY

IN A 2011 TALK TITLED "TASTE THE APPLES OF THE FUTURE," CORNELL University professor Susan Brown, one of only three commercial apple breeders in the United States, began with an enticing glimpse of how tomorrow's apples might look: pink-fleshed varieties, pale yellow-skinned chimeras striped with candy-cane red, and the non-browning NY-674, whose resistance to discoloration was discovered by chance during an equipment failure.

Before moving onto her own, more practical work developing higher yielding, earlier fruiting varieties that are resistant to cold storage "scald," Brown also mentioned that in Japan, farmers were already growing apples with built-in branding—the Japanese symbol for "good health" tattooed onto their skin by the sun.

Japan is the home of the $200 square watermelon; it is a country legendarily obsessed with the aesthetics of fruit. In 2007, Cincinnati-based artist Jane Alden Stevens spent four months in Aomori Prefecture, in Japan, documenting the extraordinary attention its orchardists put into growing perfectly beautiful apples. In addition to culling blossoms to reduce over-crowding and ensure regular, large fruit, and then hand-pollinating them using powder-puff wands, Japanese farmers put a double-layer of wax paper bags around their baby apples for most of the growing season.

The bags do double duty, shielding the apples from pests and weather damage while also increasing the skin's photosensitivity. In the autumn, a few weeks before harvest, the bags are removed—first, the outer one, and then, up to ten days later, the translucent inner ones, whose different colors are chosen to filter the light spectrum in order to produce the desired hue on the fruit's sun-deprived pearly white skin.

As they are finally exposed to the elements for the few remaining weeks before harvest, the most perfect of these already perfect apples are then decorated with a sticker that blocks sunlight, in order to stencil an image onto the fruit. This "fruit mark" might be the Japanese kanji for "good health," as Susan Brown mentioned. Others have brand logos (including that of Apple, the company), and some, according to Stevens, are "negatives with pictures.

One Japanese pop star put his picture on apples to give his entourage for presents."

Far from being the apple of the future, however, Stevens told the University of Cincinnati magazine that apple bagging and stenciling is in decline. When she visited Japan in 2007, apple bagging was applied to about thirty percent of the crop, "but fifty years ago, it affected seventy percent," Stevens says. "Farmers do it themselves, but their children aren't following in their footsteps, and there aren't enough laborers to do the work."

What's more, fruit-marking is not even a recent—or an exclusively Japanese—development. I first came across mention of it in Suzanne Freidberg's wonderful book, *Fresh*, which describes the efforts of the nineteenth century fruit-growers of Montreuil to "brand" their apples for the novelty-seeking Parisian luxury market. Wives and children spent their winters folding and gluing thousands of paper bags, and their springtime covering up each individual apple at a rate of up to 3,000 per hour.

The introduction of fruit stencils followed quickly behind, initially applied to the fruit using egg white or bave d'escargot (snail slime). According to Freidberg, particularly ambitious growers also developed negatives on their apples, in a kind of "fruit photography":

> *The marked fruit of the Montreuillois first won renown at the 1894 Saint Petersburg exhibition, where they presented the tsar of Russia with an apple stenciled with his own portrait. King Leopold of Belgium, Edward VII of England, and Teddy Roosevelt received similar fruits.*

The practice of fruit-marking may well have an even earlier source, Freidberg notes, mentioning a reference in an Arabic treatise on agriculture from the twelfth century. Nonetheless, by the 1930s, the practice was all but extinct in France, as Montreuil was absorbed into the Parisian suburbs and an industrializing agricultural sector produced ever-cheaper mass-market fruit.

Today, however, the Société Régionale d'Horticulture de Montreuil appears to be successfully reviving the lost art for today's hobbyists and home gardeners. Their album of recent successes includes swirling dragons and tribal imagery worthy of any would-be Ink Master; a twenty-first century apple is more likely to sport a Che tattoo than a king or tsar.

While bulk growers are unlikely to re-introduce fruit bagging and photography, the technique seems ripe for rediscovery by today's artisanal producers and urban arborists. Banksy could market a line of stencils with which to tag London's fruit trees, small-scale New York growers could develop photographs of local landmarks on their heirloom varieties, and suburban families could entice their children into choosing apples over sweets by imprinting their backyard harvest with cartoon characters.

After all, an apple is art—the raw material of nature sculpted over millennia by humankind's sensory perception and aesthetic appreciation. Why not gild the lily?

Millenniums of Intervention

AMY HARMON

EVEN IN THE HEYDAY OF FROZEN CONCENTRATE, THE POPULARITY of orange juice rested largely on its image as the ultimate natural beverage, fresh-squeezed from a primordial fruit. But the reality is that human intervention has modified the orange for millenniums, as it has almost everything people eat.

Before humans were involved, corn was a wild grass, tomatoes were tiny, carrots were only rarely orange and dairy cows produced little milk. The orange, for its part, might never have existed had human migration not brought together the grapefruit-size pomelo from the tropics and the diminutive mandarin from a temperate zone thousands of years ago in China. And it would not have become the most widely planted fruit tree had human traders not carried it across the globe.

The varieties that have survived, among the many that have since arisen through natural mutation, are the product of human selection, with nearly all of Florida's juice a blend of just two: the Hamlin, whose unremarkable taste and pale color are offset by its prolific yield in the early season, and the dark, flavorful, late-season Valencia.

Because oranges themselves are hybrids and most seeds are clones of the mother, new varieties cannot easily be produced by crossbreeding—unlike, say, apples, which breeders have remixed into favorites like Fuji and Gala. But the vast majority of oranges in commercial groves are the product of a type of genetic merging that predates the Romans, in which a slender shoot of a favored fruit variety is grafted onto the sturdier roots of other species: lemon, for instance, or sour orange. And a seedless midseason orange recently adopted by Florida growers emerged after breeders bombarded a seedy variety with radiation to disrupt its DNA, a technique for accelerating evolution that has yielded new varieties in dozens of crops, including barley and rice.

Its proponents argue that genetic engineering is one in a continuum of ways humans shape food crops, each of which carries risks: even conventional crossbreeding has occasionally produced toxic varieties of some vegetables. Because making a G.M.O. typically involves adding one or a few genes, each containing instructions for a protein whose function is known, they argue, it is more predictable than traditional methods that involve randomly mixing or mutating many genes of unknown function.

But because it also usually involves taking DNA from the species where it evolved and putting it in another to which it may be only distantly related—or turning off genes already present—critics of the technology say it represents a new and potentially more hazardous degree of tinkering whose risks are not yet fully understood.

If he had had more time, Mr. Kress could have waited for the orange to naturally evolve resistance to the bacteria known as *C. liberibacter asiaticus*. That could happen tomorrow. Or it could take years, or many decades. Or the orange in Florida could disappear first.

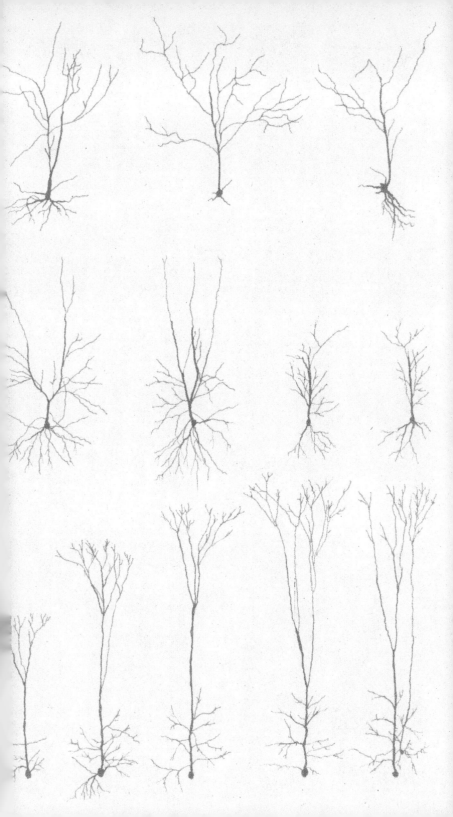

Cacao

The World Tree and Her Planetary Mission

JONATHON MILLER WEISBERGER

HOW CAN A RELATIVELY INCONSPICUOUS UNDERSTORY TREELET BE SO pregnant with wholesome goodness, so full of virtues, and so charged with mythologies? Why is cacao so revered that it has been used as money, medicine, antioxidant-rich superfood, incense, and for a variety of ceremonial offerings—to invoke responses from supernatural beings; to celebrate special moments and calendar markers such as the solstice and equinox; to sanctify weddings and births; to consecrate times of initiations and rites of passage; and as funeral offerings to accompany the dead on the afterlife voyage? When we stretch our imagination to contemplate ancient creation myths that consider cacao not just a gift from the gods to humanity, but an actual component of our identity as humans, we can begin to understand. In the Popol Vuh, the K'iche' Mayan holy book, the gods created humans from Maize and Cacao, along with other foods such as the White Cacao, known as Pataxte, *Theobroma bicolor*; the Soap Apple, known as Zapote, *Manilkara zapota*; Hog Plum or Jocote, *Spondius purpurea*; Golden Spoon, known as Nance, *Brysonima crassifolia*; and the White Sapote, that is Matasano, *Casimiroa edulis*. These narratives speak to the role of plants as an intimate part of the human fabric. Many other Central American creation myths postulate human origins in Cacao. Ancient pottery depicts the Maya great mother Ix Chel, Lady of Translucent Rainbow Light, goddess of medicine, weaving, fertility, and the crescent moon, exchanging Cacao with the rain god Chaac, the patron of agriculture.

This iconography is rooted in the tree's reputation as a conduit between heaven and Earth. To the ancient peoples who grew and adored Cacao, this sacred crop was a Tree of Life uniting the quotidian world with the supernatural realms. The ceremonial consumption and offering of Cacao symbolically connected individuals with the powers that govern their existence, with renewal and rebirth, and with the deities of creation. The bounty of the Cacao tree in Mesoamerica represents abundance, and her rounded fruit symbolize fertility. The deep spiritual meaning of Cacao crystalized her importance in all pre-Colombian societies that knew her. Cacao is a blessed, scrumptious elixir that has shaped and formed societies, igniting creation and urging us to evolve.

Don Memo Morales, an elder of the Costa Rican Brunka tribe, once shared a story with me. *"After the cataclysm, when the Earth was burned by fire, heaven had compassion for humanity, and from the sky dropped seeds of Cacao. From these seeds grew the Cacao tree, and from its ripe pregnant fruit was born the first woman, who gave birth to the first man, and from there the first people came."* Softly, Memo continued, *"In compassion for humanity, the Creator gave the first people three types of Cacao so they could live well: a sweet variety to share and to enjoy in festivals, a simple variety to eat every day as food, and a bitter variety for healing all illness."*

Cacao represents the fragile and delicately interconnected web of life, the majesty of biological diversity. She is the emblem for many great cultures. There are many things that she knows.

Over 3,800 years ago in Central America, Olmec people began cultivating Cacao, which they called Kakawa in their language that seems to be of the Mixe-Zoque family. Though far younger than the Amazonian Mayo-Chinchipe people, the Olmecs were one of the Mesoamerican mother cultures, remembered by colossal stone head carvings and less recognized as the Cacao connoisseurs that they were.

From the Olmecs, the Maya learned skills including jade carving and the cultivation and use of this fascinating plant. The Maya adopted the Olmec name and glyph of Cacao, which shows a head with a fish fin ear looking up, with another fin before the glyph's main features to double accentuate the concept. The word "kakawa" sounds like the Mayan phrase "two fish."

Cultural anthropologist Dr. Michael J. Grofe, in his paper "The Recipe for Rebirth: Cacao as Fish in the Mythology and Symbolism of the Ancient Maya," illuminates a parallel between the self-sacrifice of the Hero Twins, depicted in the the Popol Vuh, and the processing of Cacao. The Hero Twins' entrance into the underworld represents burial and fermentation of Cacao seeds; their burning is the roasting; the grinding of their bones is Cacao seeds ground on a metate, a stone mortar; and their being poured into water represents hydrating the fermented, dried, roasted and ground Cacao into a beverage. The twins are reborn as two fish, offering a provocative insight into the metaphor of Cacao as a potent symbol for rebirth, movement, and water. Fins allow a fish to swiftly move through water as Cacao allows a person to swiftly rise, and Cacao grows in the regions of highest rainfall. The Maya adored Cacao as a primordial element of their way of life, calling it the "World Tree" and the "First Tree." The Mayan beverage chocol'ha gave rise to the modern word, "chocolate."

As full as Cacao is with cultural lore and history, it is with nutrients and minerals. Containing anandamide, a chemical that has almost identical makeup as THC, known as the "bliss molecule," is why drinking Cacao makes you feel happier, while boosting your energy levels. Another peculiar alkaloid in Cacao is theobromine, having similar components as caffeine, but working more on relaxing our hearts. Cacao is also rich in phenethylamine, another alkaloid that our bodies transform into serotonin, that has come to be known as the "good mood hormone," that helps alleviate depression. Cacao's flavonoids make for an ally in the health of the heart, combating heart disease by mending degradation caused by free radicals. These same flavonoids also aid in lowering blood pressure and act as a blood thinner preventing the risk of blood clots.

Driven by a passion for Cacao as a sacred crop, more and more small chocolate-producing companies are transforming the landscape. Appropriately sourced Cacao is filled with the zest of life, rich in antioxidants and minerals, and highly beneficial for human health. Cacao originates in the most biodiverse environment, not to be grown in monocultural plantations, but rather as a member of a diversified garden system. Kallari, as a case example, is an Indigenous people's farmer-owned Cacao cooperative in Amazonian Ecuador, whose mission is "to sustainably improve the economic conditions of local partners and producers through the production, transformation and marketing of mixed agricultural garden products, called chakras, while urging for the preservation of culture and the environment." Cacao calls for an integral restoration and regeneration of humanity's relationship with nature, with the Earth, among people and with our selves. She lends herself as a conduit for an ancient future, one that reaches forward to heal landscapes and redirects our present course by inspiring unity of ancient wisdom with the best of modern-day science.

Cacao's teachings are clear for all to see. Born at the summit of biological megadiversity, she exhorts that we must reach the peak of consciousness—to feel the joys and sorrows of others and of nature as if they were our very own. She teaches that without biological and cultural diversity, we parch the Earth of her essence. That the Earth's divine abundance slips between our fingers back into the void, if taken for granted. This abundance that blesses so many must be cultivated. She gives and wants us to give back. In her silent invigorating essence, she whispers a vital message: Return to a heart-centered way of reciprocity. Who does not serve, does not live. She holds this truth, trembling with humility and compassion, uneased that we risk failing to see things for how they simply are. That we might fall short in awakening our hearts to universal love and appropriate righteous passion, so needed for us to grow, heal and create solutions. These are the healing salves allowing us to remedy the economic, sociocultural, and ecological wounds suppressing humanity and the Earth. Without diversity, there cannot be fertility, nor stability; the triad is fluent and indivisible.

In *The Diversity of Life*, ecologist E.O. Wilson stated, "*The sixth great extinction spasm of geological time is upon us, grace of mankind. Earth has at last acquired a force that can break the crucible of biodiversity.*" We also face tremendous cultural erosion as languages fade from memory.

Cacao whispers a subtle warning: If we don't evolve, we risk certain catastrophe. She has witnessed the rise and fall of many societies and cautions of apocalypse.

From the ancient perspective of the animistic worldview that sees all beings as having a sentient and energetic soul, I imagine that the meditation mat of Kakawa is revealed, in its brilliant patterns highlighted in golden yellow and neon blue. Streaks of richly saturated sapphire, emerald green, glowing red, yellow and silver white light swiftly blow around all sides.

And there are people sitting upon this mat reflecting upon all that Kakawa teaches. And these people are inspired to rise in alignment with universal order, becoming allies to life, being truly human—awake in our fullest potential.

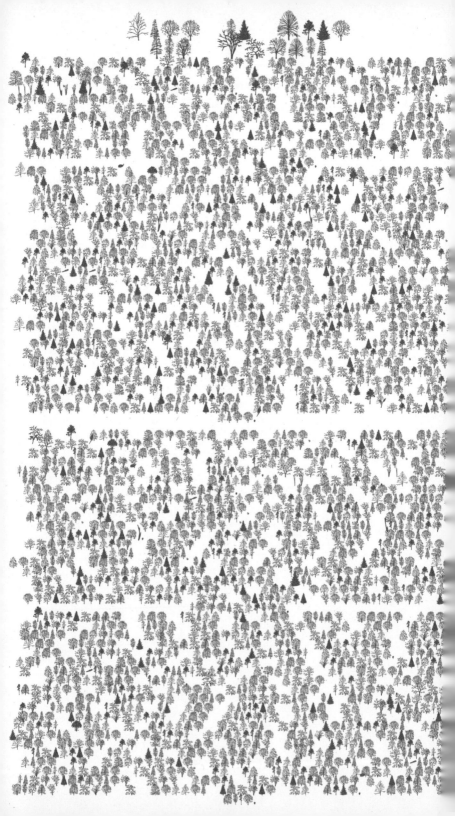

Tree of Life

ROZ NAYLOR

IT WAS EARLY MARCH AND THE RAINS STILL HAD NOT COME. IN THE town of Kalalé in northern Benin, West Africa, the temperature had reached 113°F (45°C) by mid-morning. In quiet desperation, I sought shelter from a nearby moringa tree. To me, it was a small and simple tree, arched toward a field where women with babies on their backs picked weeds from rows of leafy greens. Others, tall and erect, carried plastic buckets of water on their heads. To these women, the moringa tree was anything but simple. It was the tree of life.

The moringa's journey to Benin spans thousands of years. The tree orig- inated in India and spread slowly throughout the tropics and sub-tropics, adapting to local climatic conditions. Today, thirteen species of moringa have been identified around the world (most commonly *M. oleifera*), ranging in size from small herbs to massive trees. Moringa grows quickly, even during droughts and in poor soils. What distinguishes moringa from many other trees is its exceptionally high nutritional value. On a gram-for-gram basis, its leaves contain seven times the vitamin C of oranges, four times the vitamin A of carrots, four times the calcium of milk, and three times the potassium of bananas. Moringa is rich in protein and micronutrients, including iron that protects against anemia.

The list of nutritional and medicinal benefits from the moringa tree reads like a utopian encyclopaedia. It is used to treat conditions as diverse as cholera, diabetes, anxiety, and wounds. Adding moringa leaves to cattle and dairy feeds can increase the daily weight gain of animals by one-third and augment milk production by up to 65%. Other parts of the tree are used in fertilizer and biogas. It is no wonder researchers call the plant a "miracle tree."

As I stood beneath the tree, my local host "Mama" joined me and began to pick leaves and place them in a small bowl. Later, she would grind them into paste to add to her grandchildren's yam porridge. Mama was 51 years old and had given birth to 15 babies. Ten of them were still alive. The others died young, mostly from hunger-related diseases. Throughout the village of Kalalé, small children wore little, if any, clothing, exposing round bellies that were distended from kwashiorkor (protein deficiency). They lived in a world where malnutrition began in the womb and persisted year after year, spiking during the long dry seasons when much of the land was fallow. This type of malnutrition causes permanent physical and cognitive disabilities. For villages like Kalalé, malnutrition of this extent impedes educational gains and economic development for generations.

Ironically, the parts of the world where the moringa tree grows are the same as the places where hunger and malnutrition are most severe. The women of Kalalé are now actively moving the moringa into their farming systems. Only two years before my visit, the village acquired a solar-powered irrigation system to water their vegetable plots. At the same time, they planted moringa trees around the gardens. Mama and her friends were unaware of how farmers in other parts of the tropics, such as Nicaragua, were cultivating the moringa tree as a row crop. Using just a little water and fertilizer, those farmers were reaping multiple harvests each year. The women in Kalalé would soon figure this new practice out for themselves. With the moringa tree in abundance, along with their year-round vegetable gardens, it is possible that their grand-children, and their grandchildren's children, would have a better chance at life. There was hope.

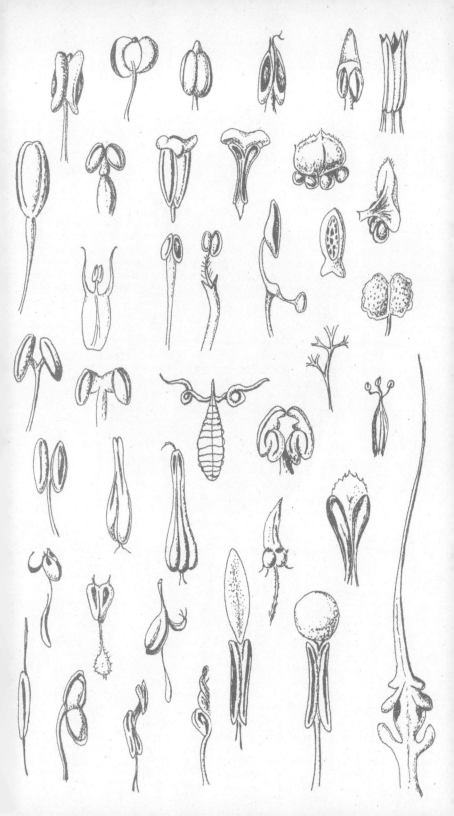

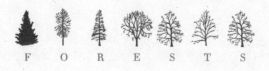

FORESTS

Two Trees Make a Forest

JESSICA J. LEE

I ASKED MY MOTHER TO WRITE OUT THE NAMES OF OUR FAMILY. ON a scrap of paper, she shaped three names:

The first was my grandfather's, Tsao Chung-chin, his name topped with 山 shan, the mountain radical. My grandmother's name, Yang Kwei-lin, was replete with trees: the wood radical 木 mu stood scattered through its syllables. The third name was my own, my surname crowned with its arboreal root 李 li (for "plum"), and my Chinese name, Jie-ke. A stone washed clean by water.

The trees are so tall I can hardly see their branches, their green foliage hanging in flat sprays that droop ever so slightly near their crowns, the way shaggy hair might drape around one's neck. The greenery's sloping shape, held against the military exactitude of the trunks, resembles to me the Chinese character that builds forests: 木 mu (the wood radical). Arboreal 木 spreads wide and tall. And like timber set to work, 木 builds all the words around it: 樹 shu ("tree"), 林 lin ("grove, woods, or forest"), and 森林 senlin ("forest"), the multiplicity of tree shapes indicating the scale of the woodland. 木 carries a vastness of possibility, like the giants in these hills. And at their scale, just two trees would make a forest.

The name of the Swedish botanist Carl Linné—often dubbed the father of modern taxonomy—is rendered in Chinese with the characters 林奈, pronounced "lin nai," meaning "someone related to the forest" or "someone who endures the forest." It seems a small satisfaction that, while in English we have taxonomized his name—calling him Carl Linnaeus—the Chinese, instead, layered in his name a meaning true to botany itself. I think of the wood radical in my own name, 李, and the many that stand in my grandmother's. I find a quiet ease in the notion that forests can be built into who we are.

THE
WORD
FOR
WORLD
IS
FOREST

URSULA K. LE GUIN

from

How Forests Think

EDUARDO KOHN

IF THOUGHTS ARE ALIVE AND IF THAT WHICH LIVES THINKS, THEN perhaps the living world is enchanted. What I mean is that the world beyond the human is not a meaningless one made meaningful by humans.[1] Rather, meanings—means-ends relations, strivings, purposes, telos, intentions, functions and significance—emerge in a world of living thoughts beyond the human to define and control these.[2] More precisely, the forests around Ávila are animate. That is, these forests house other emergent loci of meanings, ones that do not necessarily revolve around, or originate from, humans. This is what I'm getting at when I say that forests think. It is to an examination of such thoughts that this anthropology beyond the human now turns.

If thoughts exist beyond the human, then we humans are not the only selves in this world. We, in short, are not the only kinds of we. Animism, the attribution of enchantment to these other-than-human loci, is more than a belief, an embodied practice, or a foil for our critiques of Western mechanistic representations of nature, although it is also all of these as well. We should not, then, just ask how some humans come to represent other beings or entities as animate; we also need to consider more broadly what it is about these that make them animate.

In many respects the rubber boom that swept through the Amazon was the product of a variety of techno-scientific, "natural-cultural," and imperial conjunctures. That is, the discovery of vulcanization coupled with the invention and mass production of automobiles and other machines catapulted rubber onto an international market. For the Upper Amazon this boom was a sort of

---

1 See Roy Rappaport (1999: for the position that the human species lives "in terms of meaning it must construct in a world devoid of intrinsic meanings but subject to physical law.")

2 That I insist on the centrality of telos as an emergent property inherent to the "enchanted" living world that extends beyond the human puts me at odds with Jane Bennett's (2001) recent reappropriation of enchantment.

second conquest, given that outsiders were dependent, for the most part, on exploiting local populations to extract this increasingly valuable commodity that was dispersed throughout the forest. The boom, however, ended abruptly after rubber seedlings, which had been removed from the Amazon basin by British naturalists, began to take hold in Southeast Asian plantations (see Brockway 1979; Hemming 1987; Dean 1987). This story, told in terms of such interactions among humans, and even among human and nonhuman beings, is well known. Here, I want to discuss something not often noticed: namely, the ways in which the peculiar properties of form mediated all these interactions and made this extractive economic system possible.

Let me explain what I mean. Rubber falls into a form. That is, there is a specific configuration of constraints on the possible distribution of rubber trees. The distribution of rubber trees throughout the Amazon forests— whether the preferred *Hevea brasiliensis* or a few other latex-producing taxa—conforms to a specific pattern: individual rubber trees are widely dispersed throughout the forest across vast stretches of the landscape. Plant species that are widely dispersed stand a better chance of surviving attacks from species-specific pathogen,[3] such as, in the case of *H. brasiliensis*, the fungal parasite *Microcyclus ulei*, which causes the disease known as South American leaf blight. Because this parasite is endemic throughout rubber's natural range, rubber could not be easily cultivated in high-density planta- tions there (Dean 1987: 53–86). An interaction with this parasite results in a particular pattern of rubber distribution. Individual rubber trees are, for the most part, widely and evenly distributed and not clumped in single-species stands. The result is that rubber "explores," or comes to occupy, landscape in a way that manifests a specific pattern. Any attempt to exploit rubber *in situ* must recognize this.[4]

The distribution of water throughout the Amazonian landscape also conforms to a specific pattern or form. This has a variety of causes. Due to a number of global climactic, geographic, and biological factors, there is a lot of

---

3 See Janzen (1970); Wills et al. (1997).

4 My argument about the ways in which the rubber economy was formally constrained is at odds with, but ultimately not inconsistent with, what Steven Bunker has written. Bunker (1985: 68–69) argued that the fungal parasite is not enough to make rubber cropping in the Amazon impossible. Successful grafting and close planting techniques were developed in the Amazon, but these are labor-intensive, and what was lacking in this region was labor. Labor shortages, not parasites, according to Bunker, were what prevented plantation cropping. Surely, the form propagating tendencies that the rubber boom reveals are weak ones, and with sufficient labor they might well become dampened or even irrelevant. But the shortage of labor at this time allowed for certain formal properties to become amplified and to propagate across a variety of domains, and to thus play a central role in the rubber economy.

water in the Amazon basin. Furthermore, water only flows in one direction: downhill. Thus small creeks flow into larger streams, which in turn flow into small rivers that flow into larger ones, and this pattern repeats itself until the enormous Amazon disgorges into the Atlantic Ocean.

For largely unrelated reasons there exist, then, two patterns or forms: the distribution of rubber throughout the landscape and the distribution of waterways. These regularities happen to explore landscape in the same way. Therefore, wherever there is a rubber tree it is likely that nearby there will be a stream that leads to a river.

Because these patterns happen to explore landscape in the same way, following one can lead to the other. The Amazon rubber economy exploited and relied on the similarities these patterns share. By navigating up the river network to find rubber and then floating the rubber downstream, it linked these patterns such that these physical and biological domains became united in an economic system that exploited them thanks to the formal similarities they share.

Humans are not the only ones who link floristic and riverine distribution patterns. The fish known in Ávila as quiruyu,[5] for example, eats fruits of the aptly named tree quiruyu huapa[6] when these fall into rivers. This fish, in effect, uses rivers to get at this resource. In doing so it also potentially propagates the patterned similarities—the form—that floristic and riverine distributions share. If in eating these fruits the fish were to disperse its seeds along the course of the river, then the pattern of this plant's distribution would come to match that of the rivers even more closely.

The Amazon riverine network exhibits an additional regularity crucial to the way rubber was harnessed via form: self-similarity across scale. That is, the branching of creeks is like the branching of streams, which is like the branching of rivers. As such, it resembles the compound ferns that people in Ávila call chichinda, which also exhibit self-similarity across scale. Chinda refers to a haphazard pile, especially to a tangled mass of driftwood such as the kind that might snag around the base of a riverbank tree after a flood. By reduplicating a part of this word—chi-chinda—this plant name captures how in a compound fern the pattern of divisions of the frond at one level is the same as that of the next higher-order level of divisions. Chichinda, which alludes to a tangled

---

5 *Salminus hilarii.*

6 *Virola duckei*, Myristicaceae.

mass nested within another tangled mass, captures this fern's self-similarity across scale; a pattern at one level is nested within the same pattern at a higher more inclusive one.

The river network's self-similarity is also unidirectional. Smaller rivers flow into larger ones, and water becomes increasingly concentrated across an ever smaller expanse of landscape as one moves down the hydrographic network. Da Cunha (1998: 10–11) has highlighted a curious phenomenon in the Juruá River basin during the rubber boom period. A vast network of creditor-debt relations emerged, which assumed a nested self-similar repeating pattern across scale that was isomorphic with the river network. A rubber merchant located at one confluence of rivers extended credit upriver and was in turn in debt to the more powerful merchant located downriver at the next confluence. This nested pattern linked indigenous communities in the deepest forests to rubber barons at the mouth of the Amazon and even in Europe.

Humans, however, are not the only ones who harness the unidirectionally nested riverine pattern. Amazon river dolphins, like traders, also congregate at the confluences of rivers (Emmons 1990; McGuire and Winemiller 1998). They feed on the fish that accumulate there due to this nested characteristic of the river network.

Being inside form is effortless. Its causal logic is in this sense quite different from the push-and-pull logic we usually associate with the physical effort needed to do something. Rubber floated downstream will eventually get to the port. And yet a great amount of work was required to get rubber into this form. It took great skill and effort to find the trees, extract and then prepare the latex into bundles, and then carry these to the nearest stream.[7] More to the point, it took great coercive force to get others to do these things. During the rubber boom, Ávila, like many other Upper Amazonian villages, was raided by rubber bosses looking for slave labor (Oberem 1980: 117, Reeve 1988).

Although stable, form is fragile. It can emerge only under specific circumstances. I was reminded of this when I took a break from writing this chapter to prepare a pot of cream of wheat for my sons. Before my very eyes, the

---

7 For a description of rubber tapping and initial processing and the skill and effort required to get latex to rivers, see Cordova (1995).

tell-tale self-organizing hexagonal structures known as Bénard cells, which form as liquid is heated from the bottom and cooled from the top under just the right conditions, spontaneously emerged across the surface of the simmering cereal. That these hexagonal structures promptly collapsed back into the sticky gruel is testament to form's fragility. Life is particularly adept at creating and sustaining those conditions that will encourage such fragile self-organizing processes to predictably take place (see Camazine 2001). This, in part, is why I have focused here on the ways in which complex multispecies associations cultivate form in ways that also think their ways through us when we become immersed in their "fleshliness."[8]

---

8 There are also all-too-human contexts in which form propagates. Late Soviet socialism provides one such example (see Yurchak 2006, 2008; and my comment on the latter [Kohn 2008]). Here, the severing of official discursive form from any indexical specification—a form that was nevertheless sustained by the entire might of the Soviet state—allowed a certain kind of invisible self-organizing politics to emerge sponta- neously and simultaneously throughout various parts of the Soviet Union. Yurchak appropriately calls this a "politics of indistinction," alluding to the way it harnessed and proliferated official discursive forms (for some sort of an end, however undefined) rather than acquiescing to or resisting them.

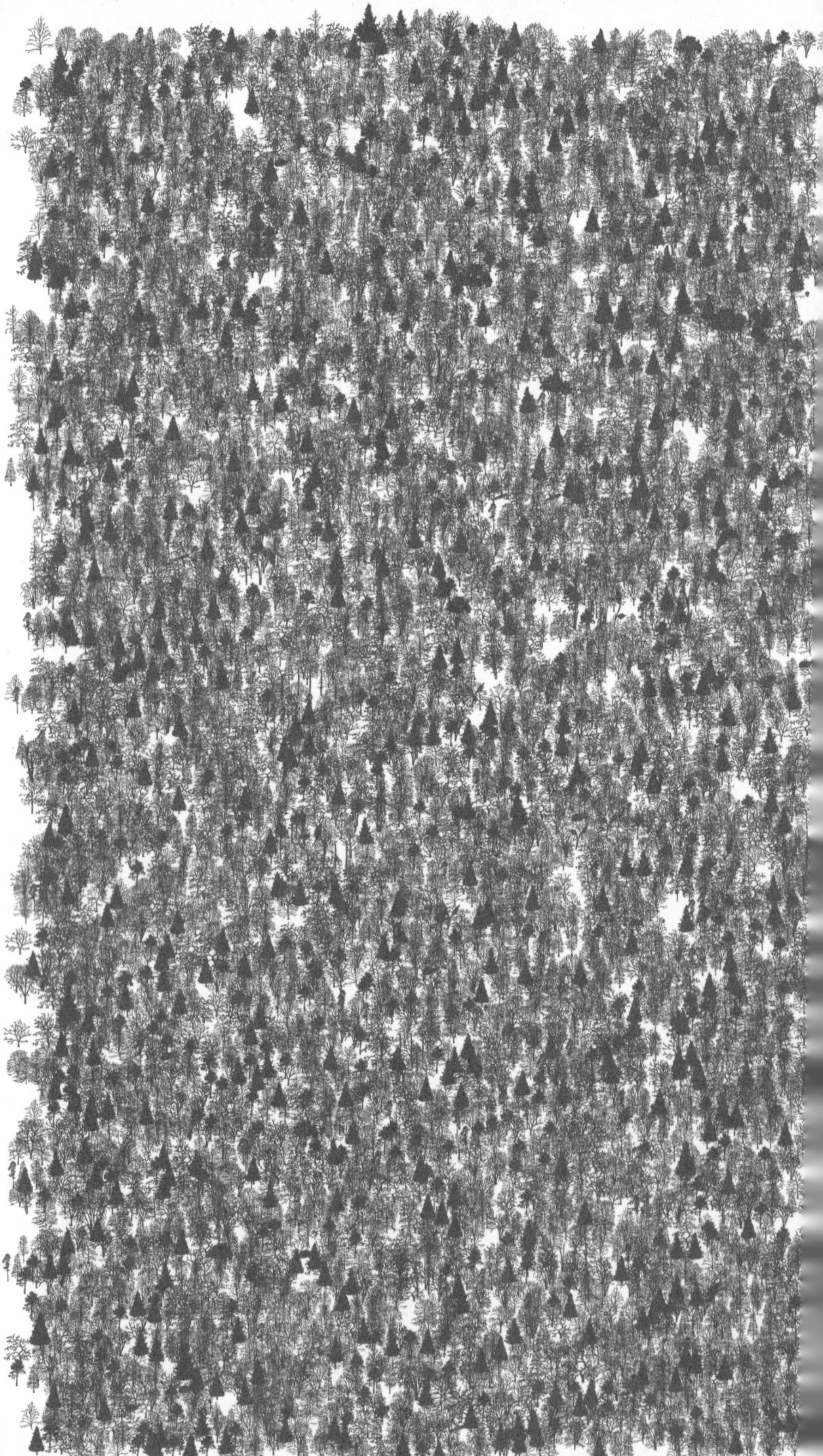

from

Forests

GAIA VINCE

THE PREDICTIONS FOR FOREST COVER DURING THE ANTHROPOCENE are dire—just when we need more rather than fewer trees to soak up humanity's greenhouse gases. Indeed the situation is so critical that some scientists are saying that instead of planting more trees, we need to improve on the tree design altogether, to find a more efficient way of soaking up carbon dioxide from the air. Nature's method, photosynthesis, was developed some three billion years ago, when a type of bacteria first evolved the ability to directly eat the sun, using the energy to make sugars out of the carbon dioxide in the air. It proved a hugely useful adaptation and the bacteria multiplied swiftly and prolifically, filling the air with their poisonous waste product, oxygen. Those organisms that weren't killed by the oxygen soon evolved and profited from it, giving rise to the life on Earth today. Plants relied on the products produced by these bacteria until, at some point 2.6 billion years ago, a plant incorporated the bacterium into its cell, where it carried out the photosynthesis as a part of the plant. Almost all life—including human—relies on the photosynthetic ability of plants to absorb carbon, the essential building block of life, from the air, using the sun for fuel. And the Holocene climate our human civilization evolved into depends on forests to modulate the levels of greenhouse gases in the atmosphere.

I travel to New Jersey to meet a man who believes he can better this process with a forest of artificial trees. Klaus Lackner, director of the Lenfest Center for Sustainable Energy at Columbia University, is an enthusiastic German-born scientist, who, like James Lovelock, came to the field of Earth systems management after a stint at NASA. (Perhaps there is something about studying outer space that makes people realize the preciousness of our home planet.) Klaus is looking at ways to modulate the global temperature by removing carbon dioxide directly from the air just like a leaf does. If it works, it would be one of the few ways of geoengineering the planet with multiple benefits, beyond simply cooling the atmosphere—oceans would become less acidic, for example.

In recent years there have been attempts to remove the carbon dioxide from its source in power plants using scrubber devices fitted to the chimneys. The carbon dioxide can then be cooled and pumped for storage in deep underground rock chambers, replacing the fluid in saline aquifers, for example. Another storage option is to use the gas to replace crude oil deposits, helping drilling companies to pump out oil from hard-to-reach places, in a process known as advanced oil recovery. Removing greenhouse gas pollution from power plants—called carbon capture and storage—is a useful way of preventing additional carbon dioxide from entering the atmosphere as we continue to burn fossil fuels. But what about the gas that is already out there? In a power-plant chimney, carbon dioxide is present at concentrations of as much as 12% of a relatively small amount of exhaust air. Removing the gas takes a lot of energy, so it is expensive, but possible. The problem with removing carbon dioxide from the atmosphere is that it is in such low concentration—just 0.04% of all the gas by volume (or 400 ppm)—and so enormous amounts of air must be processed to remove enough to make a difference, and it would require long-term commitment.[9] As a result, most scientists baulk at the idea.

But Klaus has come up with a technique that could solve the problem. He has designed an artificial tree that soaks up carbon dioxide from the air using 'leaves' that are 1,000 times more efficient than natural leaves. "We don't need to expose the leaves to sunlight for photosynthesis like a real tree does," Lackner explains. "So our leaves can be much more closely spaced and overlapped—even configured in a honeycomb formation to make them more efficient."

The leaves look like sheets of papery plastic and are coated in a resin that contains sodium carbonate, which pulls carbon dioxide out of the air and stores it as a bicarbonate (baking soda) on the leaf. To remove the carbon dioxide, the leaves are rinsed in water vapor and can dry naturally in the wind, soaking up more carbon dioxide.

Klaus calculates that his tree can remove one tonne of carbon dioxide a day. Ten million of these trees could remove 3.6 billion tonnes of carbon dioxide a year—equivalent to about 10% of mankind's annual carbon dioxide emissions. "Our total emissions could be removed with 100 million trees," he says, "whereas we would need 1,000 times that in real trees to have the same effect." Not only are natural trees struggling to grow in the Anthropocene,

---

9   Cao, L., & Caldeira, K., 'Atmospheric carbon dioxide removal: long term consequences and commitment,' Environmental Research Letters 5 (2010), 024011.

planting so many would mean taking up valuable land that could be used to grow food. If the artificial trees were mass-produced they would each cost around the same as a car, he says, pointing out that 70 million cars are produced each year. And each would fit on a truck to be positioned at sites around the world. "The great thing about the atmosphere is it's a good mixer, so carbon dioxide produced in an American city could be removed in the Arabian desert," he says.

The carbon dioxide from the process could be cooled and stored, he says. Many scientists are concerned that even if we did remove all our carbon dioxide, there isn't enough space on Earth to store it securely in saline aquifers or oil wells. But geologists are coming up with alternatives. For example, peridotite, which is a mixture of serpentine and olivine rock, is a great absorber of carbon dioxide, sealing the gas as stable magnesium carbonate mineral. In Oman alone, there is a mountain that contains some 3,000 cubic kilometers of peridotite. Another option could be basalt rock cliffs which contain holes—solidified gas bubbles from the basalt's formation from volcanic flows millions of years ago. Pumping carbon dioxide into these ancient bubbles causes it to react to form stable limestone—calcium carbonate. These carbon dioxide absorption processes occur naturally, but on geological timescales. To speed up the reaction, scientists are experimenting with dissolving the gas in water first and then injecting it into the rocks under high pressures.

However, Klaus thinks the gas is too useful to petrify. His idea is to use the carbon dioxide to make liquid fuels for transport vehicles. Carbon dioxide can react with water to produce carbon monoxide and hydrogen—a combination known as syngas because it can be readily turned into hydrocarbon fuels such as methanol or diesel. The process requires an energy input, but this could be provided by renewable sources, such as wind energy, Klaus suggests.

We have the technology to suck carbon dioxide out of the air—and keep it out—but whether it is economically viable is a different question. Klaus says his trees would do the job for around $200 per tonne of removed carbon dioxide. At that price, it doesn't make financial sense even for oil companies who would pay in the region of $100 per tonne to use the gas in enhanced oil recovery. Ultimately, we have to decide whether the cost of the technology is socially worth the price—and this will continue to be the decider as we innovate more ways to carry out the tasks that the natural world performs for us for free.

Currently, photosynthesis, whether by rainforests, artificial trees or the algal forests of the oceans, represents the only way to return our carbon dioxide levels back to Holocene norms. Further into the Anthropocene, it will become easier and cheaper to remove carbon dioxide at source, and more necessary. We may well see enormous forests of artificial trees cleaning our air. But, as I leave Klaus's lab, my mind carries me back to the huge Amazonian trees that sing with insects and birdlife. Rosa's forest is so much more than an array of carbon-sucking trees—it is life itself. How fickle will our care for forests be, once we discover artificial replacements for these services?

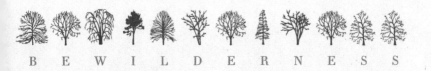

BEWILDERNESS

E.J. MCADAMS

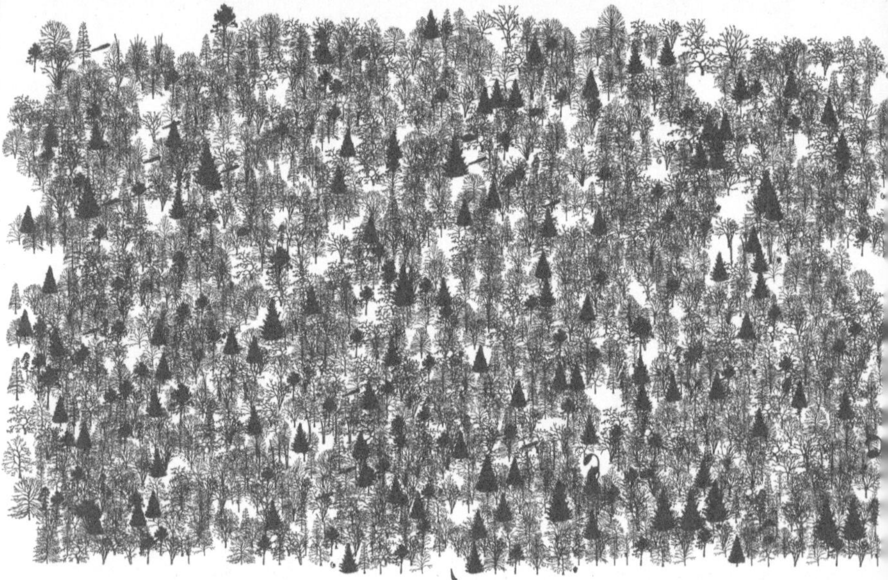

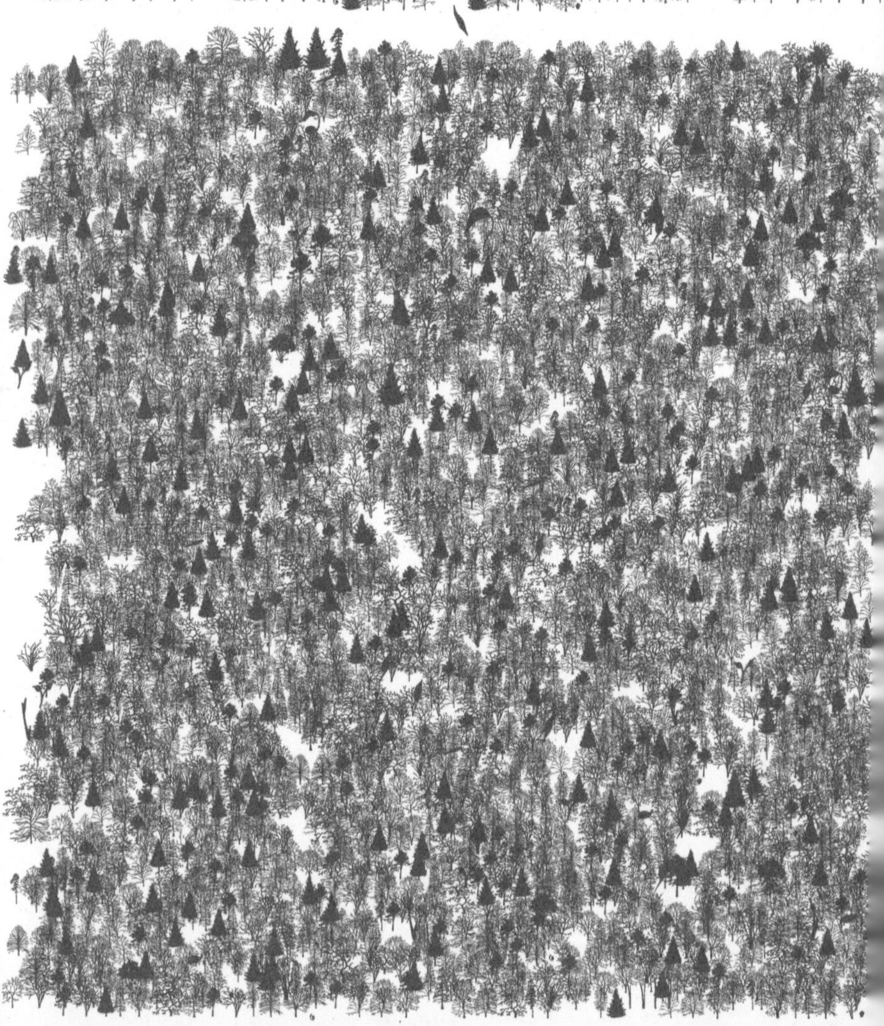

from

Islands on Dry Land

ELIZABETH KOLBERT

BR-174 RUNS FROM THE CITY OF MANAUS, IN THE BRAZILIAN STATE of Amazonas, more or less due north to the Venezuelan border. The road used to be lined with the wreckage of cars that had skidded off to one side or the other, but since it was paved, about twenty years ago, it has become easier to navigate and now, instead of burned-out hulks, there's an occasional café catering to travelers. After an hour or so the cafés give out, and after another hour, there's a turnoff to a single-lane road, ZF-3, that heads due east. ZF-3 remains unpaved, and, owing to the color of the dirt in Amazonas, it appears as a bright orange gash tearing through the countryside. Follow ZF-3 for another three-quarters of an hour and you reach a wooden gate closed with a length of chain. Beyond the gate, some cows are standing around looking sleepy, and beyond the cows is what's known as Reserve 1202.

Reserve 1202 might be thought of as an island at the center of the Amazon. I arrived there on a hot, cloudless day in the middle of the rainy season. Fifty feet into the reserve, the foliage was so dense that even with the sun directly overhead, the light was still murky, as in a cathedral. From a nearby tree came a high-pitched squeal that made me think of a police whistle. This, I was told, was the call of a small, unassuming bird known as a screaming piha. The piha screamed again, then fell silent.

Unlike a naturally occurring island, Reserve 1202 is an almost perfect square. It is twenty-five acres of untouched rainforest surrounded by a "sea" of scrub. In aerial photos it shows up as a green raft bobbing on waves of brown.

Reserve 1202 is part of a whole archipelago of Amazonian islands, all with equally clinical-sounding names: Reserve 1112, Reserve 1301, Reserve 2107. Some of the reserves are even smaller than twenty-five acres; a few are quite a bit bigger. Collectively, they represent one of the world's largest and longest-running experiments, the Biological Dynamics of Forest Fragments Project or, for short, the BDFFP. Pretty much every square foot of the BDFFP has been studied by someone: a botanist tagging trees, an ornithologist banding birds, an entomologist counting fruit flies.

The BDFFP is the result of an unlikely collaboration between cattlemen and conservationists. In the nineteen-seventies, the Brazilian government set out to encourage ranchers to settle north of Manaus, an area that was then largely uninhabited. The program amounted to subsidized deforestation: any ranchers who agreed to move to the rainforest, cut down the trees, and start raising cows would get a stipend from the government. At the same time, under Brazilian law, landholders in the Amazon had to leave intact at least half the forest on their property. The tension between these two directives gave an American biologist named Tom Lovejoy an idea. What if the ranchers could be convinced to let scientists decide which trees to cut down and which ones to leave standing? "The idea was really just one sentence," Lovejoy told me. "I wondered if you could persuade the Brazilians to arrange the fifty percent so you could have a giant experiment." In that case, it would be possible to study in a controlled way a process that was taking place in an uncontrolled fashion all across the tropics, indeed across the entire world.

Lovejoy flew to Manaus and presented his plan to the Brazilian officials. Rather to his surprise, they embraced it. The project has now been running continuously for more than thirty years. So many graduate students have trained at the reserves that a new word was coined to describe them: "fragmentologist." For its part the BDFFP has been called "the most important ecological experiment ever done."

Currently, about fifty million square miles of land on the planet are ice-free, and this is the baseline that's generally used for calculating human impacts. According to a recent study published by the Geological Society of America, people have "directly transformed" more than half of this land—roughly twenty-seven million square miles—mostly by converting it to cropland and pasture, but also by building cities and shopping malls and reservoirs, and by logging and mining and quarrying. Of the remaining twenty-three million square miles, about three-fifths is covered by forest—as the authors put it, "natural but not necessarily virgin"—and the rest is either high mountains or tundra or desert. According to another recent study, published by the Ecological Society of America, even such dramatic figures understate our impact. The authors of the second study, Erle Ellis of the University of Maryland and Navin Ramankutty of McGill, argue that thinking in terms of biomes defined by climate and vegetation—temperate grasslands, say or boreal forests—no longer makes sense. Instead, they divide the world up into "anthromes." There is an "urban" anthrome that stretches over five hundred thousand square miles, an "irrigated cropland" anthrome (a million square miles), and a "populated forest" (four and a half million square miles). Ellis and Ramankutty count a total of eighteen "anthromes," which together extend over thirty-nine million square miles. This leaves outstanding some eleven million square miles. These areas, which are mostly empty of people and include stretches of the Amazon, much of Siberia and northern Canada, and significant expanses of the Sahara, the Gobi, and the Great Victoria deserts, they call "wildlands."

But in the Anthropocene it's not clear that even such "wildlands" really deserve to be called wild. Tundra is crisscrossed by pipelines, boreal forest by seismic lines. Ranches and plantations and hydroelectric projects slice through the rainforest. In Brazil, people speak of the "fishbone," a pattern of deforestation that begins with the construction of one major road—by this metaphor, the spine—that then leads to the creation (sometimes illegal) of lots of smaller, riblike roads. What's left is a forest of long, skinny patches. These days every wild place has, to one degree or another, been cut into and cut off. And this is what makes Lovejoy's forest fragment experiment so important. With its square, completely unnatural outline, Reserve 1202 represents, increasingly, the shape of the world.

Ghost Forest

MAYA LIN

THROUGHOUT THE WORLD, CLIMATE CHANGE IS CAUSING VAST tracts of forested lands to die off. They are called ghost forests; they are being killed off by rising temperatures, by extreme weather events that yield saltwater intrusion, forest fires, infestation by insects whose populations thrive in these warmer temperatures, and trees that, overstressed from these rising temperatures, are more susceptible to beetles. In southwestern Colorado, where my family and I live in the summer, these forests—killed off by beetles—are all around us.

As I approached thinking about a sculptural installation for Madison Square Park, I knew I wanted to create something that would be intimately related to the park itself, the trees, and the state of the Earth. Being more accustomed to making permanent large-scale works out of earth and grass, I felt a different path had to be taken, to create something transient and temporal rather than like my permanent works. It is not a time frame I am familiar with in my outdoor installations.

I had first considered bringing a living willow walk to the park—but the more I explored and thought about this, I could not stop looking at the ghost forest right outside my Colorado studio, which looks out onto national forest lands. I wanted to bring a ghost forest to the heart of Manhattan—and to find trees that were as close to Manhattan as possible. I wanted to connect you to something that was affected by climate change nearest to us.

I wanted to be respectful of the distance we would need to travel the trees and the team. I also did not want to bring a non-native tree into the city, and each tree was carefully inspected for insects before being transported to the site.

In the Pine Barrens of New Jersey we were able to locate large stands of Atlantic white cedars that had died off because of extreme weather events related to climate change, wind, fire, sea-level rise, saltwater infiltration, and bad forestry practices. Atlantic white cedars, once a dominant species along the Atlantic seaboard, have been reduced to under ten percent of their original habitat. Foresters we were working with located an area that was about to be cleared as part of a restoration project on private lands of just such a forest stand. The owner had chosen to clear the dead or compromised cedars to allow for regeneration of the trees, since cedars need open light to repopulate.

We have very little time left to alter our climate change emission patterns and our way of living within the natural world. I wanted to bring awareness to a die-off that is happening all over the world. I feel that a potential solution lies in nature-based practices—changing our forestry practices, reforming our agricultural and ranching practices, and increasing our wetlands. These nature-based solutions can offset and sequester more than fifty percent of the world's emissions and would help protect and ensure that the Earth's biodiversity is increased and restored.

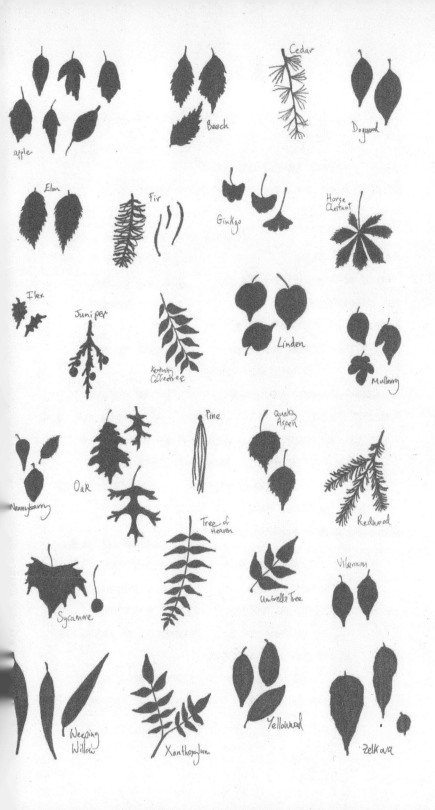

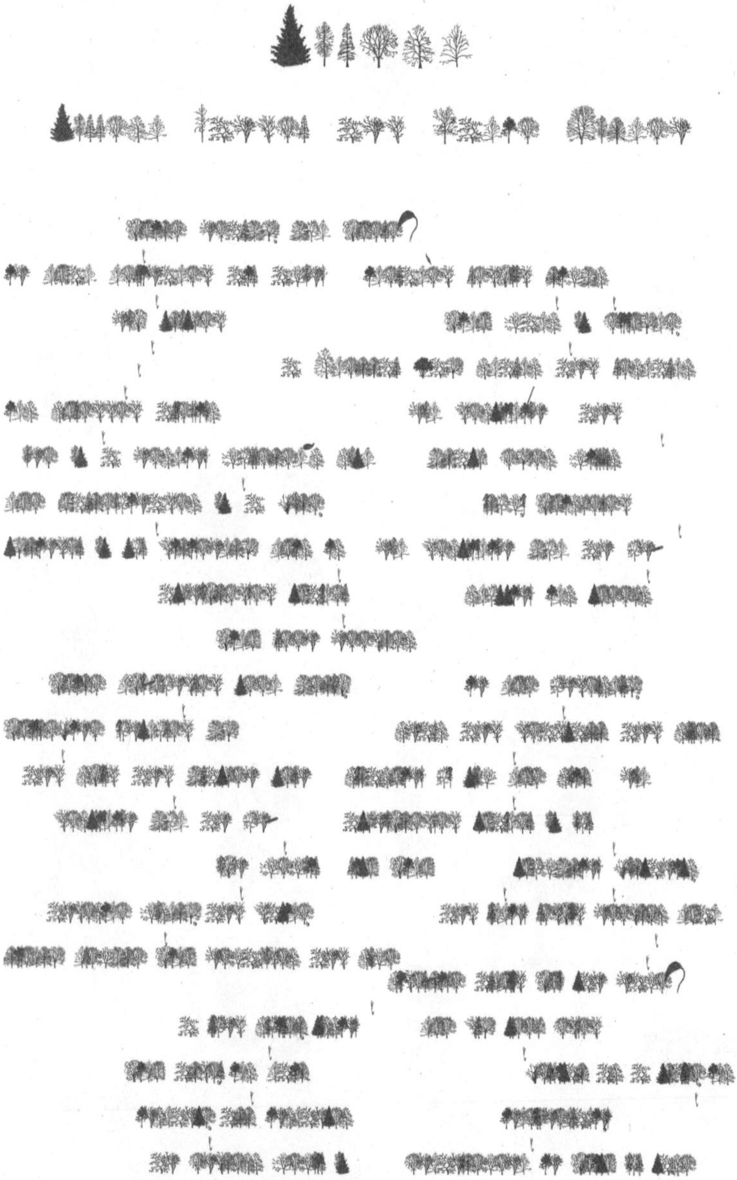

Forest

FORREST GANDER AND KATIE HOLTEN

while nearby, but where?
/ \
in that terpinated air among   iterated redwood limbs
\   / \
now flocked   with mats of epiphyte,
/ |
/   a Stellar jay starts and restarts
/   /
its shredded arpeggios—   *not description*— and
\   \
one of a nesting murrelet's soft   black eyes mirrors
/
the harlequinades of a vole,   plump, whiskered
\ |
cylinder of fur diligently— *this is*   *not description but an un-*
\   /
acknowledged chapter—   stuffing its cheeks
/
with green needles

while two-hundred feet below,   in the understory,
/   /
whipplevine punctured by   snags and deadfall and sorrel
| /
and sword and bracken fern   splashing up from the soil— *not*
\   \
description but an un-   *acknowledged chapter of our*
\   /
own memoir— rich with   chumbling volcanics,
/   \ /
andesite mostly, and dacite,   and rotting redwood needles that
\   /
lightly tremble with nematodes and some   /
spider-like arthropod who can name?

\
a ground squirrel, crossing   the dry creek edged
/   \
with alder, its tail   vertical as a flagpole, *its*
/   \
instance, all instances   *interpenetrating,*
\   /
an endless memoir of   *entanglement in which our case*
\   \
likewise has been underwritten—   \
| /
careens between   its burrow and fire caves in
/   /
the massive redwood trunks   glistening with slug trails, rimmed
\ |
by rooting mushrooms

FAMILY

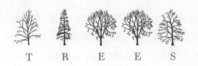

TREES

Being

TANAYA WINDER

Wake up, greet the sun, and pray.
Burn cedar, sweet grass, sage—
sacred herbs to honor the lives we've been given,
for we have been gifted these ways since the beginning of time.
Remember, when you step into the arena of your life,
think about those who stand beside you, next to, and with you.
Your ancestors are always in your corner, along with your people.
When we enter this world we are born hungry,
our spirits long for us to live out our traditions
that have been passed down for generations.
Prayer, ceremony, dance, language—our ways of being.
Never forget you were put on this Earth for a reason—
honor your ancestors.
Be a good relative.

Brutes

Meditations on the myth of the voiceless

AMITAV GHOSH

SCIENTISTS NOW ACCEPT THAT TREES IN A FOREST ARE ABLE TO communicate with one another in certain circumstances—they can send help, in the form of carbon, to ailing members of their group; and they can warn one another about pestilence and disease. It is now thought that certain plants can even emit sounds that are inaudible to the human ear but are audible to some other living things. So it is only in that they lack language—a human attribute—that trees are mute. But in that humans lack the ability to communicate as trees do, could it not be said that for a tree it is the human who is mute?

It may seem obvious to humans that their ability to destroy trees and forests endows them, and them alone, with the capacity to act. But intentional action can also unfold over completely different scales of time. Trees have inhabited Earth much longer than human beings, and their individual life spans are, in many cases, far greater than those of people: some live for thousands of years. If trees possessed modes of reasoning, their thoughts would be calibrated to a completely different timescale, perhaps one in which they anticipate that most humans will perish because of a planetary catastrophe. The world after such an event would be one in which trees would flourish as never before, on soil enriched by billions of decomposing human bodies. It may appear self-evident to humans that they are the gardeners who decide what happens to trees. Yet, on a different timescale, it might appear equally evident that trees are gardening humans.

But perhaps this is all wrong? After all, trees and humans are not—or not just—adversaries competing for space. They are also linked by innumerable forms of cooperation. Perhaps what is at fault here is the very idea of a single species. It is now known that the human body contains vast numbers of microorganisms of various kinds; biologists estimate that 90 percent of the human body consists of bacteria, rather than human cells, and one microbiologist has suggested that under a microscope a human body looks like a coral reef, "an assemblage of life-forms living together." It is known also that micro-organisms influence moods, emotions, and the human ability to reason. So if it is true that the human ability to speak, and think, can only be actualized in the presence of other species, can it really be said that these faculties belong exclusively to humans?

Recent research in biology has shown that many species do not evolve singly: bacteria are critical to the survival of animals of all kinds, including humans. "More and more," according to a team of biologists, "symbiosis appears to be the 'rule,' not the exception. Nature may be selecting 'relation-ships' rather than individuals or genomes." Many organisms are born without the bacteria that are essential for them to attain adulthood; they must encounter those bacteria in the world—and without those meetings they are unable to fully realize their potential.

Could it not be said of humans too that the presence of certain other species, in specific moments of encounter, has enabled *Homo sapiens* to transcend their limitations? Take for instance that landmark moment in the history of consciousness when the Buddha attained Enlightenment: this event occurred, as is well known, while the Buddha was meditating under a Bodhi tree. Within the Buddhist tradition, for more than two thousand years, the presence of this tree has been inseparable from that moment. This is not to say that the tree transmits illumination, or even that it is an active participant in the process. Nor is it at all the case that everyone who meditates under a Bodhi tree will achieve Enlightenment.

Yet it has long been accepted, by many millions of people, that a trans-species encounter, at a specific historical juncture, was essential to the Enlightenment of one particular human, Prince Siddhartha Gautama. The Buddha himself believed the tree to be essential to his attaining Enlightenment, which is why millions of Buddhists consider the Bodhi tree sacred to this day. In the words of the Dalai Lama:

> *Under a tree was the great Sage Buddha born.*
> *Under a tree, he overcame passion*
> *And attained enlightenment*
> *Under two trees did he pass into Nirvana.*

It would seem then that the idea that humans are the only storytelling animals is by no means an unproblematic reflection of reality. It is something that some people like to believe, just as some once believed that most humans were brutes and thus incapable of making meaning. It is, in other words, a construct, one that is intimately connected with structures of power and with the forceful repression of the awareness of nonhuman forms of agency and expression. Not surprisingly, in this matter, too, the hand of power has often fallen hardest on Indigenous people.

It is perfectly possible, then, that far from being an exclusively human attribute, the narrative faculty is the most *animal* of human abilities, a product of one of the traits that humans indisputably share with animals and many other beings—attachments to place. Perhaps, then, storytelling, far from setting humans apart from animals, is actually the most important residue of our formerly wild selves. This would explain why stories, above all, are quintessentially the domain of human imaginative life in which nonhumans had voices, and where nonhuman agency was fully recognized and even celebrated. To make this leap may be difficult in other, more prosaic domains of thought, but it was by no means a stretch in the world of storytelling, where anything is possible.

The shrinking of the possibilities of this domain, and the consequent erasure of nonhuman voices from "serious" literature, has played no small part in creating that blindness to other beings that is so marked a feature of official modernity. It follows, then, that if those nonhuman voices are to be restored to their proper place, then it must be, in the first instance, through the medium of stories.

This is the great burden that now rests upon writers, artists, filmmakers, and everyone else who is involved in the telling of stories: to us falls the task of imaginatively restoring agency and voice to nonhumans. As with all the most important artistic endeavors in human history, this is a task at once aesthetic and political—and because of the magnitude of the crisis that besets the planet, it is now freighted with the most pressing moral urgency.

Trophic Cascade

CAMILLE T. DUNGY

After the reintroduction of gray wolves
to Yellowstone and, as anticipated, their culling
of deer, trees grew beyond the deer stunt
of the mid century. In their up reach
songbirds nested, who scattered
seed for underbrush, and in that cover
warrened snowshoe hare. Weasel and water shrew
returned, also vole, and came soon hawk
and falcon, bald eagle, kestrel, and with them
hawk shadow, falcon shadow. Eagle shade
and kestrel shade haunted newly-berried
runnels where mule deer no longer rummaged, cautious
as they were, now, of being surprised by wolves. Berries
brought bear, while undergrowth and willows, growing
now right down to the river, brought beavers,
who dam. Muskrats came to the dams, and tadpoles.
Came, too, the night song of the fathers
of tadpoles. With water striders, the dark
gray American dipper bobbed in fresh pools
of the river, and fish stayed, and the bear, who
fished, also culled deer fawns and to their kill scraps
came vulture and coyote, long gone in the region
until now, and their scat scattered seed, and more
trees, brush, and berries grew up along the river
that had run straight and so flooded but thus dammed,
compelled to meander, is less prone to overrun. Don't
you tell me this is not the same as my story. All this
life born from one hungry animal, this whole,
new landscape, the course of the river changed,
I know this. I reintroduced myself to myself, this time
a mother. After which, nothing was ever the same.

Catalpa Tree

Catalpa speciosa

AIMEE NEZHUKUMATATHIL

A CATALPA CAN GIVE TWO BROWN GIRLS IN WESTERN KANSAS A green umbrella from the sun. *Don't get too dark, too dark*, our mother would remind us as we ambled out into the relentless midwestern light. Every day after school, the bus dropped me and my younger sister off at Larned State Hospital, and every day, our classmates stared at us as the bus pulled away. I'd unlock the door to the doctor's quarters with a key tied to my yarn necklace and we'd go inside, fix ourselves snacks, and finish worksheets on fractions or spelling. We'd wait till our mom called to say we could meet her in her office, a call that meant she was about ten minutes away from being done for the day. We'd click off the TV and scramble to get our plastic jelly sandals on for the block-long walk to the hospital's administration building. Catalpa trees dotted the wide prairie grounds and watched over us as we made our way to Mom's office. My sister and I knew not to go anywhere near the fence line of the patients' residence because they sometimes were given basketball privileges outside, behind three layers of barbed wire. But occasionally I allowed myself to look at them when I rode my maroon three-speed bike, and sometimes an inmate would wave as I passed.

Catalpas stand as one of the largest deciduous trees at almost sixty feet tall, and dangle long bean pods and flat seeds with wings to help them fly. These bean pods inspire some to call the catalpa cigar tree, trumpet creeper, or catawba. Catalpa trees can help you record the wind as it claps their giant heart-shaped leaves together—leaves with spit curls, not unlike a naughty boy from a fifties movie, whose first drag race ends in defeat and spilled milkshakes. But these leaves can make a right riot of applause on a particularly breezy day. A catalpa planted too close to a house is a calamity just waiting to happen, but perhaps some people think the danger isn't too menacing since catalpas also yield good tone wood for guitars. And who would challenge that song out there on the plains?

All those songs call out to the sphinx moth, who lays about five hundred half-millimeter eggs at a time on the catalpa's leaves. These leaves are the moth's only source of food, and if left unchecked, the caterpillars can completely defoliate a single mighty tree. Kids in the Central Plains know these "worms" as good spending money. The sphinx caterpillars (also known as "catfish candy") make prized fishing bait; catfish and bluegill gobble them without seeming to get the least bit suspicious about their sudden appearance in the water.

Sometimes, before we left to pick up our mom, my sister and I gathered coins for the vending machine in the lobby of her office. In 1986, a Little Debbie brownie cost a precious thirty-five cents—precious because what little allowance we received was inconsistent, and so we couldn't count on it for gummy bracelets stacked up my arm in imitation of Madonna, or for the occasional ninety-nine-cent ice cream sandwich at Dairy Queen, or to save up for another colorful pair of jelly sandals. We were known as the daughters of the new doctor in that sleepy little county, but my mom made sure we weren't spoiled, unlike most of her coworkers' kids—children who had six or seven pairs of the latest high-tops, or were already talking about what luxury sports car would be their first. Extravagance, then, was the occasional afternoon when my sister and I found just enough to split a brownie between us. After greeting the receptionist, riding the elevator up a few stories, and walking past the patients' pool tables and lounge, we'd greet our mother with bits of chocolate in our smiles. *Cavities, cavities!* she'd cluck at us, dropping whatever she was doing to hug and kiss us hello. I only pieced it together years later—how her day was spent trying to help patients who often hurled racist taunts and violent threats against her, like *Get out of here, Chink*, or *I'll choke you with my own hands!*

I can't believe how she managed the microaggressions of families who told her that they couldn't understand her accent, who spoke loud and slow at her, like she—the valedictorian of her class, the first doctora of her tiny village in northern Philippines—was a child who couldn't understand. But my mother always kept her calm, repeating recommendations and filing reports without losing her temper. How did she manage to leave it all behind in that office, switching gears to listen to the ramblings of her fifth and sixth-grade girls with their playground dramas, slights, and victories? I don't remember her talking about work while she walked home, changed out of her stylish suits, or fixed us hot meals from scratch. I only knew of what she regularly had to suffer because I'd sneak into and skim over her journals while she was in the shower or brushing her teeth. If not for those little peeks, I never would have known what she had to endure that year.

Thirty years later, I find myself underneath the largest catalpa tree in Mississippi. This tree is one of the centerpieces of the famous "tree walk" at the University of Mississippi, where I now teach. Its branches stretch horizontally to nearly the length of a bus, and have to be reinforced by metal supports in several areas so the branches that are soft and starting to get mushy at the center don't fall on an unsuspecting coed. The foot-long leaves of catalpa trees like this one, for me, always meant shade from persistent sun and shelter from unblinking eyes. When I moved to the South, I thought I'd need to make use of those wide leaves constantly, but for the first time in my life, I haven't had to. And for the first time in their young lives, my kids see brown people other than me on a daily basis. Nobody stares at me here in the South. No one stares at my parents when they visit, or when they're at home now in central Florida. In their backyard, my parents spend their retirement crafting an elaborate garden, planting trees with much smaller leaves, and one of their great joys is to tend to the trees after a daily walk. To tug off any dead leaves or branches, pruning them just so, more orderly than any haircut they've ever given me. When I visit, one of my favorite things is to walk among the fruit trees with my mother while she regales me with all the tree-drama that's occurred since I was last there: *Can you believe all the flowers fell off this tree during the last hurricane? Too bad—no mangoes this year. Here is the tree where the vanda orchid grows best, remember? I told your father the birds are going to steal everything on this tree and he didn't listen, can you imagine?*

On campus, when I pass the giant catalpa tree, I think of that shy sixth grader who was so nervous when people stared. But then I remember the confident clickety-clack of my mother's heels as she walked home from work with me and my sister—when people would stare at us but my mother didn't seem to mind or notice. I remember her radiant smile when we burst through her office door, and then her laugh as she listened to our tales of the lunchroom and gym dramas of the day. I hear my own heels as I rush to meet my first class. The campus catalpa offers up its creamy blossoms to the morning, already sultry and humid at nine o'clock in the morning. It still stands, even through the two or three tornado warnings we've had just this first windy year in Mississippi. As I pass the enormous tree, I make note of which leaves could cover my face entire if I ever needed them again. If I ever needed to be anonymous and shield myself from questions of *What are you?* and *Where are you from?* I keep walking. My students are waiting. My sweet southern students, who insist on calling me "Ma'am," no matter how much I gently protest. And I can't wait to see their beautiful faces.

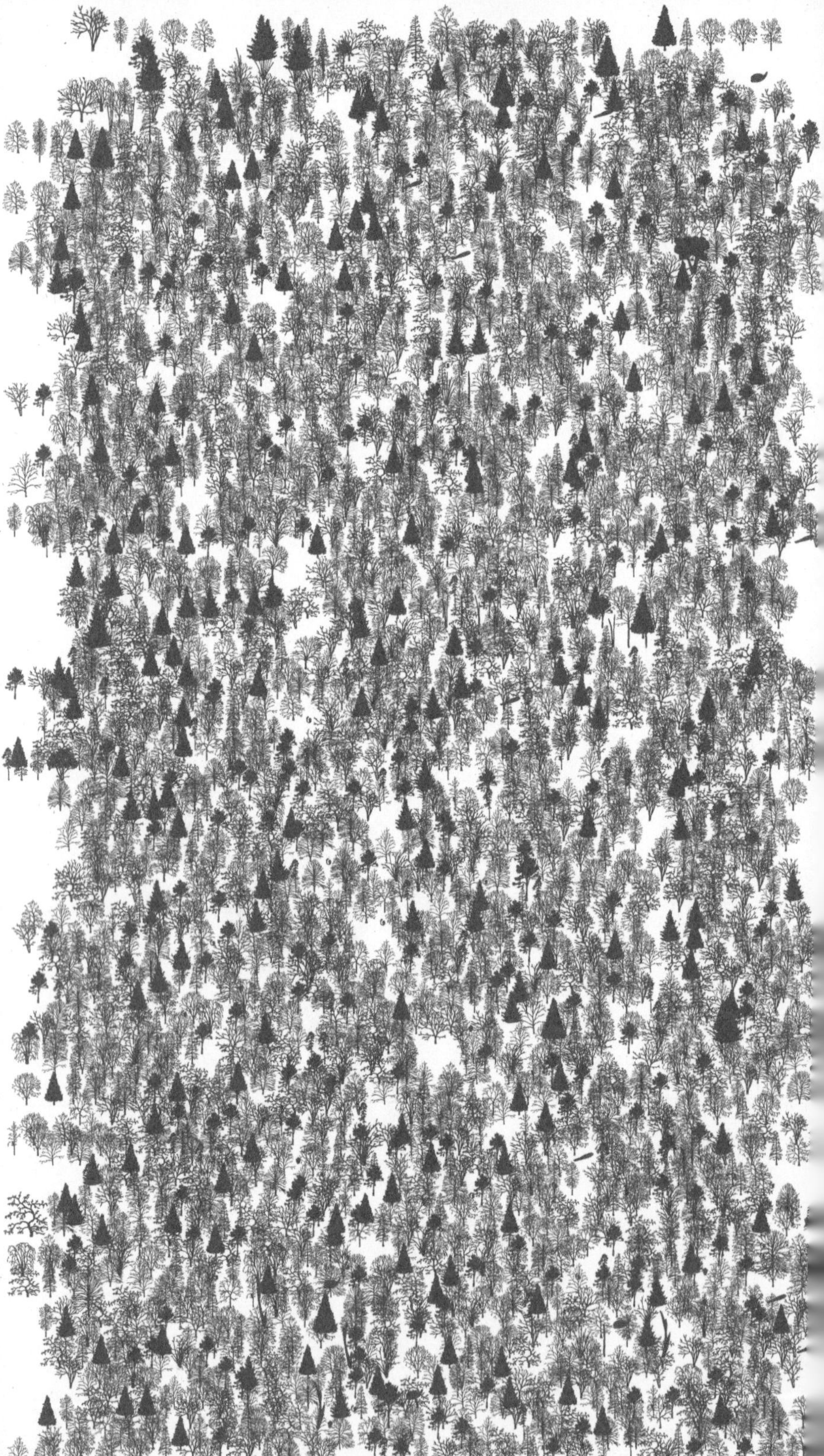

Notes for a Salmon Creek Farm Revival

FRITZ HAEG

IN 1971 SALMON CREEK FARM WAS FOUNDED AS A COMMUNE LESS than two miles from California's Mendocino coast in Albion. 33 acres of second-growth Redwoods slope to the south from a meadow and fruit orchard on top, to Big Salmon Creek in the valley. A small community cottage in the orchard is followed by seven owner-built cabins secluded on footpaths throughout the property, three small abandoned cabins hidden in the wilds across a tributary that bisects the land, an octagonal sauna on its last legs, various out-houses and out-buildings, and the remains of historic commune structures buried deep in the woods.

It was established by a group of young people looking for something else, craving more than what mainstream culture was offering them. This commune, along with many others in this region at the time, grew out of the student protest culture of the late 60s, by those disenchanted with the society they were inheriting from previous generations. They were resisting the war and general mindless consumer conformity, while promoting issues like civil rights and environmental consciousness. Turning their back on systems they no longer believed in, they learned how to build their own homes, make their own clothes, grow their own food while living communally and practicing consensus decision-making.

One by one the original founders moved away—three of whom set-tled on three sides of the property—until an official closing ceremony was held in 2012. With the purchase of Salmon Creek Farm in November 2014 we start a new chapter as a sanctuary, continuing as a place to take a step back from contemporary society. An informal colony of an extended expanding revolv-ing community of artists, crafts-people, cooks, dancers, designers, farmers, gardeners, makers and writers help to revive the wild and cultivated land and 11 cabins while pursuing their own projects responding to the unique qualities of the place.

Building upon its special legacy, visiting artists are offered an experi-mental home away from home with a critical distance from their daily lives, to take a breath, to gather their thoughts, to consider other ways of living, to engage more deeply with the land and each other. Instead of a fixed group of permanent residents, there is a steady flow of friends coming, going, and returning, from distinguished elders to curious youth. Their experiences, work and contributions constantly building on those who came before. New arrivals and ideas breathe life into the place, while those departing take a piece of it back home with them. The precise nature of Salmon Creek Farm is ultimately determined by whoever happens to be together there at any given moment.

The revival begins with researching its social and ecological history, exploring the land and structures to understand what is there, fixing up the cabins, establishing food gardens and generally bringing new life to the place. Visiting builders, carpenters, crafts-people, farmers, gardeners, makers, permaculturists, woodworkers stay in cabins while contributing to the revival of the structures and land. Also ceramicists, cooks, dancers, foragers, furniture makers, musicians, oven builders, sign makers, textile artists, weavers, wood carvers, etc. But right now the first priorities are the cabins, waiting to be brought back to life.

Later we'll welcome book-makers (to revive a version of Times Change Press, which was housed in one of the structures in the 70s) and archivists (to create an on-site archive of both our new life on the land and the historic commune, with materials, artifacts and accounts from the original communards). I'm not exactly sure what this place will become, but it will be determined in large part by these early pioneering visitors.

We Are the ARK

MARY REYNOLDS

ONE FINE MORNING LAST YEAR, I WAS SITTING AT MY DESK LOOKING out over my garden when something happened that made me realize how we can all become part of the solution to the crisis we are facing with nature.

A fox ran across the garden. Then two hares. Soon after, I lifted my head to see a family of hedgehogs scuttle along the edge of the hedgerow. All these creatures were running away from something and it was like the reverse of the Ark stories I had heard as a kid. When I went to investigate what was happening, it turned out that the neighboring field across the road was being cleared by a digger. A house was being built at the top of the field and the owners had gone in and cleared out years of growth. Brambles, bracken and a thicket of thorny trees and plants that was a home for many families were wiped out in an instant. All these families had suddenly lost their homes and they had to move into a wild field beside my garden which already housed a lot of creatures with little room and resources. This cleared ecosystem across the road was to be replaced with a monoculture of grass lawn that would get no use, support no life and would require constant maintenance. The owners were completely oblivious to the destruction they had caused to countless creatures.

I immediately realized I had done the same thing myself many times over. At that moment, *We Are the ARK* was born.

ARK = Acts of Restorative Kindness

We are losing countless species to extinction every single day. Each species lost, is lost FOREVER.

An ARK is a restored, native ecosystem, a local, small, medium or large rewilding project. It's a thriving patch of native plants and creatures that have been allowed and supported to re-establish in the Earth's intelligent, successional process of natural restoration. Over time this becomes a pantry and a habitat for our pollinators and wild creatures who are in desperate need of support. This takes time to happen but it begins to re-establish itself as a simple ecosystem very quickly and over time it becomes a strong wildlife habitat and eventually a multi-tiered complex community of native plants, creatures and microorganisms.

Some Extra Creature Supports

The aim of *We Are the ARK* is to create habitats and maximize the diversity and sanctuary available on your land. Some people may have the time and energy to strengthen the ecosystem services offered by their land.

Tufty grasses. Leave some areas of grassy ARKness which you don't cut back. Bumblebees, shrews, field mice and many more will Thank You for the accommodation. Leave the seed heads on everything, as this is the winter and early spring larder and habitat for many wild creatures.

Wildlife pond. If you can take the time and energy to install a small wildlife pond, do! It's a huge help and support to wildlife. It's very hard for our wild kin to find clean sources of water these days.

Log, twig and leaf pile. Throw a pile of logs somewhere quiet and create a log, twig and leaf pile if you can get hold of them. Lots of creatures will make homes here. Rotting wood and leaves create warmth for many families.

Lagoon. A container of water with some rotting leaves and inserted twigs for ramped escape routes. Lots of insects need this kind of habitat for their life cycle. (Not the best idea if you live in a part of the world where mosquitoes might cause problems for you.)

Sand or earth bank. Most of our bees are solitary bees. They often live in these places in little bee burrows.

Rock pile or dry stone wall. Many wild plants like lichens and mosses as well as a host of wild creatures will love you for the perfect home for their needs.

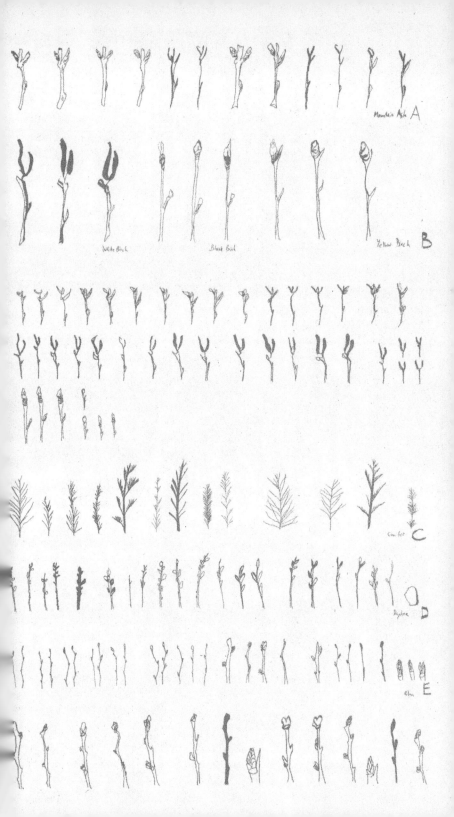

Among the Trees

CARL PHILLIPS

WHAT HAPPENED BACK THERE, AMONG THE TREES, IS ONLY AS untenable as you allow yourself or just decide to believe it is. It happened, and now it's over. And the end feels—to you, at least—both like the end of a long pilgrimage and like the end of a well-reasoned, irrefutable argument, which is its own form of pilgrimage: don't both depend on stamina and faith, in the right proportions? Wasn't the point, at the end, persuasion?

I used to speak in terms of shadowlands, by which I meant, I think, some space where what transpires between two bodies and what gets transacted almost look the same. I'd say a thing like

> *There's a kind of shadowland that one body makes, entering*
> *another; and there's a shadowland the body contains always*
> *within itself, without resolution—as mystery a little more*
> *often, perhaps, should be ...*

and I'd call it a poem, and it looked like one, but how it felt was more like saying aloud the words "rescue me" long enough that it almost seemed plausible that mere saying could turn the light to twilight, and the twilight dark. I lived in the world that, for lack of a prettier word, I'd call tangible, where risk meant risk, it seemed, and violation, not psychological but solid things, for they each cast a shadow as only a solid thing, so I'd been told, could, though I had tried to touch them—violation, risk—and each time my hands touched nothing.

My earliest memory of trees is of a particular fig tree in the yard of the first house I remember, in Portland, Oregon. I was five, at the most. Sometimes what I remember is playing in the shade of it, and at other times the bees that seemed to bloom from inside the windfalls—though it seems now to have been less the wind that brought the fruit down but the weight of ripeness itself, as if sweetness, too much sweetness, meant mistake, punishment therefore; for hours, I'd watch the bees enter and leave the split-open sides, and how the figs looked lonely, once the bees had gone, as if to be plundered meant at least not being alone ...

One evening, instead of coming inside when called, I climbed the fig tree, wearing only a tee shirt and underpants. It seemed like a game, to be up in the tree, and my parents not able to find me, calling my name as they wandered the yard. And then somehow, I fell, and then suddenly stopped falling: my underwear had caught on a branch, saving me from hitting the ground, but holding me in midair, unable to get down. The way I remember it, my mother told my father to get a ladder.

What's very clear in memory is my father saying I should hang there in the tree for a bit, to learn a lesson about disobeying my parents.

I find no evidence, in my sixty years of knowing him, that my father is particularly attentive to historical resonances when it comes to our daily lives, but I can't help thinking about the place of trees in African-American history, as the site for lynching. How strange for my father, an African American, to find it a fitting punishment to leave his son hanging in a tree at night.

My earliest memory of humiliation is of a particular fig tree in the yard of the first house I remember. Who can say how related this is to my refusal, all my life, to believe forgiveness exists?

Some trees are compasses, and some are flags. If a flag tells you where you are, a compass can potentially tell you how to get there or how to find someplace else. A flag, in marking a spot, seems more definitive, a form of punctuation; a compass implies movement, navigation. I know a man who, whenever he needs to write, or cry, or think—*really* think—goes to a willow in his local park and hides beneath its draped branches. He goes there so often, you could almost say he's become *part* of the willow; he seems a willow himself; he marks a place in my life where I stopped to rest, once, but I couldn't stay. Then there's another man, long ago now. His body a forest when seen from the air in a small plane, so that it's possible to get close enough to see where the oaks give way to poplar trees, or where, if you follow the pines far enough, they'll open out to a field across which you can see the ocean. I couldn't have found my way here without him.

Despite my childhood mishap with the fig tree, and despite fairy tales, in which the forest so often contains danger—witches ready to shove children into ovens, wolves masquerading as harmless grandmothers—I've had a love of trees all my life. Throughout high school, I lived in a house in the woods in Massachusetts, and even on the darker mornings of winter what kept me from being frightened was the trees themselves—mostly scrub pines, as we called them there, with struggling oaks scattered among them. Unlike the kids at school, the trees remained silent as I passed, and I took this as a sign of acceptance. Irrational, sure—but in my feeling so unlike everyone else at school, in my confused wrestling with what I felt was real but I couldn't name precisely, why not take silence for acceptance? Among the trees loneliness could be itself, in the open—so could strangeness—even as both remained hidden from the rest of the world for the time it took me to pass through the woods to the bus stop. As I walked, I'd sing to the trees, loudly at first, then more and more softly the closer I got to where the woods gave out, until all I could hear was whatever wind there was through the leaves and needles. A sound like the trees unable to sing back, but trying to.

As with myth, fairy tales often seem designed to explain something very real in surreal terms. The story of Red Riding Hood might as easily be a way to warn about the fact of dangerous animals in the woods as to suggest that potential criminals might be encountered. The secrecy that a forest provides makes it the perfect setting for crime. Also for intimacy, which has often been deemed a crime. It makes sense that woods and forests have long been a queer space.

Queer, not just in the sense of strangeness or alienation—going back to my relationship to the woods in high school—but in terms of sexuality, the woods as a space in which to hunt for sex. What is cruising, if not a form of hunting, if not to pass, as animal (the act of sex is perhaps our most animal manifestation, as humans), in pursuit of another human who has chosen for the moment to yield more entirely to the animal that each of us carries inside?

Was like when the body surrenders to risk, that moment when an unwillingness to refuse can seem no different from an inability to, though they are not the same—inability, unwillingness. To have said otherwise doesn't make it true, or even make it count as true. "Yes, but what does the truth matter now," I whispered, stepping further inside what, by then, was night, almost. The tamer animals would soon lie down again, and the wild go free.

It's not just the convenience of the woods—its ability to conceal, to keep a secret—that makes it a likely site for sexual behavior that isn't societally condoned. Trees are utterly natural, or the collections of trees called woods and forests tend, anyway, not to have been artificially constructed (as compared with parks or public gardens). And this natural context for sexual intimacy can give, if not a sense of wholesomeness exactly, then a sense of permission, at least, to what can feel like—what we've been made to feel *is*—transgression; if only temporarily, the trees erase the shame that drove us to seek hiddenness in the first place. Or if shame didn't drive us there, a reasonable fear likely did. And then—remember?—that well-worn path where we found one another, the trees to either side like a lengthy convoy of fears that kept diminishing, the more south they shuffled—until there *was* no fear.

At this point in my life, I'm not always sure how much of what I think about my life among trees—in forests, in woods—actually happened, how much is imagined, and how much is what I've read and somehow superimposed over my own actual experience—everything from *Sir Gawain and the Green*

Knight—the forest as the site of quest and conquest, riddle and answer—to those passages in Tolkien's *The Hobbit* and *The Lord of the Rings* where so much travel is done under cover of night through forests. In the Tolkien, especially, while there is plenty of potential danger, so many of the scenes have to do with camaraderie and trust and an intimacy that isn't sexual at all. Or I think about Randall Jarrell, whose poetry often revisits fairy tale, and seems especially fascinated with what goes on in the woods—specifically, Jarrell seems to want to rewrite fairy tale and the psychology of it. The forest is an example of "the lost world" that he's always seeking, where the witch who would kill children is transformed. Here's the end of his "The House in the Wood":

> *Here at the bottom of the world, what was before the world*
> *And will be after, holds me to its black*
>
> *Breasts and rocks me: the oven is cold, the cage is empty,*
> *In the House in the Wood, the witch and her child sleep.*

The house is held by the wood, the mother and child are held by the house, perhaps the mother is holding her child. Which is to say the poem's in part about enclosure as a form of security, and about nurture, the very opposite of what the witch conventionally stands for. The wood, in effect, reverses evil to the good it began as, or that's the wish, a human one, with which the wood in the end has very little to do. In that same poem, Jarrell reminds us that

> *after the last leaf,*
> *The last light—for each year is leafless,*
>
> *Each day is lightless, at the last—the wood begins*
> *Its serious existence: it has no path,*
>
> *No house, no story; it resists comparison ...*

So there are the trees of literature, floating somewhere in my head, always. Then there are all of my actual adventures and misadventures among trees throughout my life. And then there are the stories that maybe began with a shred of fact but got transformed in the course of my making a poem. Jarrell, again: "Which one's the mockingbird? which one's the world?"

They moved together in groups, and singly.
They moved among the trees as among the parts of a language they'd forgotten they knew.
Pitch pine, sycamore, maple, oak, and birch.
Humiliation, loneliness, permission, sex, and shame.
Memory, innocence, forgiveness. Willow. Willow.

Another way of thinking, though, about this interplay between reality and imagination when it comes to memory is that I've lost track of what happened, versus what serves as *camouflage* for what happened—camouflage in the form not just of trees but of the context they become for the stories that I tell in poems. In a sense, the poems themselves are trees, or tree-like, in that they become a place where what's difficult and/or forbidden can have a place both to be hidden and within which to feel free to unfurl and extend itself. Here's how I spoke of the forest once:

> *I lived, in those days, at the forest's edge—*
> *metaphorically, so it can sometimes seem now, though*
> *the forest was real, as my life beside it was. I spent*
> *much of my time listening to the sounds of random, un-*
> *knowable things dropping or being dropped from, variously,*
> *a middling height or a great one until, by winter, it was*
> *just the snow falling, each time like a new, unnecessary*
> *taxonomy or syntax for how to parse what's plain, snow*
> *from which the occasional lost hunter would emerge*
> *every few or so seasons, and—just once—a runaway child*
> *whom I gave some money to and told no one about,*
>
> *having promised ...*

And here is a different way since then:

There's a forest that stands at the exact center of sorrow.
Regrets find no shelter there.
The trees, when they sway,
sway like the manes of horses when a storm's not far.
There's no reason to stay there,
nothing worth going to see,
but if you want to, you can pass through the forest
in the better part of a long day.
Who would want to, though?

Story, versus information. Lyric, versus didactic. Long, periodic sentences, versus clipped, straightforward ones. Catalpa trees aren't hawthorns. I'm not the man I was.

They lay where they'd fallen, beneath the forest's canopy. And at first when they woke, it was as if the forest, besides containing them, was itself contained, as in a snow-globe when it's been shaken and just now set down, except instead of snow, just shadows falling, *like* snow, in pieces that it was as useless to try to hold on to as catching snow on the tongue—"to catch us is at once to know us and to lose us," said the shadows, falling like snow, gathering in shadowy, steep banks on which the light, being light, depended.

To know where we came from—and what we came through—doesn't have to mean we know any more clearly where we are, except not *there*, anymore. The forest begins where civilization ends, so I'd been told. Past here be monsters. Past the meadow; past harvest. Past daylight into forest light—for it's never all darkness, beneath the trees, not even at night; not even on a moonless night. Song travels differently in forest light. Everything's different.

That the forest itself contains no apology doesn't mean you're not hurt. Or I'm not sorry. Or I didn't hurt you.

Toward the end of Marilyn Nelson's poem "My Grandfather Walks in the Woods," the grandfather asks the trees a question, and "They answer / with voices like wind / blowing away from him." That's one way of putting it, for their voices can sound like wind. What matters more, I think, is that in the language of trees there's no grammatical mood: questions, statements, commands—it's all song, stripped of anything like judgment, intention, or need. This makes translation especially difficult. Though I know parts of many of their songs, I've only three by heart: "Yes, you can tell me anything," and "No, even we can't help you," and "If I were you, I'd be the lostest, lostest boy I know."

In the dream, I'd bought a large house in a large city, a house that came with a backyard so thick with trees that by summer, by then in full leaf, they blocked all views of the high-rises to the north, of the neighbors to the west, while to the east through the leaves of an old pear tree I could see the cathedral dome, on top of it a cross caught the sunlight and tossed it back. Besides the pear, there's a high-rise-sized pin oak, two dogwoods, two catalpas, a chestnut, before the yard ends in a stand of bamboo I'll eventually lose almost all of, as the dream continues. When I wake, it's as if to another dream, though it feels no different: I become briefly silver, as in what the leaves mean, beneath. Bells are ringing. No, the leaves are falling. Now the bells start ringing. Sudden scattering, all around me, of leaves, all gold.

WHEN MOTHER TREES — THE
MAJESTIC HUBS AT THE CENTER
OF FOREST COMMUNICATION,
PROTECTION, AND SENTIENCE —
DIE, THEY PASS THEIR WISDOM
TO THEIR KIN, GENERATION
AFTER GENERATION, SHARING
THE KNOWLEDGE OF WHAT
HELPS AND WHAT HARMS, WHO
IS FRIEND OR FOE, AND HOW
TO ADAPT AND SURVIVE IN AN
EVER-CHANGING LANDSCAPE.
IT'S WHAT ALL PARENTS DO.

SUZANNE SIMARD

T R E E

T I M E

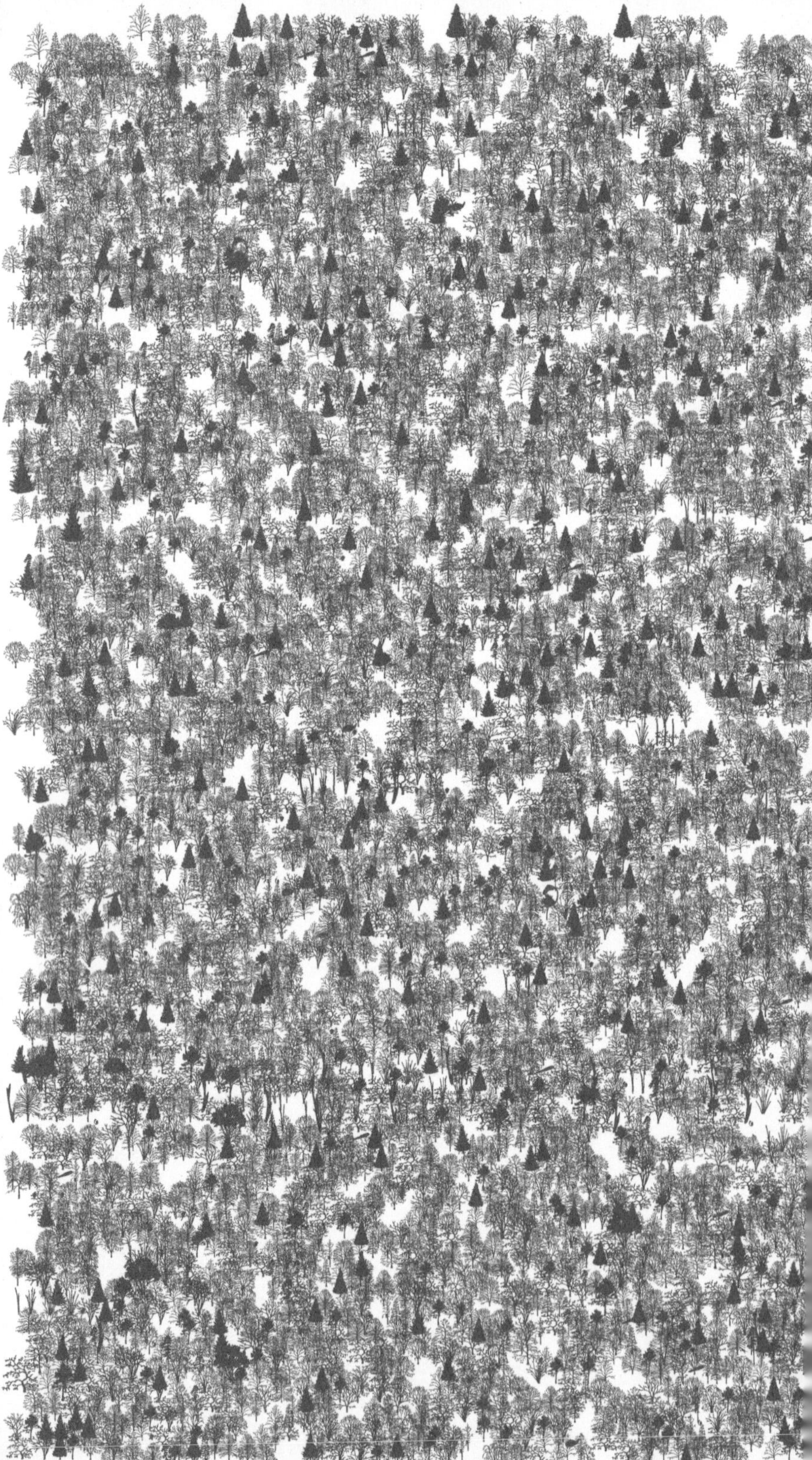

Tree Clocks and Climate Change

NICOLE DAVI

TREES START GROWING IN THE SPRING, MOST TREES THAT IS, CELL-by-cell. In the fall, the wall of each cell thickens, darkens, and eventually the tree stops growing for a time. When that happens a tree ring forms.

Trees do this year after year after year.

I study tree rings—how the width of each ring varies from year to year. I measure that variation to 1/1000 of a millimeter from one ring to another, and another, and so on for hundreds, sometimes thousands of rings in one small sample from one tree. I repeat this process for as many samples as I have taken, which can be 20 to 200 depending on the study site and how many trees we sampled. I have spent an obscene amount of time looking through a microscope and have measured hundreds of thousands of rings.

Old trees are what I'm after, especially those that have had tough lives. These grow near the very edge of where trees can even exist: on mountain treelines, in the subarctic regions of the Northern Hemisphere, or in very arid regions, such as the American Southwest. In these places trees grow very, very slowly. We would describe these trees as "climate sensitive," meaning that their ring widths reflect the conditions of the growing seasons every year that the tree is alive.

There is a principle familiar to scientists that states the present is the key to the past. It's called the uniformitarian principle and it means we can expect that natural processes operated similar in the past as they do today. Tree-ring science builds on this principle by using the past to understand the future. We can use tree-ring records (and other natural recorders of climate) to study the past and learn what's possible in terms of drought or temperature on timescales of hundreds and thousands of years. Knowing what has happened gives us a baseline to understand what can happen. In this way, we see the future in the past. From trees, we have learned much about how our climate system works. We have been able to understand recent global warming trends in the context of the past 2,000 years or more.

For more than a decade I traveled to remote, exotic places in search of climate-sensitive trees. The trips were usually arduous, exploring the backcountry by bush plane or by some old Russian-made vehicle for days and searching by foot up and down mountains. We would usually find the trees we sought, and when we did, I would pause. To be in the presence of these trees—it was peaceful and stunningly beautiful. I would just breathe it all in for a few minutes before unwrapping my hand drill and beginning the very physical process of extracting non-destructive, pencil-sized samples from the trees. Without this fieldwork, I never would have experienced these sites, so far off the road and, furthermore, off the beaten path. These are incredibly special and sensitive areas of the world that tell us about the past and remind us how vulnerable we are.

Trees growing at approximately 6,000 feet, west of Mongolia's Lake Khövsgöl are only accessible after extensive road travel and three days on horse-back through the mountains. One living tree at this site dated back to 1405 A.D. It had a diameter of only 36 cm (14 in) or an average annual ring growth rate of only approximately 0.3 mm per year. Such trees are extremely sensitive to changes in their environment. Hiding under their bark are crucial records of environmental conditions for that spot over centuries and millennia.

In the cores we took at this pristine, high-elevation site, wide rings reflect years with better growing conditions—in particular, warm summers. The narrowest rings represent less-than-optimal growing conditions: cooler summers. The cores didn't come from living trees only. We found many dead trees scattered around this site, and because the conditions here are so harsh, the wood decays very, very slowly. Some trees we sampled had toppled over eight hundred years ago. By using a combination of living and dead trees we were able to get a picture of summer temperatures for the past 1,300 years. In this rich data record, we could see unprecedented warming in the twentieth and twenty-first century, and we could also see a volcanic signature. Some past tropical volcanic eruptions were so explosive that they cooled average temperatures around the world, causing the trees in northern Mongolia to form very narrow rings for the years A.D. 935 (Eldgja, Iceland), 1177 (Haku-San, in Honshu, Japan and Katla in Iceland), 1258 (likely Samalas, Indonesia), 1454 (likely Kuwae in Vanuatu), 1601 (Huaynaputina in Peru), 1783 (Laki, Iceland), 1884 (Krakatoa, Indonesia), and 1912 (Katmai, Alaska).

New Jersey, where I grew up, was essentially clear-cut of trees in the 18th and 19th centuries to grow food, heat homes and to make charcoal to fuel iron mines throughout the state.

Old-growth trees are rare in the Northeastern US. You might not even know you were among them should you be lucky to wander into a stand.

They are not terribly impressive forests, not compared to the iconic old-growth Redwood forests in the West, but sacred nonetheless. In central New Jersey, we have white oak trees that date back to the 1600s, although, sadly, Hurricane Sandy blew down many of the oldest trees in 2012. On a private property hidden in West Milford, New Jersey a colleague sampled a stand of chestnut oak trees that date back to 1577. In New Paltz, New York I have seen ancient hemlocks growing on a rocky outcrop, but an infestation of the aphid-like woolly adelgid is literally sucking the life (and sap) out of them and most other hemlocks across the Northeastern US. At High Point State Park, in a bog near the highest part of New Jersey, we can visit old-growth Atlantic white cedar trees.

I want to believe there are more such stands, spared from metal blades, growing in some hard to get to ravine or swamp, where felling a tree would have been very difficult. The adventure is in trying to find them, akin to stumbling into a library of ancient scrolls, connecting us to another time, helping us navigate what's to come.

from

Alphabet

INGER CHRISTENSEN

1   apricot trees exist, apricot trees exist

2   bracken exists; and blackberries, blackberries; bromine
exists; and hydrogen, hydrogen

3   cicadas exist; chicory, chromium, citrus trees; cicadas
exist; cicadas, cedars, cypresses, the cerebellum

4   doves exist, dreamers, and dolls; killers exist, and doves,
and doves; haze, dioxin, and days; days exist, days and
death; and poems exist; poems, days, death

5   early fall exists; aftertaste, afterthought; seclusion and
angels exist; widows and elk exist; every detail exists;
memory, memory's light; afterglow exists; oaks, elms,
junipers, sameness, loneliness exist; eider ducks, spiders,
and vinegar exist, and the future, the future

Translator's note: The length of each section of Inger Christensen's alphabet is based on Fibonacci's sequence, a mathematical sequence beginning 0, 1, 1, 2, 3, 5, 8, 13, 21..., in which each number is the sum of the two previous numbers.

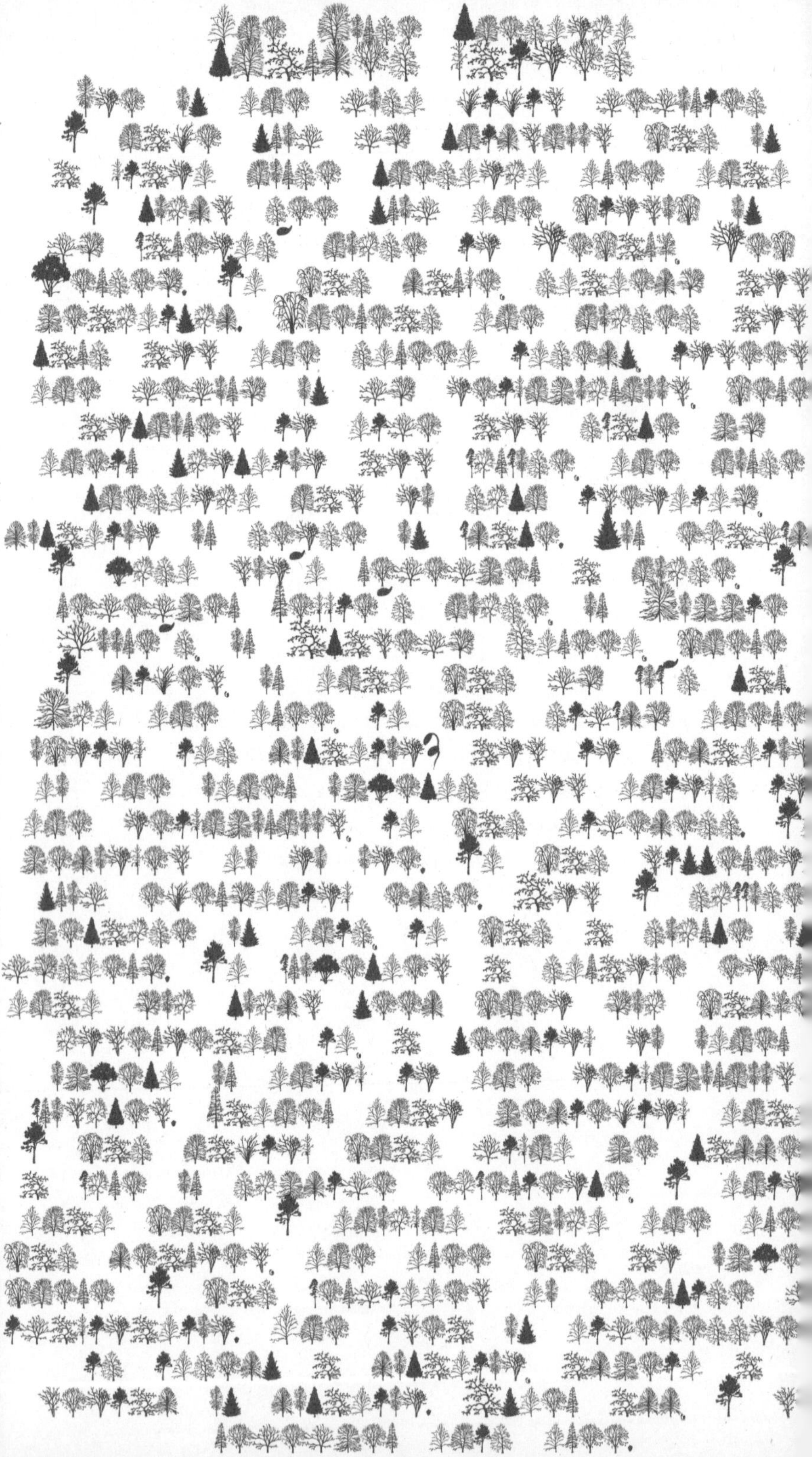

The Horse Chestnut

CHARLES GAINES

ONE OF THE MOST VIVID MEMORIES I HAVE FROM MY CHILDHOOD was of a giant horse chestnut tree that I could see from the window of my parents' house in Newark, New Jersey. It was large, stately and beautiful. Whereas the houses and cars and the street itself, indeed the memory of my neighbourhood, were anchored in time and space by their function and purpose, the horse chestnut had no such identity, location or sense of place. For example, I don't just remember a house, I remember Reggie's house, or Bobbie Moore's, or Academy Street, where I lived, or that was my pop's car. But the tree, it was simply there, owning its location; and in relation to the other objects and things in the neighborhood, it was timeless. It belonged to no one. It was different from everything else. And I suppose because of this, it was a source of mystery. It projected a strange energy that you could feel when you walked underneath it, a feeling no other object or thing in the neighborhood produced. Rather than believing that I was having what might be called a pure or sublime experience, I think that what I thought about the tree was learned, the tree was an object where I was permitted to exercise my imagination. The idea of timelessness is itself a location, albeit a denial of location. After all, I do remember this tree.

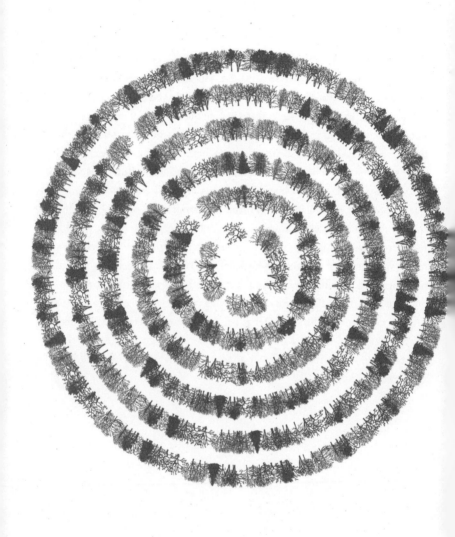

Future Library

KATIE PATERSON

A THOUSAND TREES HAVE BEEN PLANTED IN NORDMARKA, A FOREST just outside Oslo, which will supply paper for a special anthology of books to be printed in one hundred years' time. Between now and then, one writer every year will contribute a text, with the writings held in trust, unpublished, until 2114. Tending the forest and ensuring its preservation for the 100-year duration of the artwork finds a conceptual counterpoint in the invitation extended to each writer: to conceive and produce a work in the hopes of finding a receptive reader in an unknown future.

The manuscripts will be held in trust in a specially designed room in the Deichman Public Library in Bjørvika, Oslo. Intended to be a space of contemplation, this room is lined with wood from the forest. The authors' names will be on display, but none of the manuscripts will be available for reading—until their publication in one century's time.

Liberty Trees

ROBERT SULLIVAN

WHEN THE BRITISH CUT DOWN THE GIANT OLD ELM TREE IN BOSTON, Massachusetts at the end of the summer in 1775, it wasn't a strategic gain in a pure tactical sense, but at the same time it was an immense defeat. The tree wasn't just symbolic; it was supercharged with symbolism. A number of elm trees were similarly charged in North America at the time, as they are today, and in considering these trees, we get to consider all the possible motives of the humans who created the first cities. Were cities settled as a response to some human impulse to herd, or did people come together for, say, ritualistic or religious reasons, creating shrines and crop festivals or sacrifices? Either way, at the heart of most cities are certain instruments of civic infrastructure that aren't exactly man-made and aren't exactly not man-made either. Good examples are the elm trees of Boston and Cambridge, Massachusetts, just across the Charles River.

The elm that the British cut down in 1775 is thought to have been planted 129 years earlier. The elm itself was a meeting point, as well as a civic altar of celebration and remonstrance. It is reported that in 1765, on a summer market day, an effigy of the stamp agent was left at the foot of the elm, as well as a large boot that was meant to represent Lord Bute, the First Lord of the Treasury, who Bostonians mistakenly believed authored the tax. For Royalists, the tree was, as one noted, "consecrated as an Idol for the Mob to worship." The group that Royalists described as a mob was Boston's Liberty Boys, primarily dockworkers and nautical craftsmen who were, generationally speaking, the Founding Fathers' fathers. They decorated the branches with flags and bunting, filled the limbs with lanterns, and, for the Stamp Act, placed at the center an obelisk, specially designed for the protest, covered with poems and drawings, all declaiming tyranny, proclaiming liberty. A few weeks later a copper plate was attached to the tree, golden letters naming it: The Liberty Tree.

Liberty Trees had sprung up all along the Atlantic Coast of North America during the years that the British colonies were splitting off from Great Britain, the trees versions of European protests and celebrations and combinations thereof. In seventeenth century France, the mai was a tree, its upper branches pruned, that served as a community gathering point. The mai was associated with fertility rights (and it seems a short stretch from the public use of the mai to the Northern European tradition of dousing orchards with drink, at the turn of the year, to ensure fruit in the summer, the tradition known as wassail.) Sometimes, the branches of the mai were decorated, with objects or candles or luminaries. Sometimes, the tools of dead laborers dangled from the branches, to entice wandering souls. Sometimes, the trees were poles or a ship's mast, and if a collection of poles was placed before a manor house, wine sprinkled liberally about, it was meant as a community ransom note, a threat, the crowd assembled awaiting its dû, or payment.

By 1790, the mai had become known as the arbre de la liberté, and in larger European cities where trees might be rare, citizens used masts. This was often the case in Connecticut and New York, where ships' masts were frequently used as Liberty Trees. New York City had a ship's mast that New Yorkers referred to as The Liberty Pole, and it can be argued that the first bloodshed in the American Revolution was not in Boston, during the skirmish that became known as the Boston Massacre, but during the Battle of Golden Hill, a street brawl between a group known as the Liberty Boys—a group of sailors, oystermen, sail makers and other waterfront workers—and the British troops, who routinely took waterfront jobs—they were often given priority—when not on duty. The descendant of New York's Liberty Pole still stands in City Hall Park.

Thomas Paine wrote a poem called "Liberty Tree," and Irish Republicans sang a song with the same title. Toussaint L'Ouverture, the leader of the Haitian revolution, which began in 1791, said: "By overthrowing me, you have succeeded in cutting down the tree of liberty of the blacks in Santo Domingo, but have failed to destroy the roots that are deep and strong. The tree will grow again." In an essay entitled "Liberty Tree: A Genealogy," Arthur M. Schlesinger described the Liberty Tree as "silent propaganda," adding that "no single venture paid richer dividends than the Tree of Liberty." The last surviving Liberty Tree from the time of the Revolution was on the campus of St. John's College in Annapolis, Maryland. It died from damage suffered during Hurricane Floyd in September 1999. A scion from the tree was planted to replace it.

Trees are markers. Sometimes trees mark ancient boundaries. Sometimes trees mark memories; their roots hold time, or grow down into it. People mark their lives with trees, taking photos of children near saplings, for example, though maybe more frequently people plant trees in memory of the deceased. In cities, plaques explaining trees are hiding everywhere, some with trees that are still alive, some that are long gone. A tree that survives a storm or disaster is a corollary of a tree planted in commemoration of someone or something. It is a tree that is in a sense inaugurated by the event it survives. A street tree that survived the destruction of the old World Trade Center Towers in 2001 was taken off the site shortly after September 11, nurtured back to health in the Bronx and then replanted in the memorial area. Today, it is referred to as the Survivor Tree, and people who lost family members in the World Trade Center disaster have hung yellow ribbons in its branches, laid wreaths at its roots, placed pictures of the deceased in the branches, dangled photographs from the limbs.

Elm trees in particular were revered in New England towns, and linked to important historical moments, or in some cases revered purely for their longevity, for having been alive throughout the life of the community. Andrew Jackson Downing, the renowned nineteenth century landscape architect, called them America's pyramids, the link to antiquity—"not less instructive and poetical than the ruins of a past age." In *Republic of Shade*, a book that surveys New England's long relationship with American elms, Thomas Campanella cites Charles Joseph Latrobe, the English author of *The Rambler in North America*, published in 1835. Latrobe, seeing these old elms still standing in Connecticut Valley towns, characterised them as nearly human: "sole survivor of the original forest, and boundary-mark of the first colonists."

In the midst of researching *Republic of Shade*, Campanella published an author's query in *The New York Times Book Review*, asking for people to send him reminiscences of elm trees. "The response was overwhelming. Week after week I received letters—more than a hundred in all—from addresses across the United States. My respondents ranged from cooks and shopkeepers and nursing home residents to poets and Ivy League professors. They sent me photographs from family albums, yellowed newspaper clippings, extracts of diaries and snippets from love letters; they sent poems and eulogies and sermons. And all for a tree!"

Over the years, I have enjoyed looking for the oldest trees in a city, and I have marveled at how many of the sites of the old trees are marked by plaques. One of my favorite places to look for trees or plaques marking the sites of old trees is in Massachusetts, a state that seems to me to be innately tree-interested, though more likely this has to do with the commonality of town commons, places owned by the community and thus preserved in an essential sense. On a rainy day about five years ago, I took a bus up to Boston, with trees in mind. I had read about the old elm tree in Boston, on Boston Common—The Great Elm, as it was called—and I was interested in finding the plaque marking its site. I was also interested in seeing the site of a tree in nearby Cambridge—a tree called The Washington Elm. The Washington Elm was a witness tree, and the event it was said to witness was the moment George Washington first took command of the troops, in 1776.

My bus got in at South Station, and on the walk over to the Boston Common, I stopped at Essex Streets and Washington Streets, to visit the site of Boston's Liberty Tree. I was there for a couple of minutes looking around in the street because I did not think to look up—over the entrance to the T, over the donut shop, over the state motor vehicle registry on the second floor—to what was a bas relief of a tree that filled in the space of a large third-floor window. The inscription: "Sons of Liberty, 1765." I later learned that this neighborhood was once known as the "Neighborhood of Elms," making the Liberty Tree marker a sort of before, a marker even in its tree-less state, over-the-Dunkin-Donuts-state of what the landscape was, a still cherished witness and survivor.

The Common was a few blocks away, and, thanks to the rain, I nearly had the place to myself. I did not know exactly where the Great Elm stood, so I made my way blindly through the park, noting all the small plaques. It was like walking through an old church, reading notes on former pastors and congregants. An example of an individual:

THIS TREE WAS DONATED BY
THE FRIENDS AND COLLEAGUES OF
WILLARD R. POPE
GENERAL COUNSEL (1975–1981)
MASSACHUSETTS DEPARTMENT OF
ENVIRONMENTAL PROTECTION
TO HONOR BILL FOR THE COMMITTED WORK
ON BEHALF OF THE NATURAL ENVIRONMENT

I read it a few times, and considered the life of a man I had never before heard of: a young strong tree stood behind Pope's small stone marker. Then, not far away, another plaque, this one planted by a group, marking a faraway disaster:

REMEMBER CHERNOBYL, UKRAINE

26 APRIL 1986

DONATED BY

UKRAINIAN AMERICANS

TO COMMEMORATE

THE 5TH ANNIVERSARY

There were dozens, I think, and I photographed a bunch and wrote down some inscriptions. And then I made my way to some big old elm trees in one corner of the park, a row of them kept alive during the elm blight by chemical infusions—a ranger told me that he hoped he was fairly confident they would live for a while longer. But the marker for the Great Elm was difficult to find, until I found it, a lone little plaque out in a field, marking a tree that was not there:

SITE OF THE GREAT ELM

HERE THE SONS OF LIBERTY ASSEMBLED

HERE JESSE LEE, METHODIST PIONEER, PREACHED IN 1790

THE LANDMARK OF THE COMMON,

THE ELM BLEW DOWN IN 1876

When it stood, the Great Elm was revered by the community as its oldest living thing. A poet described it as a vestige of the raw wilderness: "These forty acres, more or less... / Where Yankees walk, and brag and guess, / Were but a howling wilderness / Of wolves and bears." Scientists saw it as a "visible relic," as the president of the Boston Society of Natural History put it in 1855, "of the Indian Shawmut..." In 1860, when a limb fell, the tree was judged to be 190 years old, but some speculated it could possibly have sprung out of the Earth after the Bible's Great Flood. Most miraculous, though, was that it had survived the times that the Common has been used as a field for cattle.

When the Great Elm blew down, on June 29, 1876, during a "storm of no ordinary character," the community mourned. A new tree was planted, officials officiating, a box buried beneath it listing citizens deemed important by the powers that were. But the replacement tree was never adored, and I would argue that a list of important people chosen by officials alone is bad for your roots. A few years later, it was learned that two policemen had grabbed a seedling from the roots of the old elm and planted it quietly in the park. That tree, a true descendant, was moved closer to the site of the Great Elm, an affidavit sworn to by the police officers discovered in the city auditor's office in 1909. I like to think the old elms the park ranger had talked to me about are related to the Great Elm, though I don't think anyone knows for certain.

Some webpages and guidebooks can cause you to believe that the Washington Elm still stands, though the website for the city of Cambridge helpfully points out that this is not the case. When it did stand, world rulers and royalty visited the tree, and it's image is still today on the Cambridge city seal, where residents associate with patriotism, the place where, as tradition would have it, Washington drew his sword, vowing to fight for liberty. That idea—that Washington took command in the old elm's view—was what is referred to as an invented tradition, as no proof exists that Washington took command beneath the tree and the proof of his whereabouts at the time (July 3, 1775) that does exist indicates he was likely elsewhere.

As for why this tradition was invented, scholars point to an influx of immigrants to Cambridge in the 1840s, primarily Irish immigrants, fleeing famine, at which point long-time residents sought to distinguish themselves by their long-time connections to the American Revolution. "The Washington Elm tradition was invented, as it were, to provide continuity with a past under siege by the forces of modernity," writes Campanella. The tradition invention worked. Washington Irving invoked the elm, in *Life of Washington*, one of the most widely read books in America at the time—I still see old copies of the multi-volume work turn up at garage sales, especially in New England; it's like old rocks that turn up in a field in spring.

As traffic increased in the roads around it, the tree was fenced off for its own protection, and then when the tree came down in the fall of 1923, there was civic hysteria. The last witness to the revolution was mourned around the country. Cubes were cut up and sent to governors, to representatives of 32 countries, to Mount Vernon, George Washington's home. In 1925, a Cambridge historian debunked the myth of the tree. Today, the city's website has a page of frequently asked questions. One question is: Did George Washington take command of the American Army under the Washington Elm? The City of Cambridge's official response:

> This popular legend became part of American popular culture as early as the 1830s. The story was made famous during the centennial year of 1876, with the publication of a fictitious "eye-witness" journal, The Diary of Dorothy Dudley. The tree itself was indeed real and stood in the middle of Garden Street at the intersection of Mason Street. In 1923, the diseased and very fragile trunk was accidentally pulled over by a city worker. A plaque embedded in the street's pavement marks the original location of the tree.

In the common, I found a bas-relief marker, unveiled on July 3, 1950. There is no mention of the tree in the text on the marker—by then the debunking had sunk in among historians, at least—but a tree stands behind Washington in the sculpture, watching. I found a stone tablet nearby, an earlier marker, this one mentioning Washington's command. And then I went out into the intersection to look for a spot in the pavement marking the site of the long-gone tree.

Looking for a marker in the road was not an easy thing to do. The middle of the intersection was the middle of three streets, and four lanes of traffic. I could see it, but I could not examine it. It was the end of the day. I had to catch a bus back to New York. I was tired. I gave up. But for weeks after, I kept thinking about the idea of the old site of a tree as a manhole cover. I fell in love with the idea, and it began to seem almost like a conceptual art piece: the roots of the city, its electrical or maybe watery infrastructure, marked where historic roots were also marked. A constitutional overlap! A couple of months later I returned, and on a slow traffic morning saw it: a beautiful manhole cover, featuring Washington and an elm, as best as I can recall.

I say as best as I can recall because when I went out into the street to look for it again a few months ago—it's getting more difficult, traffic what it is, my legs what they are becoming—the marker was gone. What's there now is what appears to be a manhole cover covered in asphalt. Was it accidentally paved over? Was it paved over intentionally? I wrote to the Cambridge public works department and (impressively) they got back to me with alacrity. "I know this manhole," the engineer said. "It is very historical. I think it is still there." He asked me to let him check. He said it would take some time. I am waiting for him to get back to me, and I am hopeful. I feel as if the tree is still there, one way or another, maybe a plaque waiting to be exhumed from the tar, and anyway in the city we always manage to work things out.

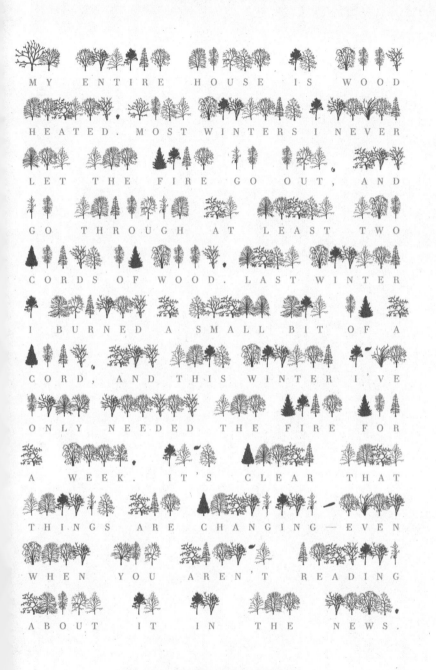

MY ENTIRE HOUSE IS WOOD
HEATED. MOST WINTERS I NEVER
LET THE FIRE GO OUT, AND
GO THROUGH AT LEAST TWO
CORDS OF WOOD. LAST WINTER
I BURNED A SMALL BIT OF A
CORD, AND THIS WINTER I'VE
ONLY NEEDED THE FIRE FOR
A WEEK. IT'S CLEAR THAT
THINGS ARE CHANGING—EVEN
WHEN YOU AREN'T READING
ABOUT IT IN THE NEWS.

ANDREA ZITTEL

A Matter of Time

AMY FRANCESCHINI

WHILE WALKING DOWN A LONG, DARK HALLWAY A SLIVER OF LIGHT escaped from a doorway ahead of us—a bright beam of light that made everything that was dark even darker. As we neared the light source, our eyes adjusted enough to see into a small room where a woman's face was illuminated by the light of a copy machine as she scanned a daily comic. Our guide told us that the woman was Vera Rubin. Vera Rubin, the American astronomer who confirmed the existence of dark matter—a kind of matter that cannot be seen by the naked eye or telescopes, but that makes up most of the matter in the universe—95.1% in fact. Humans, trees, air and the text printed on this paper are less than 5% of all matter in the universe.

As our eyes recovered from this vignette, the details in the dark hallway resumed and we made our way to the brightly lit offices of the Geophysical Laboratory.

In 2009, during a research visit for an exhibition at the Baltimore Contemporary Museum we visited the Carnegie Research Institute in Washington D.C. Our wish there was to ask one of the researchers what we might find if we were to do a core sample of a wooden floorboard harvested from an abandoned row house in Baltimore.

What would it tell us? We knew that trees are the greatest archivists and we were hoping our friend's trained eyes and tools would help us see its holdings.

The first thing our host said with an obvious conjecture, "Well, you would find out if the tree was pre-bomb or post-bomb, of course. And then you would probably find DNA from blood, asbestos from brake-pad lining. You would also see the evolution of the city to some extent, meaning you would find evidence of dirt from when the roads were dirt and then stone from cobble stones and finally asphalt. All of this history would have been brought in on the soles of the inhabitants' shoes."

These are "marker layers," or some call these stories the human dust print. For example, everything that was growing on the Earth's surface at the moment the atomic bomb was tested has been inscribed with what scientists call the isotopic fingerprint—a permanent record of this event.

The floorboards we had collected were stamped on the underside: ELKINS WEST VIRGINIA OAK FLOORING. These boards were sourced from trees grown four hours away from Baltimore in what is now Monongahela National Forest. Since most row houses were built between 1810 and 1900, the wood in our hands was "pre-bomb."

Between October 14 and 25 in 2009, Futurefarmers acquired over fifty boards from twelve different rowhouses in Baltimore. With this material a set of five oars were made and installed in the gallery and were the main protagonists of our project, *The Reverse Ark*: A temporary school built with Baltimore-specific, reclaimed materials; floorboards from abandoned row houses, fallen trees, surplus paper rolls from the *Baltimore Sun* and surplus fabric from the textile industry. Content for the school was informed by the political, social and economic history of the materials. Giant oars made from salvaged floorboards of (abandoned) row houses penetrated the walls of the museum—blades inside the museum and handles out onto the street, begging one to ask, *Who is rowing the boat?* The museum became a vessel, an ark with a sail that doubled as a massive loom inviting visitors to become weavers. A pedestrian press enabled daily printing by foot whereby an entire tree was turned into an alphabet. Each letter carved into a slice of the tree and tied to one's foot. Collectively, a printing march would roll out daily news. The gallery was handed over to Baltimore students, community groups and passersby who created weekly public programs for three months.

These oars made from the floorboards of Baltimore rowhouses are looking for a home. This year we created the *Reverse Ark Trade Agreement*. If you have wooden floors and would like a Futurefarmers artwork in your home, please contact us.

info@futurefarmers.com

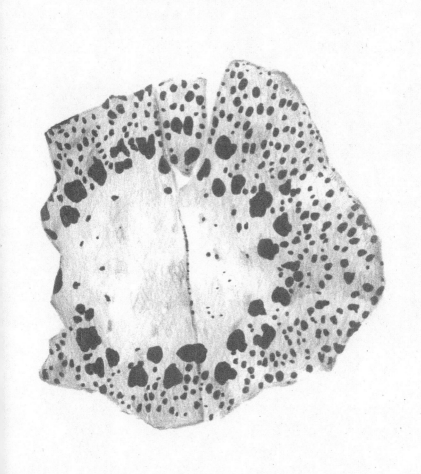

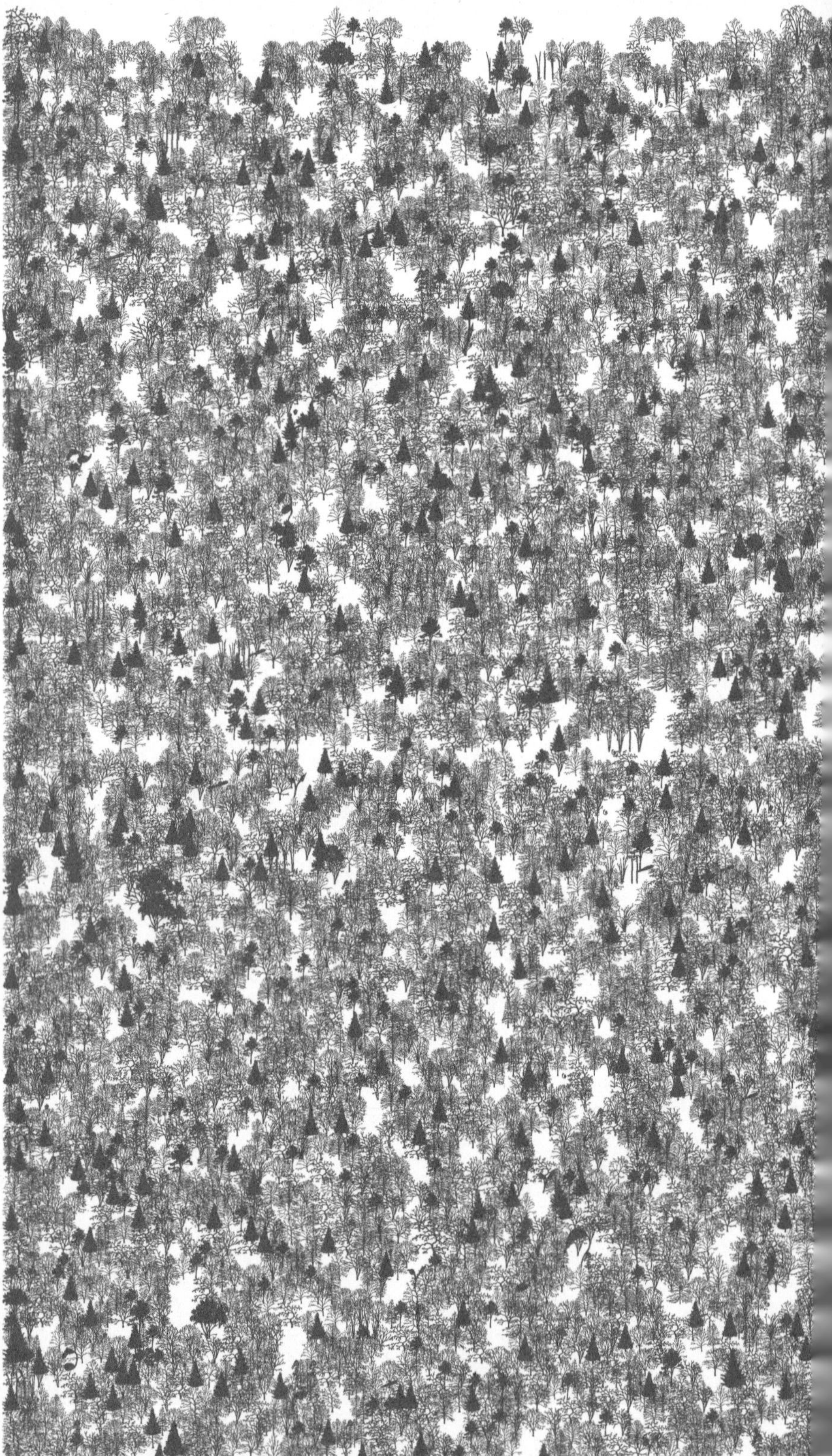

All the Time in the World

RACHEL SUSSMAN

THE TREE HAD BEEN ON FIRE FOR OVER A WEEK BEFORE ANYONE noticed. On January 16, 2012, The Senator, one of the oldest cypress trees in the world, collapsed and died, engulfed in flames. It was 3,500 years old.

It was my art and science project, *The Oldest Living Things in the World*, consisting of research, travel, photographing, and writing about continuously living organisms 2,000 years old and older, that brought me to Florida in search of The Senator. I had recently returned from Africa, where I'd driven around the Limpopo in search of ancient Baobab trees, visited an underground forest in Pretoria amidst a morning threat of "smash and grabs," and taken a road trip from Cape Town up through Namibia to find the genuinely odd *Welwitschia Mirabilis*, which looked more like a science-fictional sea creature than a primitive conifer punctuating the vast and empty Namib-Naukluft. And then I flew to Orlando—a trip that had failed to ignite my imagination.

The Senator was the primary attraction at the aptly named Big Tree Park, just twenty minutes' worth of strip malls away from downtown Orlando. In fact, it was the original Orlando attraction, BD ("Before Disney," if you will), visited via horse and carriage. Named for Senator Overstreet in 1927, it was impressively tall and robust while not overly gnarly.

I snapped a digital shot for a couple who asked that I take their picture in front of the tree. I then took out my medium format film camera and made some photographs of my own. I make large-scale fine art prints of my images, and feel that I get the best of both worlds by shooting film, and making high resolution scans of the negatives and making archival pigment prints. When I got the film back I knew I had missed my mark: there were some interesting compositions, but I hadn't captured the spirit of this remarkable being. I was coming to see my subjects as individuals, and as such I wanted to make portraits of them rather than landscapes; to encourage anthropomorphism, and create a means to connect to Deep Time—thousands of years of a life distilled into 1/60th of a second.

And with that, I made an unceremonious decision to return to The Senator when opportunity allowed. In the intervening years I traveled to Greenland for lichens that grow only 1 cm every hundred years, to Chile for the strange and wonderful llareta plant growing at 15,000 feet and a desert-cousin of parsley, and to Western Australia for the stromatolites, tied to the oxygenation of the planet and the very beginnings of all life on Earth. I went to Tasmania in search of a 43,000-year-old shrub that is the last of its species left on Earth, rending it both critically endangered and theoretically immortal. But in five years, despite having visited Florida a couple of times to see family, I did not make it back to The Senator. It was too easy. It would always be there. Surely, if The Senator had been around for 3,500 years, it was going to be around for 3,505 years.

But it wasn't.

Extreme longevity can lull us into a false sense of permanence. We fall into a quotidian reality devoid of long-term thinking, certain that things which have been here "forever" will remain, unchanging. But being old is not the same as being immortal. Even second chances have expiration dates. The comparative ease of access and the seeming lack of urgency bred a certain complacency in my return to The Senator.

On February 8, 2012, just days before I was to ship out for Antarctica in search of the 5,500-year-old moss, I returned to what remained of the ancient tree. I met Jim Duby, program manager of the Seminole County Natural Lands Program, at the locked gate of the park. Jim had been to the site every day since the fire. At the time, the cause of the fire had not yet been determined, and natural causes, like a lightning strike, were still on the table. After speaking with him, it was hard for me to consider the cause of death to be anything but human intention. There was no lightning recorded in the area during the weeks in question, and the tree had been newly fitted with a lightning rod. Another idea that it had spontaneously combusted under its own auspices simply seemed absurd. On the other hand, the tree had been visibly hollow before the fire, and an opening at the base of the trunk, once filled with concrete, had become large enough for a person to squeeze through and stand inside. Or to drop a match into, and run. The Senator was likely spared the long-ago ax of the logging industry because it was hollow, but the very same defect ultimately sparked its death.

After spending over a decade of my life researching, photographing, and traveling all over the world in search of ancient life, it has put my own mortality into perspective. I have a more immediate understanding of the briefness of a single human life in the face of the incomprehensible vastness of "forever," and at the same time, when standing in front of these organisms, I feel a connection to the moments, small as molecules, that shape a constantly unfolding narrative on both a micro and macro scale. Any given moment matters.

So what did kill The Senator? Some kids in their twenties who snuck into the park and climbed inside the tree, high on methamphetamine. They lit matches or a lighter to "see the drugs better," and just like that The Senator's hollow trunk was transformed into a towering chimney and fuel source in one. In June of 2014 Sara Barnes was convicted of the crime, and ultimately sentenced to probation.

For The Senator, there is a chance at a second life: clippings from the tree were taken years ago and successfully propagated in a nursery. In February 2013, after a careful root-stabilization process, a forty-foot grafted tree was successfully transplanted back into The Senator's original spot and has already sprouted fresh growth and gained in height. The stump has been incorporated into the playground area.

Seminole County held a contest to name the newly planted clone. The community chose "The Phoenix."

T R E E

P E O P L E

Mujer Waorani / Waorani Women

NEMO ANDY GUIQUITA

WE WANT TO TELL THE WORLD THAT THE JUNGLE, OUR HOME, IS bleeding from the presence of extractive mining and oil companies that are destroying the only forests we have left; today as we are here, thousands of hectares are being cut down and our culture and identity is in danger. We want the banks and governments to understand once and for all the immense damage that they continue to cause to our peoples when they finance the trade of Amazon crude; today they have the opportunity to show the world that they are on the side of humanity's survival, and finally stop the devastation of the planet.

It hurts me to see the little that is left of our rainforest inside this protected area. We should be fighting to protect our rainforest in Ecuador, but instead they are granting more oil concessions. The oil spill has reached the banks of the Coca River. The situation is critical because more than 60,000 people depend on water from this river.

The rainforest for us is home. It is our life, our pharmacy, our everything.

For us, the sounds of the rainforest are music, representing peace and harmony.

Oil drilling in our Amazon has brought contamination, disease, deforestation, destruction of our cultures, and the colonization of our territories. It is an existential threat for us and violates our fundamental rights as Indigenous peoples. We are calling for an end to all new extraction on our lands, and as our ancestors and science now affirm, we must keep fossil fuels in the ground.

The Amazonian territories and ecosystems are at a tipping point. It's now or never. We need to ensure protection of 80% of the Amazon rainforest before 2025 or we risk planetary peril.

There is hope because the women of the rainforest are rising up.

TREE X OFFICE

NATALIE JEREMIJENKO

HISTORICALLY, THE CAPACITY TO OWN PROPERTY HAS BESTOWED political agency, independence and even personhood to the property owner. "40 acres and a mule" were reparations granted to (and then re-seized from) freed slaves; a well-known example of the suturing of recognition and territorial control. However, even today the capacity to own and inherit property diverges markedly with gender. If non-human organisms own property, will that change their explicit value in a market-based participatory democracy?

This transaction took place between 1820 and 1832. According to the newspaper article, the deed read:

> *I, W. H. Jackson, of the county of Clarke, of the one part, and the oak tree... of the county of Clarke, of the other part: Witnesseth, That the said W. H. Jackson for and in consideration of the great affection which he bears said tree, and his great desire to see it protected has conveyed, and by these presents do convey unto the said oak tree entire possession of itself and of all land within eight feet of it on all sides.*

Under the new property ownership regime of UP2U urban plan, in which the trees have deeded themselves and the property they stand on, trees can of course exploit their property for their own purposes. Moreover, trees assume personhood through the 14th amendment which is now assumed to grant personhood to corporations. Applying this to trees, by virtue of their shareholder and board status in the OOZ corporation, trees themselves become corporate/persons, or active agents—new citizens.

Further, the current technological opportunity transforms trees' capacity to self-monitor and report, tweet, and account for their use by people and other organisms. They themselves account for the variety of uses and services they provide, and they themselves monetize these services, exploit their own assets, and capitalize on their capital. Using simple, inexpensive sensors, the trees assume their own voice and capacity to exert corporate personhood within this new structure of ownership.

Further to this, other uses develop these Trees as amenities. Including: International Tree Climbing Sport and Aerial Yoga class. TREE X OFFICE will continue to incubate other explicit uses. And will also be an x Clinic field office for this time.

Want to set up a co-working space in a tree in your neighbourhood? Contact us for the TREE X OFFICE kit that includes legal template (for the tree to own itself) and tips for how to enlist the local community board and/or Parks Department, and sensors for putting your tree on the Internet-of-Things and making it a sentient being, investment guide for trees (i.e. how the tree can invest profits most profitably, including BIOchar soil augmentation and College Fund for sending saplings to college), high-speed internet (Free Network Foundation have done the hard work of figuring how to support the information commons), Pirate Box instructions for local area network, OS treebooking software, inexpensive recycled mezzanines custom made for your tree, recycled office furniture coupon from GreenBuild and a white paper outlining the strategy to exploit private property laws for public good and the relationship to the Rights of Earth declaration.

Occupy Trees!
treexoffice@gmail.com

THIS IS NOT

OUR WORLD WITH

TREES IN IT.

IT'S A WORLD

OF TREES,

WHERE HUMANS

HAVE JUST

ARRIVED.

RICHARD POWERS

I Want to Be a Tree

SUMANA ROY

You discover an autograph on a tree.
You know it's not the tree's—
it has no commitment to history.
Only strangers leave their names on bark.
That signature is a tease, a trace—'I was here'.
(Which tree has ever needed to say that?)
No one else has their self-importance,
the smoke billowing silhouettes of madmen and lovers.
This they share with trees, these sky-holding people—
a flattened anonymity.

It is always a surprise, the history of anonymity.
You look at the trees, their indifference to recognition,
and you begin to see the path of evolution—
the mammal's backbone needs fame. The tree trunk none.
You've seen it behave like a time bomb,
you've seen 'Anonymous' become the name of a race.
Later, when you realize that tree leaves calibrate wind speed,
you discover that anonymity also has genres.
You sit under a tree and sneeze,
and you wonder which one is more anonymous—
the tree or the sneeze.

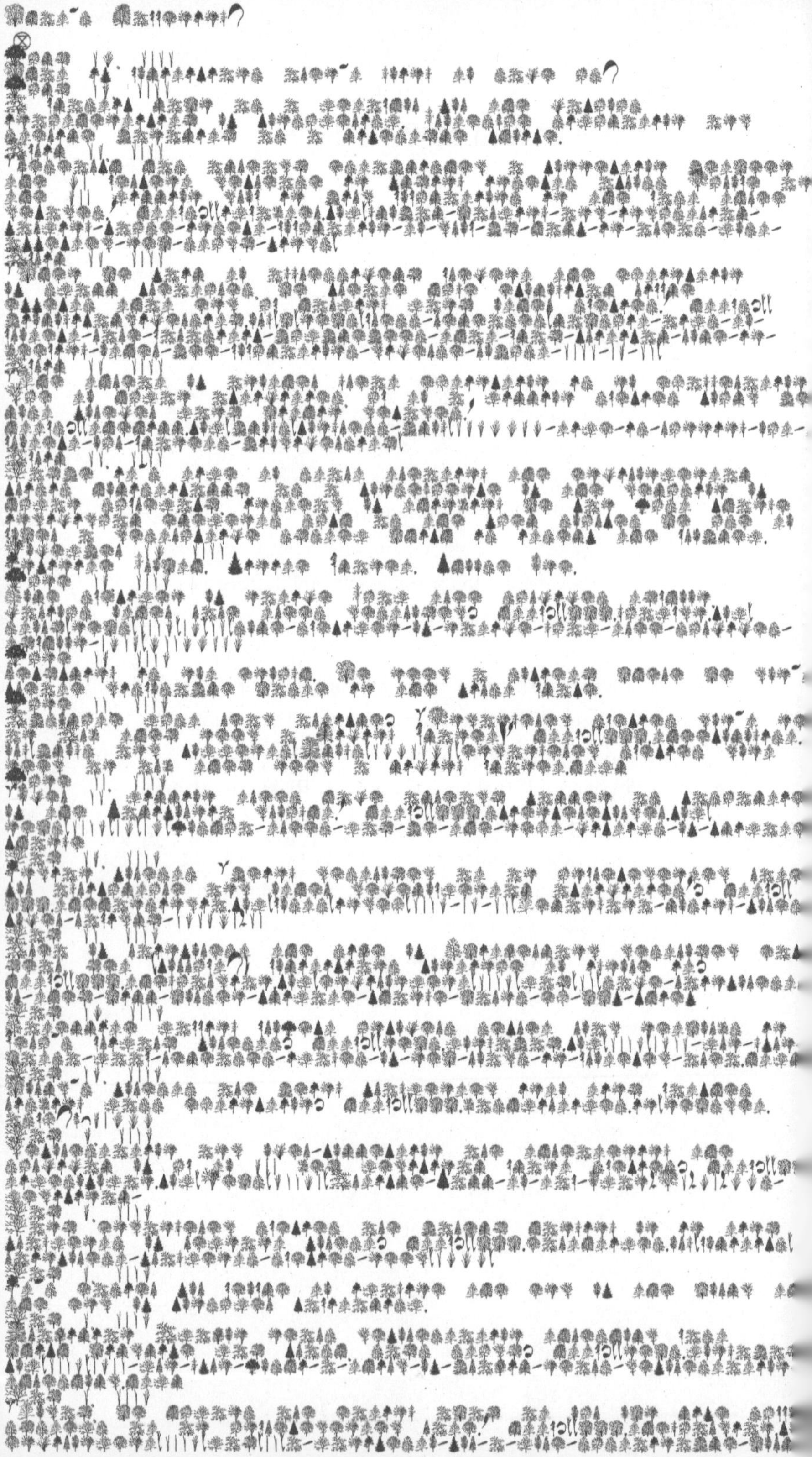

What's Happening?

JULY 29, 2022
What if politicians aren't going to save us?

JULY 15, 2022
A plastic lawn as a metaphor for the vacuous inauthenticity of consumerism. Grotesque simulation and sterile banality as a lifestyle choice.

APRIL 23, 2022
"Research has already established a connection between the 80 percent decrease in flying insects across Europe and the 400 million drop in bird populations in the past three decades." *https://impakter.com/ global-warming-and-industrial-farming-cause-insect-population-to-drop-by- half-in-areas-most-affected-new-study-finds/*

APRIL 23, 2022
"When we fail to aggressively prevent the extinction of small creatures, we create huge ecological ripple effects that end up harming many other species." *https://biologicaldiversity.org/w/news/press-releases/ lawsuit-aims-to-protect-rare-parasitic-bumblebees-that-play-critical-role-in- keeping-other-bee-populations-diverse-robust-2022-04-21/*

APRIL 23, 2022
"The threat of another great extinction is no exaggeration. Due to human activities, up to a million species could be lost forever—many within decades."
https://thehill.com/blogs/congress-blog/3459948-time-is-running-out-to- protect-our-planets-biodiversity/

APRIL 22, 2022
Maybe it's time to start treating the environmental crisis holistically, as a consequence of the delusion of human supremacy, instead of thinking we can

just change individual elements such as the fuel sources we use to power a destructive system which is itself the problem.

NOVEMBER 27, 2021
Infinite Growth. Finite Planet. Choose One.

JUNE 14, 2015
Sole specimen of native Guam tree survives typhoon, various other rare trees destroyed: *http://www.guampdn.com/story/news/2015/06/13/ sole-specimen-of-native-guam-tree-survives-typhoon-0614/71169336*

JUNE 14, 2015
Recycling is not enough. We need a society where we don't create disposable waste in the first place.

JUNE 11, 2015
Absolute must read article: "Endangered species don't need an Ark—they need a Living Planet!" *http://www.theecologist.org/blogs_and_comments/ Blogs/2882373/endangered_species_dont_need_an_ark_they_need_a_living_ planet.html*

JUNE 10, 2015
"Over 12 million trees have already fallen as casualties of the California drought." *http://www.sciencerecorder.com/news/2015/06/09/ joshua-trees-may-be-the-next-victims-of-climate-change*

MAY 24, 2015
Indian forests "being destroyed at an unprecedented rate for agriculture and other developmental activities": *http://www.thehansindia.com/posts/ index/2015-05-21/Telangana-losing-forest-cover-rapidly-152470%20*

MAY 21, 2015
Area of rainforest the size of Switzerland destroyed each year, yet (corrupt?) politicians continue to ignore it:
http://www.theguardian.com/environment/2015/may/21/ save-rainforests-or-they-will-worsen-climate-change-warns-ex-wwf-chief

MAY 18, 2015

Satellite mapping project uncovers secret road networks in Peru's primary forests: *http://news.mongabay.com/2015/0513-mrn-gfrn-watsa-maap-releases-images-of-new-roads-in-proteced-area.html*

MAY 15, 2015

World's forests are being fragmented into tiny patches—risking mass extinction: *http://www.kashmirtimes.in/newsdet.aspx?q=40978*

MAY 5, 2015

Deforestation and over-collection are threatening the survival of up to 400 key medicinal plant species: *http://www.timesofoman.com/News/51160/Article-Call-to-tap-Oman%E2%80%99s-medicinal-*

MAY 4, 2015

Many endangered species are barely hanging on in tiny fragments of remnant forest: *http://www.earthtimes.org/politics/rainforest-fragments-species-need/2878/*

MAY 3, 2015

It's easier for people to imagine the end of the world than the end of consumer capitalism.

MAY 2, 2015

Brazilian Amazon nears deforestation threshold past which wildlife may crash, says study: *http://news.mongabay.com/2015/0501-mrn-gfrn-joshi-a-third-of-brazil-nears-deforestation-threshold.html*

MAY 2, 2015

"Today, we humans are eating away at our own life support systems at an unprecedented rate." *http://www.theguardian.com/environment/2015/may/01/a-manifesto-for-a-more-sustainable-world*

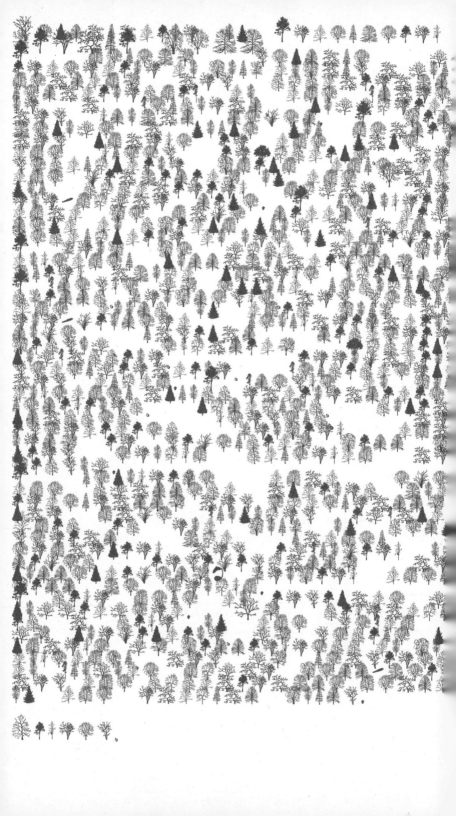

Declaration of Interbeing

KINARI WEBB

I HEREBY DECLARE MY INTENTION TO WORK TOWARD A MORE healthy and sustainable relationship to the planet on a personal, community, and global level. I will become a force for healing and change in the face of the greed, injustice, and destruction which threaten the viability of the Earth for sustaining human and non-human life. I recognize that we have little time left to switch from a path of destruction to one of thriving. I know we must all work together collaboratively to bring about change quickly.

I pledge my effort, resources, skills, knowledge, and desire. The tools of this work are non-violent reorganization, love, radical listening, wisdom, equality, justice, compassion, innovation, determination, persistence, and truth. I pledge to work together across nationalities, religions, cultures, social classes, genders, and identities, knowing that only in diversity will we find enough strength and wisdom.

I recognize that even the smallest actions—both internally and externally—can have profound impacts. This is not work of self-denial, but rather of enhancing and improving our lives individually and collectively: knowing there will be enough.

I sign here to indicate my commitment. My signature is a sign of the depth of my conviction, my desire for change, my willingness to work together, and my readiness to promote human well-being and the sustainable health of the natural world.

Signed,

R O O T S

&

R E S I S T A N C E

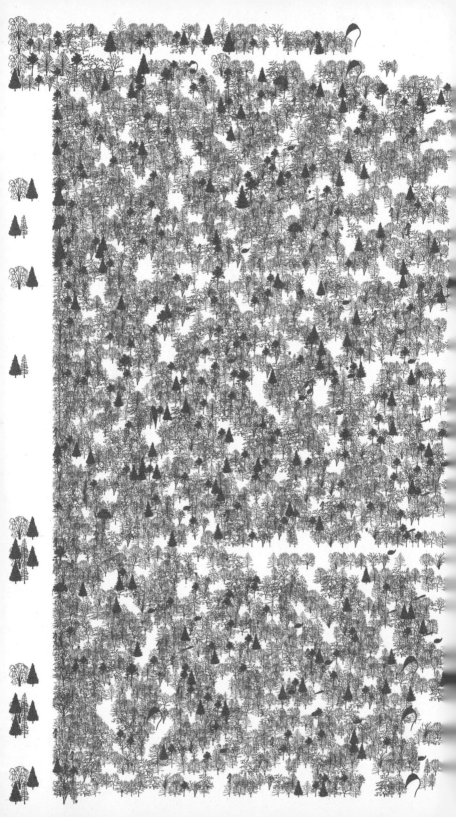

Why Are There No Trees
in Paleolithic Cave Drawings?

WILLIAM CORWIN AND COLIN RENFREW

WILLIAM CORWIN: *Why are there no images of trees in cave art?*

COLIN RENFREW: It is not just trees that do not figure in Paleolithic cave art, it is the plant world in general. In fact all that does figure, apart from quite a few rather abstract symbols, is animals—mainly quadrupeds, and indeed mainly mammals. Why that should be is not entirely clear. The link with hunting may be there—but the species depicted are not always those they hunted. Perhaps it's because they were impressed by big beasts—whether edible or not. The vivacity of those animals is the vivacity of the zoo, not the botanical garden.

WC   *I remember when I was in the caves, Combarelles and Font-de-Gaume, the guides said there were several things they did not represent besides plants—constellations or themselves.*

CR   In general, there are just a few representations of humans in the Paleolithic painted and engraved caves of France and Spain, but they are very few, and they don't have the same vivacity as the representations of the animals.

WC   *The one thing I noticed was a connection between vegetation, constellations and humans, and this is a very practical consideration, in that they don't run away from you, they don't avoid you, they don't need to be captured visually. It seems that perhaps they were drawing animals because unless you killed an animal, you couldn't spend time observing it. If you wanted to see an animal in the wild, it would only be there briefly.*

CR   Well, I think it's natural if you're living in a hunting community to find animals exciting—I mean it's also true in the modern world; you get more thoughtful people going to a botanical garden. But children don't ask to go to the botanical garden, they ask to go to the zoo! And then they're interested in seeing animals that can be pets and domestic animals, or in seeing wild and savage animals.

It is a circumstance that they do move, which is clearly a quality of animals that is part of their fascination, but it is very difficult to say why they didn't show the animals in a vegetational environment which they obviously could have done, you could have the animals rushing through trees as you see in wonderful Renaissance paintings, but you just don't see animals rushing through trees in Paleolithic art.

WC   *They gathered food and used various plants for healing or even religious purposes...*

CR   Undoubtedly yes...

WC   *It seems odd that they wouldn't ever represent them.*

CR   Well it may seem odd, but clearly they focused on animals, and the subject matter is animals, and signs, as we were saying. There are symbols of various kinds, or we call them symbols—they are signs that re-occur, but they're usually not very large and they don't impress us very much visually because they're quite simple. They look as if they might be a sort of proto-writing but really aren't. Whereas some of the depictions of the animals impress us greatly, they seem brilliantly immediate, don't they?

WC   *Yeah. I noticed those designs—some of them were very geometric, some of them almost look like the cross-section of a house or something, they're triangles...*

CR   Yes, those tectiforms.

WC   *Does anyone have any idea what those are? Or what they're about?*

CR   There are theories, but there's no very persuasive theory, but it is clear that they did have a repertoire of signs, so you do find some signs which get repeated. But it's not really very clear what they are or what they're doing.

WC   *Do you have a personal opinion as to what you think the tectiforms are?*

CR   No.

Speaking of Nature

ROBIN WALL KIMMERER

Finding language that affirms our kinship with the natural world

We have a special grammar for personhood. We would never say of our late neighbor, "*It* is buried in Oakwood Cemetery." Such language would be deeply disrespectful and would rob him of his humanity. We use instead a special grammar for humans: we distinguish them with the use of *he* or *she*, a grammar of personhood for both living and dead *Homo sapiens*. Yet we say of the oriole warbling comfort to mourners from the treetops or the oak tree herself beneath whom we stand, "*It* lives in Oakwood Cemetery." In the English language, a human alone has distinction while all other living beings are lumped with the nonliving "its."

As a botany professor, I am as interested in the pale-green lichens slowly dissolving the words on the gravestones as in the almost-forgotten names, and the students, too, look past the stones for inky cap mushrooms in the grass or a glimpse of an urban fox.

For me, this story began in another classroom, in another century, at the Carlisle Indian School where my Potawatomi grandfather was taken as a small boy. My chance of knowing my native language and your chance of ever hearing it were stolen in the Indian boarding schools where native children were forbidden to speak their own language. Within the walls of that school, the clipped syllables of English replaced the lush Potawatomi sounds of water splashing on rocks and wind in the trees, a language that emerged from the lands of the Great Lakes. Our language hovers at the edge of extinction, an endangered species of knowledge and wisdom dwindling away with the loss of every elder.

So, bit by bit, I have been trying to learn my lost language. My house is spangled with Post-it notes labeling wiisgaak, gokpenagen, and ishkodenhs.

It's a very difficult language to learn, but what keeps me going is the pulse of animacy in every sentence. There are words for states of being that have no equivalent in English. The language that my grandfather was forbidden to speak is composed primarily of verbs, ways to describe the vital beingness of the world. Both nouns and verbs come in two forms, the animate and the inanimate. You hear a blue jay with a different verb than you hear an airplane, distinguishing that which possesses the quality of life from that which is merely an object. Birds, bugs, and berries are spoken of with the same respectful grammar as humans are, as if we were all members of the same family. Because we are. There is no it for nature. Living beings are referred to as subjects, never as objects, and personhood is extended to all who breathe and some who don't. I greet the silent boulder people with the same respect as I do the talkative chickadees.

It's no wonder that our language was forbidden. The language we speak is an affront to the ears of the colonist in every way, because it is a language that challenges the fundamental tenets of Western thinking—that humans alone are possessed of rights and all the rest of the living world exists for human use. Those whom my ancestors called relatives were renamed *natural resources*. In contrast to verb-based Potawatomi, the English language is made up primarily of nouns, somehow appropriate for a culture so obsessed with things.

At the same time that the language of the land was being suppressed, the land itself was being converted from the communal responsibility of native people to the private property of settlers, in a one-two punch of colonization. Replacing the aboriginal idea of land as a revered living being with the colonial understanding of land as a warehouse of natural resources was essential to Manifest Destiny, so languages that told a different story were an enemy. Indigenous languages and thought were as much an impediment to land-taking as were the vast herds of buffalo, and so were likewise targeted for extermination.

Linguistic imperialism has always been a tool of colonization, meant to obliterate history and the visibility of the people who were displaced along with their languages. But five hundred years later, in a renamed landscape, it has become a nearly invisible tool. We forget the original names, that the Hudson River was "the river that runs both ways," that Devils Tower was the sacred Bear Butte of the Lakota. Beyond the renaming of places, I think the most profound act of linguistic imperialism was the replacement of a language of animacy with one of objectification of nature, which renders the beloved land as lifeless object, the forest as board feet of timber. Because we speak and live with this language every day, our minds have also been colonized by this notion that the nonhuman living world and the world of inanimate objects have equal status. Bulldozers, buttons, berries, and butterflies are all referred to as it, as things, whether they are inanimate industrial products or living beings.

English has come to be the dominant language of commerce, in which contracts to convert a forest to a copper mine are written. It's just the right language for the purpose, because the forest and the copper ore are equivalent "its." English encodes human exceptionalism, which privileges the needs and wants of humans above all others and understands us as detached from the commonwealth of life. But I wonder if it was always that way. I can't help but think that the land spoke clearly to early Anglo-Saxons, just as it did to the Potawatomi. Robert Macfarlane's wonderful book *Landmarks*, about land and language, documents myriad place names of great particularity that illuminate an ancient Anglo-Saxon intimacy with the land and her beings. It is said that we are known by the company we keep, and I wonder if English sharpened its verbal ax and lost the companionship of oaks and primroses when it began to keep company with capitalism. I want to suggest that we can begin to mend that rift—with pronouns. As a reluctant student of the formalities of writing, I never would have imagined that I would one day be advocating for grammar as a tool of the revolution.

Some of the students in the cemetery have read the chapter in my book *Braiding Sweetgrass* that invokes the grammar of animacy. They are taken aback by the implicit assumption of the hierarchy of being on which English grammar is built, something they had not considered before. They dive headfirst into the philosophical implications of English-language pronouns.

One student, Carson, writes in his essay that *it* is a numbing word: "*It* numbs us to the consequences of what we do and allows us to take advantage of nature, to harm it even, free of guilt, because we declare other beings to be less than ourselves, just things." He echoes the words of Wendell Berry who writes, "People exploit what they have merely concluded to be of value, but they defend what they love, and to defend what we love we need a particularizing language, for we love what we particularly know."

While it's true that words are simply vessels for meaning, without meaning of their own, many cultures imbue the utterance of words with spirit because they originate with the breath, with the mystery of life itself. In her book *Becoming Wise*, Krista Tippett writes, "The words we use shape how we understand ourselves, how we interpret the world, how we treat others. Words make worlds."

I don't mean to say that we are constrained to act in a certain way because of our grammar. I've been saying *it* for most of my life and so far I have not clearcut a forest. (I can't even bring myself to litter, although I tried once, just to see what it would feel like.) Nor does a language of animacy dictate that its speakers will behave with respect toward nonhumans. After all, there are leaders of indigenous nations, raised speaking a grammar of animacy, who willingly surrender their homelands to the use of mining or timber companies. And the Russian language, while embracing animacy in its structure, has not exactly led to a flowering of sustainability there. The relationship between the structure of a language and the behavior characteristic of a culture is not a causal one, but many linguists and psychologists agree that language reveals unconscious cultural assumptions and exerts some influence over patterns of thought.

As we talk beneath the oaks, one of the students emphatically disagrees: "Just because I say *it* doesn't mean I disrespect nature. I grew up on a farm and we called all of our animals *it*, but we took great care of them. We just said *it* because everyone knows that you don't give a name to the thing that you're going to eat." Exactly! We use *it* to distance ourselves, to set others outside our circle of moral consideration, creating hierarchies of difference that justify our actions—so we don't feel.

In contrast, indigenous philosophy recognizes other beings as our relatives, *including* the ones we intend to eat. Sadly, since we cannot photosynthesize, we humans must take other lives in order to live. We have no choice but to consume, but we can choose to consume a plant or animal in a way that honors the life that is given and the life that flourishes as a consequence. Instead of avoiding ethical jeopardy by creating distance, we can embrace and reconcile that tension. We can acknowledge food plants and animals as fellow beings and through sophisticated practices of reciprocity demonstrate respect for the sacred exchange of life among relatives.

The students we walk with in the cemetery are primarily environmental scientists in training. The practice of *it*-ing everything in nature is not only prevalent, but is required in scientific writing. Rachel points out that in her biology class, there are "strict taboos governing personification of nature, and even a whisper of anthropomorphism will lose you a grade on a paper."

I have had the privilege of spending my life kneeling before plants. As a plant scientist, sometimes I am collecting data. As an indigenous plant woman, sometimes I am gathering medicine. These two roles offer a sharp contrast in ways of thinking, but I am always in awe, and always in relationship. In both cases the plants provide for me, teach me, and inspire me. When I write as a scientist, I must say, "An 8 cm root was extracted from the soil," as if the leafy beings were objects, and, for that matter, as if I were too. Scientific writing prefers passive voice to subject pronouns of any kind. And yet its technical language, which is designed to be highly accurate, obscures the greater truth.

Writing as an indigenous plant woman I might say, "My plant relatives have shared healing knowledge with me and given me a root medicine." Instead of ignoring our mutual relationship, I celebrate it. Yet English grammar demands that I refer to my esteemed healer as *it*, not as a respected teacher, as all plants are understood to be in Potawatomi. That has always made me uncomfortable. I want a word for beingness. Can we unlearn the language of objectification and throw off colonized thought? Can we make a new world with new words?

Inspired by the grammar of animacy in Potawatomi that feels so right and true, I've been searching for a new expression that could be slipped into the English language in place of *it* when we are speaking of living beings. Mumbling to myself through the woods and fields, I've tried many different words, hoping that one would sound right to my leafy or feathered companions. There was one that kept rising through my musings. So I sought the counsel of my elder and language guide, Stewart King, and explained my purpose in seeking a word to instill animacy in English grammar, to heal disrespect. He rightly cautioned that "our language holds no responsibility to heal the society that sought to exterminate it." With deep respect for his response, I thought also of how the teachings of our traditional wisdom might one day be needed as medicine for a broken world. So I asked him if there was a word in our language that captured the simple but miraculous state of just being. And of course there is. "*Aakibmaadiziiwin*," he said, "means 'a being of the Earth.'" I sighed with relief and gratitude for the existence of that word. However, those beautiful syllables would not slide easily into English to take the place of the pronoun *it*. But I wondered about that first sound, the one that came to me as I walked over the land. With full recognition and celebration of its Potawatomi roots, might we hear a new pronoun at the beginning of the word, from the "aaki" part that means land? *Ki* to signify a being of the living Earth. Not *he* or *she*, but *ki*. So that when the robin warbles on a summer morning, we can say, "Ki is singing up the sun." Ki runs through the branches on squirrel feet, ki howls at the moon, ki's branches sway in the pine-scented breeze, all alive in our language as in our world.

We'll need a plural form of course, to speak of these many beings with whom we share the planet. We don't need to borrow from Potawatomi since—lo and behold—we already have the perfect English word for them: *kin*. Kin are ripening in the fields; kin are nesting under the eaves; kin are flying south for the winter, come back soon. Our words can be an antidote to human exceptionalism, to unthinking exploitation, an antidote to loneliness, an opening to kinship. If words can make the world, can these two little sounds call back the grammar of animacy that was scrubbed from the mouths of children at Carlisle?

I have no illusions that we can suddenly change language and, with it, our worldview, but in fact English evolves all the time. We drop words we don't need anymore and invent words that we do. *The Oxford Children's Dictionary* notoriously dropped the words *acorn* and *buttercup* in favor of *bandwidth* and *chatroom*, but restored them after public pressure. I don't think that we need words that distance us from nature; we need words that heal that relationship, that invite us into an inclusive worldview of person-hood for all beings.

As I've sent these two little words out into the world like seeds on the wind, they have fallen here and there on fertile ground. Several writers have incorporated them into children's books and into music. Readers have reported that the very sound, the phoneme pronounced "kee," has resonance with other words of similar meaning. *Ki* is a parallel spelling of *chi*—the word for the inherent life energy that flows through all things. It finds harmony with *qui* or "who" in Latinate languages. I've been told it is the name of a Sumerian Earth goddess and the root of Turkic words for *tree*. Could *ki* be a key to unlocking a new way of thinking, or remembering an ancient one?

But these responses are from nature writers, artists, teachers, and philosophers; I want to know how young people, the language makers among us, react. Our little environmental college is dominated by tree huggers, so if there were ever an audience open to *ki*, they would be it.

With *ki* and *kin* rattling around in their heads, the students walk together in the cemetery again, playing with using the words and seeing how they feel on their tongues and in their heads.

Steeped in the formalities of syntax, a fair number of student questions revolve around wanting "rules" for the use of the new words, rules that we don't have. Is there a possessive case? Where are the boundaries? "I could say 'ki' about this shrub," Renee says, "but what about the wind?"

"Yes," I tell her, "in my language, the wind is understood as animate."

As we stand beneath the stoutly branched oak, the students debate how to use the words. If the tree is *ki*, what about the acorns? They agree that the acorns are *kin*, a whole family of little beings. The ground is also littered, in this unkempt portion of the cemetery, with fallen branches. "Are these dead limbs considered *kin* too? Even though they're dead?" Evelyn asks. "Looking at the dead branches on the ground, I found myself thinking a lot about firewood," she says. "I've always spoken—and thought—as if I was the one who made firewood. But when I thought of that tree as *ki*, as a being, I suddenly saw how preposterous that was. I didn't make the firewood. The tree did. I only picked it up from the ground." In just one sentence Evelyn experiences a transfer of agency or capacity for action from humankind to the tree itself. The grammar of animacy is an antidote to arrogance; it reminds us that we are not alone. Evelyn later writes, "Using *ki* made me see everything differently, like all these persons were giving gifts—and I couldn't help but feel grateful. We call that kind of firewood *kindling*, and for me it has kindled a new understanding. And look—that word *kin* is right there in *kindling*."

Another student, Amanda, adds, "Having this word makes me regard the trees more as individuals. Before, I would just call them all 'oak' as if they were a species and not individuals. That's how we learn it in dendrology, but using *ki* makes me think of them each, as not just 'oak,' but as that particular oak, the one with the broken branch and the brown leaves."

Despite their very brief introduction to *ki* and *kin*, the students get right to the heart of the words' implications: "I imagine that this would be a challenge for most religious people," Paul says. "It kind of knocks humans off the pedestal of being the only ones with souls." Indeed, Christian missionaries were the spearhead of language suppression in indigenous cultures and were among the prime architects of the Indian-boarding-school movement. War on a language of animacy and relationship to the natural world was essential to the dual mission of religious and economic conversion. Certainly the biblical mandate for human subjugation of the creation was incompatible with indigenous languages.

Another student, Kieran, observes, "Using these words as I walk around opened my eyes to how we are all connected. When you start using *ki* and *kin*, you will feel remorseful that all of your life you took them for granted."

Ecopsychologists have suggested that our conceptions of self as inherently separate from the natural world have negative outcomes on the well-being of humans and ecosystems. Perhaps these words can be medicine for them both, so that every time we speak of the living world we breathe out respect and inhale kinship, turning the very atmosphere into a medium of relatedness. If pronouns can kindle empathy, I want to shower the world with their sound.

The most outspoken students voice some enthusiasm for the new pronouns, but the quiet skeptics save their reservations for the writing assignment when we are back in class. One student puts it this way: "This is a warm-hearted and generous idea, but it will never work. People don't like change and they will be pissed off if you try and tell them how to talk. Most people don't want to think of nature as being as good as them." One student writes in a scrawl that carries his impatience in every half-formed letter: "If changing the world is what you're after, do something real. Volunteer at the food bank, plant a tree. Dreaming up pronouns is a major waste of time."

This is why I love teaching, the way we are forced to be accountable.

The abstraction of "dreaming up pronouns" does seem fruitless during a time in our nation's history when the language of disrespect is the currency of political discourse. American nationalism, to say nothing of human exceptionalism, is being elevated as a lofty goal, which leaves little room for humility and ecological compassion. It seems quixotic to argue for respect for nonhuman beings when we refuse to extend it to human refugees. But I think this student is wrong. Words do matter, and they can ripple out to make waves in the "real" world.

The ecological compassion that resides in our indigenous languages is dangerous once again to the enterprise of domination, as political and economic forces are arrayed against the natural world and extractive colonialism is reborn under the gospel of prosperity. The contrast in worldview is as stark today as it was in my grandfather's time, and once again it is land and native peoples who are made to pay the price.

If you think this is only an arcane linguistic matter, just look to the North Dakota prairie where, as I write this, there are hundreds of people camping out in a blizzard enduring bitter cold to continue the protective vigil for their river, which is threatened by the construction of the Dakota Access Pipeline and the pipeline's inevitable oil spills. The river is not an *it* for them—the river lies within their circle of moral responsibility and compassion and so they protect *ki* fiercely, as if the river were their relative, because *ki* is. But the ones they are protecting *ki* from speak of the river and the oil and the pipe all with the same term, as if "it" were their property, as if "it" were nothing more than resources for them to use. As if it were dead.

At Standing Rock, between the ones armed with water cannons and the ones armed with prayer, exist two different languages for the world, and that is where the battle lines are being drawn. Do we treat the Earth as if ki is our relative—as if the Earth were animated by being—with reciprocity and reverence, or as stuff that we may treat with or without respect, as we choose? The language and worldview of the colonizer are once again in a showdown with the indigenous worldview. Knowing this, the water protectors at Standing Rock were joined by thousands of non-native allies, who also speak with the voice of resistance, who speak for the living world, for the grammar of animacy.

Thankfully, human history is marked by an ever-expanding recognition of personhood, from the time when aboriginals were not seen as human, when slaves were counted as three-fifths of a person, and when a woman was worth less than a man. Language, personhood, and politics have always been linked to human rights. Will we have the wisdom to expand the circle yet again? Naming is the beginning of justice.

Around the world, ideas of justice for nature are emerging in political and legal arenas. In New Zealand, when the Whanganui River was threatened, indigenous Maori leadership earned protection for the sacred waters by getting the river declared a legal "person" with rights to its own well-being. The constitutions of indigenous-led Ecuador and Bolivia enshrine the rights of Mother Nature. The Swiss amended their constitution to define animals as beings instead of objects. Just last year, the Ho-Chunk Nation in Wisconsin amended its tribal constitution, recognizing that "ecosystems and natural communities within the Ho-Chunk territory possess an inherent, fundamental, and inalienable right to exist and thrive." This legal structure will allow the tribe to protect its homelands from mining for fracking sand and fossil fuel extraction because the land will have legal standing as a person. Supported by the revolutionary initiatives of the Community Environmental Legal Defense Fund, the burgeoning Rights of Nature movement is flowering from the roots of animacy, from the personhood of all beings. We'll need a new pronoun for that.

The students comment that they'd like to use *ki* and *kin*, but stumble over the changes in phrasing. "This would be much easier if I'd learned it as a child," they say. They're right of course. Not only because language patterns are established early in development, but because children quite naturally speak of other beings as persons. I delight in listening to my grandson, who like most toddlers watching a butterfly flit across the yard says, "He is flying," or "She sits on a flower." Children speak at first with a universal grammar of animacy, until we teach them not to. My grandson is also completely smitten with bulldozers and will watch them endlessly, but despite their motion and their roar he is not confused as to their nature: he calls them "it."

I am also introducing him to Potawatomi words. In honor of the language that was taken from his great-grandfather, I want to give that language back to my grandson, so he will never be alone in the world and live surrounded by kin. He already has the basics of animacy; he hugs trees and kisses moss. My heart cracked with happiness when he looked up from the blueberries in his oatmeal and said, "Nokomis, are these minan?"

He's growing up in a time when respect among peoples has grown threadbare and there are gaping holes in the fabric of life. The mending we need will require reweaving the relationship between humans and our more-than-human kin. Maybe now, in this time when the myth of human exceptionalism has proven illusory, we will listen to intelligences other than our own, to kin. To get there, we may all need a new language to help us honor and be open to the beings who will teach us. I hope my grandson will always know the other beings as a source of counsel and inspiration, and listen more to butterflies than to bulldozers.

"Joy Is Such a Human Madness"

The Duff Between Us

ROSS GAY

OR, LIKE THIS: IN HEALTHY FORESTS, WHICH WE MIGHT IMAGINE TO exist mostly above ground, and be wrong in our imagining, given as the bulk of the tree, the roots, are reaching through the earth below, there exists a constant communication between those roots and mycelium, where often the ill or weak or stressed are supported by the strong and surplused.

By which I mean a tree over there needs nitrogen, and a nearby tree has extra, so the hyphae (so close to hyphen, the handshake of the punctuation world), the fungal ambulances, ferry it over. Constantly. This tree to that. That to this. And that in a tablespoon of rich fungal duff (a delight: the phrase fungal duff, meaning a healthy forest soil, swirling with the living the dead make) are miles and miles of hyphae, handshakes, who get a little sugar for their work. The pronoun *who* turned the mushrooms into people, yes it did. Evolved the people into mushrooms.

Because in trying to articulate what, perhaps, joy is, it has occurred to me that among other things—the trees and the mushrooms have shown me this—joy is the mostly invisible, the underground union between us, you and me, which is, among other things, the great fact of our life and the lives of everyone and everything we love going away. If we sink a spoon into that fact, into the duff between us, we will find it teeming. It will look like all the books ever written. It will look like all the nerves in a body. We might call it sorrow, but we might call it a union, one that, once we notice it, once we bring it into the light, might become flower and food. Might be joy.

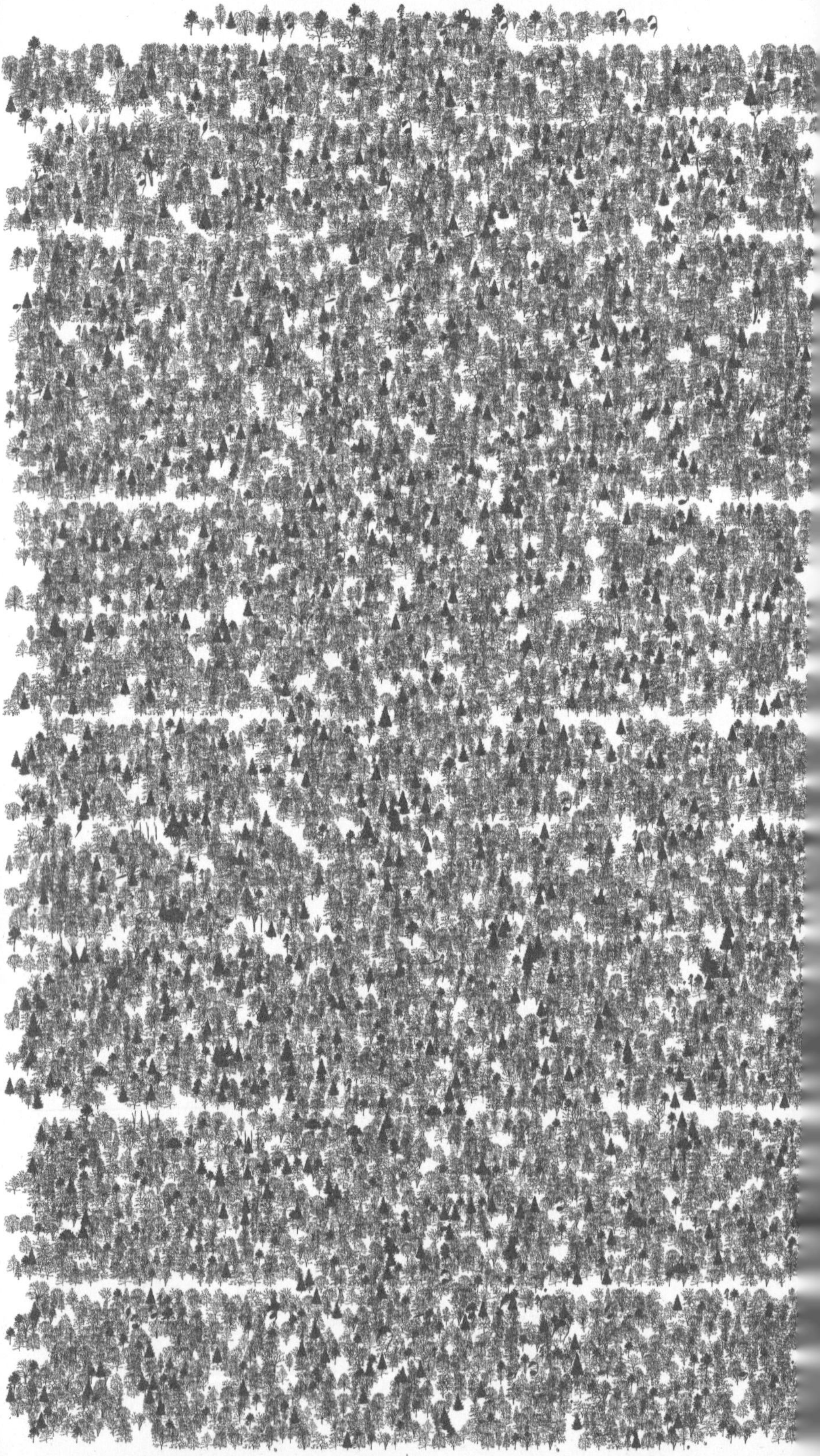

Of Trees in Paint; in Teeth;
in Wood; in Sheet-Iron; in Stone;
in Mountains; in Stars

AENGUS WOODS

BEGINNINGS

In the beginning there were stories and the stories were made of Earth. Rocks and rivers, mountains and sea, these were the gods and the gods moved within them. Of all these we may recall the Meliai, who were dryads or spirits of ash trees. The Meliai were born of Gaia, mother Earth and, so Hesiod tells us, were themselves the mothers of the third, Bronze, race of mankind. It is notable that these ash-tree sisters had also nursed the infant Zeus in Rhea's Cretan cave. And so we might say that trees have tended to the birth of mortals and immortals alike.

MYTH

In 1944, Max Horkheimer and Theodor W. Adorno write, "myth is already enlightenment; and enlightenment reverts to mythology." They tell us that enlightenment is the disenchantment of the world, "the dissolution of myths and the substitute of knowledge for fancy." Such a process of disenchantment is achieved by what they call "die Ausrottung des Animismus" or "the extirpation of animism." Extirpation: from Latin *exstirpō* ("uproot"), from *ex-* ("out of ") + *stirps* ("the lower part of the trunk of a tree, including the roots; the stem, stalk"). Myth would stand for a world infused with life, while knowledge would represent that world with all its life extracted. The things of this Earth uprooted and petrified. Such would be the fate, too, of the language of myth, drained and ossified into a language of science. But language is a thing of parts: words, and beyond that, letters. Could the parts escape the fate of the whole? What might an alphabet of myth look like?

Ogham is an early medieval alphabet, used primarily to write the Early and Old Irish languages. The earliest inscriptions date to the fourth century but some believe it to have been invented as early as the first century B.C. The script appears as a series of horizontal and diagonal strikes. The letters are grouped into four groups determined by the style of stroke involved. Strictly speaking, the word 'ogham' refers only to the script itself, or the form of the letters, while the letters themselves are known collectively as Beith-luis-nin after the letter names of the first letters (in the same manner that the modern 'alphabet' is derived from the Greek Alpha and Beta). The word 'nin' literally means 'a forked branch' but was also used to refer to a written letter in general.

The principle sources on the history and significance of Ogham are the seventh century *Auraicept na n-Éces* (*The Scholars Primer*) and the *Old Irish In Lebor Ogaim* (*Book of Ogham*). Both of these sources make a remarkable claim, that each letter in the script was named after a tree. Because Ogham is not a language but an alphabet, it was primarily a written substitute for Irish. As such, its letters were indicated by names rather than phonetic value, and these names were all derived from trees. In the *Auraicept na n-Éces* the names are given and explained by Bríatharogaim or two-word kennings, poetic devices in which compound figurative language is used to demonstrate the meaning of single-word nouns. Kenning as a literary device is most commonly seen in Old Norse sagas. There a phrase like "wave's horse" might be substituted for "ship" or "feeder of ravens" for "warrior." Thus the *Auraicept* tells us that the Ogham symbol Dair is named after the oak tree and its kenning is slechtam soíre or 'most carved of craftsmanship.' Or another example, Sail, named after the willow whose kennings are the joyous 'beginning of honey,' but also the 'pallor of a lifeless one.'

Consider now the strangeness of an alphabet of trees. Growing within it a pure figuration of meaning, a language mythological to its roots, a script in which the separation of the literal and the figurative is all but erased. Letters that look like branches of trees, named for trees, to be written on bark and on stone.

DACTYL|DÁKTYLOS|FINGER

There are three main theories concerning Ogham's origins. Some have argued that it functioned as a cryptic alphabet so that those who spoke Irish might have a secret means of written communication. Others suggest that Ogham was developed for the writing of Irish, the sounds of which poised a difficulty for its translation into the Latin alphabet. The third view, though much out of favor these days, is nonetheless the richest: R.A.S. Macalister held that Ogham was developed by Gaulish druids as a secret system of hand and finger signals. This theory is based on the fact that Ogham signs are composed of up to five strokes, hypothetically allowing for a relationship of equivalence between the lines of the sign and the fingers of one's hand. Strange it is, too, to recall that poetic meter in Latin is called the pes or foot, and that the meter of the Greek elegy is called the dactyl, from daktylos or finger.

VERBIS NATURALIBUS

On the topic of language acquisition, St. Augustine in his *Confessions* writes, "When they (my elders) named some object, and accordingly moved toward something, I saw this and I grasped that the thing was called by the sound they uttered when they meant to point it. Their intention was shown by their bodily movements, as if it were the natural language of all peoples." Macalister's theory of Ogham's origin thus, and in a most unlikely manner, brings together two senses of the notion of a natural language. Natural in that it is a language composed not of abstractions but of trees, and natural in that it is a language of the hands and fingers, and thus the body. Yet for all that, Ogham is presented by Macalister as a code, a secret language, designed not "for all peoples," but precisely for the learned few.

CYPHERS

Ogham, strictly speaking, is not so much a code as it is a cypher. The distinction between a code and a cypher is that the former works at the level of meaning while the latter works at the level of component. Thus while a codified language might consist of symbols for various words, clauses or ideas, a cypher would, by contrast, offer a symbol for each letter of the alphabet. Something that more truly exemplifies this is hobo code. Its origins are unknown but, like Macalister's claims of a secret system, hobo code served to transmit messages between initiates—tramps, vagrants and the wandering dispossessed—usually by means of signs cut into trees, fences and other wayside markers. Particular markings had specific meanings: a vertical stroke with four horizontal strokes of alternating length meant that an officer of the law lived at that location.

CODES

In a 2011 work from his *Codes* series called "Voices From Moon," the Japanese artist On Kawara used pencils to fill page after page with varying combinations of colored strikes and dashes. The work appeared to constitute a code to which the artist declined to offer any key. In 2015, during a retrospective of his work at the Guggenheim Museum, a gallery guide named Ben Slyngstad worked out that there were twenty-five possible combinations of dashes. This was one shy of the 26 needed to completely represent the English alphabet. However, Slyngstad then noticed that the letter w could be symbolised by writing two consecutive symbols for v. Using this key he translated the entire work, revealing that it consisted of the conversation, verbatim, between Buzz Aldrin, Neil Armstrong, and the space center in Houston on July 20, 1969, the day of the moon landing. Like Ogham, Kawara's code is thus, strictly speaking, a cypher.

THE IDEOGRAM

In 1919, Ezra Pound published *The Chinese Written Character as a Medium for Poetry* by Ernest Fennollosa. A highly eccentric work, it argued that the Chinese language is essentially ideographic and non-phonetic in nature. Fennollosa interpreted Chinese characters as images that offered meaning pictorially by compounding discrete parts. In his view, Chinese script presented "visual shorthand pictures of the operations of nature." What this meant was that the etymology of the language remained constantly in view, its figurative and metaphorical roots were not lost to time but remained active and visible in the characters themselves. In the written Chinese, birds might be seen, perching by water, houses and people, wood and stone; such, at least, were Fennollosa's claims. Questionable or not, they spoke to the dream of a language of nature in which the Earth might be seen giving the mind its resources and the mind might remain aware of the metaphorical and mythical foundations of its own edifice. Curiously, this tethering of language and nature in the Chinese ideogram provided the basis for Pound's ideogrammic method of composition in which ideas and images are juxtaposed without explanation, producing radically new complexities of meaning. Thus, claims about the pictorial clarity and simplicity of a language that might bear nature on its face influenced Pound's composition of the Cantos, one of the most dense, abstract and allusive poetic sequences in the history of modernism.

EMOJIS

In 2013, the entirety of the novel *Moby Dick* was translated into emojis, those little ideograms of smiling faces and pets and objects that populate our phones and number around 1000. The result goes by the pleasingly apt title *Emoji Dick*. Meanwhile, the usage of emojis in our daily messages and missives grows exponentially. Their appeal seems to be based on the strange and paradoxical combination of specificity and obscurity that they embody. The numerous face and hand emoji point to a framework of meaning in which St. Augustine's natural language is made manifest in a series of signs based around the body. Others portraying houses, cars, cakes and pets seem to draw their apparent universality from that other expansive and ever-metastasising framework of significance: capitalism. They purport to transcend cultural difference and cut a line of sincerity and clarity straight to the nebulous heart of what we mean to say. Yet for all that, emojis, particularly in combination, open wormholes of ambiguity. Their creative juxtaposition looks like Pound's ideogrammic method writ small—ideas and images side by side without explanation, meanings slippery and subjective. Few who are not adept can penetrate this mass of brightness. By times code, by times translation, by times thought or emotion expressed with remarkable directness or infinite possibility, emoji represent the twin dreams of language: semantic certainty and creative ambiguity.

OF TREES

Yet directness and certainty remain a dream despite our words, despite our codes, despite our cyphers. Who can state for sure the meaning of *Moby Dick*? "Of whales in paint; in teeth; in wood; in sheet-iron; in stone; in mountains; in stars": Ishmael, its narrator, could find them everywhere. Yet the whale itself, the white whale, *the named whale*, is elusive. What did it mean to Ahab? Why the obsession, the desire and the pursuit? Everything can mean something else, if only we could agree what. Augustine wondered whether we could decide simply by pointing and naming. Remember that *Moby Dick*, whose title names its prey, itself begins with an act of naming: "Call me Ishmael." Yet in saying that, it is clear, too, that any name would have sufficed. The willow is also 'sallow,' is also 'osier.' In such simple acts lie a world of ambiguity, and a history concealed from the eyes of the everyday. Nothing is steady. Meaning sways like the hull of a ship. Ahab, with leg of wood, and scars on his body like the "seam sometimes made in the straight, lofty trunk of a great tree," hunts over ocean and sea in a vessel of timber from which a mast extends like a great oak into the sky above. Nailed to it is a gold doubloon and at its top a man sits, in the masthead, watching the horizon, searching.

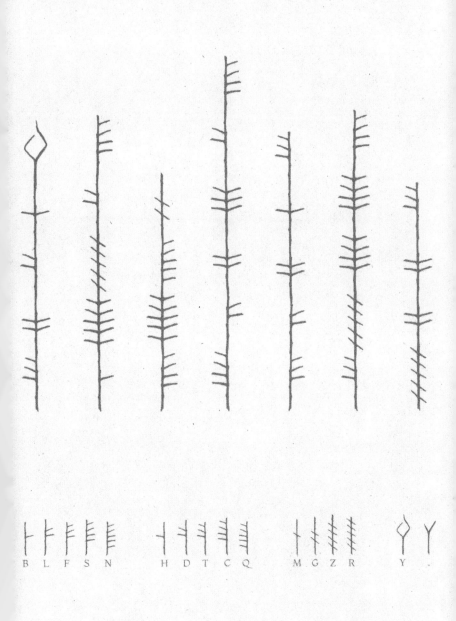

Legere and βιβλιοθήκη

The Library as Idea and Space

ANNA-SOPHIE SPRINGER

> It felt like being inside an enormous brain. Imagine
> being totally surrounded by those shelves, full of books
> in their compartments, ladders all over the place, all
> those book stands and library tables piled high with
> catalogues and bibliographies, the concentrate of all
> knowledge, don't you know, and not one sensible book
> to read, only books about books.
>
> —GENERAL STUMM, IN ROBERT MUSIL'S
> *THE MAN WITHOUT QUALITIES,* 1940

ETYMOLOGICALLY LINKED TO VOCABULARY SUCH AS THE LATIN
legere, which can mean both "collecting" and "reading," and the Greek
bibliothēkē, or "bookcase," the library—from Robert Musil and Virginia
Woolf to Jorge Luis Borges and Walter Benjamin to Alberto Manguel and
Moyra Davey—is inhabited as a space of tension between chaos and order,
a space of collecting information of and about life and the universe in an
attempt to make sense of it through organization, reading, commentary, and
interpretation. This establishes the library both as archetype and prototype
for storing knowledge, literally a device of historiography itself. The most
famous ancient library that was designed as such was, of course, the mytho-
historical Library of Alexandria. From around 300 B.C. until the beginning
of its destruction with the Roman imperial takeover under Julius Caesar,
the Library of Alexandria was the principal workplace for international
scholarship. In light of this discussion of the curatorial, it is worth noting that
this classical library was in fact incorporated into a larger complex known
as the Mouseion, or House of the Muses, which formed a multidisciplinary

study center similar to a university (etymologically, it is the source of the modern word "museum.")[10] In his erudite meditation on libraries, Alberto Manguel makes the observation that in terms of a conception of the world, the Library of Alexandria and the Tower of Babel are direct opposites. While the tower represents the "belief in the unity of the universe," the library instead embodies an understanding that the world is made up of innumerable different voices that, if somehow collected and read, would "address the whole of creation" through their very singularity and yet, as an ensemble, could never become static.[11] Expanding Manguel's comparison, it is interesting to consider the two architectures in relation to concepts of dispersal and containment. In the moment of its destruction fragments of the Tower are violently and irretrievably flung out in all directions across the Earth, whereas the Library derives its meaning as a space of proximity for gathering together such fragments. "Books are not dispersed but assembled," as Georges Perec asserts in "The Art and Manner of Arranging One's Books."[12] If we consider that the Library's assumed founder, King Ptolemy I, used to send missives around the world pleading for "every kind of book by every kind of author,"[13] the myth of an all-embracing library evokes yet another Old Testament story, that of Noah's Ark as a repository for living specimens of every existing species. While the Ark was built to survive the Great Flood, the Library of Alexandria—ancient repository of memory for the paginated world—was destroyed by flames.

The intrinsic connection between the library and grand cultural narratives still perpetuates today; reflecting such great ambitions, the Bibliotheca Alexandrina was, for instance, recently rebuilt and declared a

---

10 For an in-depth history of the Library of Alexandria, see Roy MacLeod, ed., *The Library of Alexandria: Center of Learning in the Ancient World* (New York: I.B. Tauris, 2005). On the history of cultural loss and the mass destruction of libraries, see James Raven, ed., *Lost Libraries: The Destruction of Great Book Collections since Antiquity* (New York and London: Palgrave Macmillan, 2004).

11 "The Tower of Babel collapsed in the prehistory of storytelling; the Library of Alexandria rose when stories took on the shape of books, and strove to find a syntax that would lend each word, each tablet, each scroll its illuminating and necessary place." Alberto Manguel, *The Library at Night* (New Haven and London: Yale University Press, 2006), 23–4.

12 Georges Perec, "The Art and Manner of Arranging One's Books" (1978), in *Species of Spaces and Other Places*, ed. and trans. John Sturrock (London: Penguin Books, 1997), 150.

13 Manguel, *The Library at Night*, 22; with additional references to Luciano Canfora, *La Biblioteca Scomparsa* (Palermo: Sellerio Editore, 1987).

"window" between contemporary Egypt and the rest of the world.[14] In the context of Occidental history, however, libraries are especially symbolic of a particular Enlightenment sensibility. Poignantly addressed by Victor Hugo in *The Hunchback of Notre Dame*, libraries became the new cathedrals of cities when science and the attendant desire to disseminate knowledge replaced the religious impetus of previous generations. Stories were no longer told primarily through clerical art and architecture but were instead translated, multiplied, and circulated through printed books. In Hugo's novel, this idea is summarized in the phrase "Ceci tuera cela" "this will kill that"—a provocative exaggeration, though the printing press by no means did away with architecture, just as the digital turn has not replaced printed matter. What is true, however, is that the ethos of the public library (in contrast to private, monastic, or other specialized and restricted libraries) continues to be intimately connected to democratic ideals of equality and free access to knowledge and culture. Such libraries are usually non-profit spaces, which provide citizens with material and immaterial goods and media that would otherwise have to be purchased. Therefore, one of the many ways in which the library contributes to society is by converting marketable goods into public goods. The potential of the library for making things public is furthermore reflected in its paradoxical reality as an intellectual meeting place: based on intellectual and communal values, it also lends a public platform to otherwise fundamentally private—whether mental or cerebral—activities like reading and thinking, thus connecting it with ideals such as free speech and the freedom of expression. The library is thus both a political economy and an intellectual space. In a recent essay, media studies and library scholar Shannon Mattern has emphasized this notion by discussing several recent initiatives of so-called "little libraries," that is, community or artistic endeavors of setting up alternative "para-libraries" in urban public spaces. The author addresses the role and use of such initiatives in light of the institution of the public library as their general model. While she critically questions a number of these

---

14 The institution was inaugurated in 2002 as a UNESCO project; the complex was designed by the Norwegian/American architectural firm Snøhetta Arkitektur og Landskap. The library has the capacity for eight million volumes and aims to be a center both for traditional media and digital materials, though whether the shelves will ever be filled to capacity is uncertain due to financial and other constraints.

projects as potentially counter-productive, especially when trying to hold governments accountable for their responsibilities as providers of sufficient public space, as one strong, positive example she describes the guerrilla libraries of the Occupy movement. Mattern stresses their antithetical but complimentary role in relation to online media and communication, arguing that these politicised street libraries draw their importance from the occupation of physical public space, while symbolizing the "right to knowledge" for the 99 percent. Furthermore, their collections are said to reflect and express the ideologies and intellectual culture upon which the movement is based.[15]

As a phenomenon also observed recently in the major protests in Turkey—when publishing houses and readers came together to build a street library in Istanbul's Gezi Park—and which has intensified through the news about several violent attacks on the Bibliotheca Alexandrina during the political upheavals in Egypt in August 2013, it is crucial to understand how books and libraries are embraced in political struggles for freedom.

IN THIS MADHOUSE OF BOOKS

In order to allow for our subjectivities to unfold by selecting and engaging with whatever book-fragment we request from their archival holdings (and then reanimating these fragments through individualized and intertextual reading processes), public libraries have typically been standardized in order to administer the retrieval of books in an ordered form. There are several different library classification systems currently in use, such as the Library of Congress Classification (LCC) for academic libraries (mostly in the English-speaking world), and several more varied approaches in Germany. The most widely accepted library ordering system is the Dewey Decimal Classification Scheme (DDC), originally invented in the 1870s by the American librarian and rationalist Melvil Dewey (1851–1931). Applied in general public libraries to this day, it laid the foundation for the LCC and other academic classification systems. One of the reasons the DDC has survived

---

15 See Shannon Mattern, "Marginalia: Little Libraries in the Urban Margins," *Design Observer*, 5 May 2012. On publishing houses setting up camp at Gezi Park in the summer of 2013, see "Publishing Houses to Unite in Gezi Park to Distribute Major Resistance Material: Books," *Hürriyet Daily News*, 4 June 2013.

for so long is that its mathematical sequences can be broken down infinitely in order to add new categories to the nine conceptual "classes" that Dewey initially conceived. Despite its relative flexibility and ubiquity, Dewey's invention has been criticized for reflecting a culturally narrow interpretation of objectivity, privileging white, Anglo-Saxon, and Christian worldviews, and thereby excluding a range of alternative perspectives on human knowledge.[16] But the imposition of a particular standpoint is not unique to the DDC. Since it is usually possible to assign one book to multiple categories at once, any chosen library system whether in a private, "individual bureaucracy" (Georges Perec) of free associations, or in a public context, will reflect particular assumptions, while operating through a combination of various classificatory modes. Library classification systems are rational structures inherently motivated by a "fear of being engulfed by this mass of words,"[17] and yet, even if they are powerful enough to suppress this fear, in so doing they proliferate other limits, cracks, and misguided trajectories.

"How do you find your way in this madhouse of books?" asks Robert Musil's General Stumm of the librarian. The following reasoning suffices to inform the General: "The secret of a good librarian is that he never reads anything more of the literature in his charge than the titles and the tables of contents. 'Anyone who lets himself go and starts reading a book is lost as a librarian!' ... 'He's bound to lose perspective!'"[18] As a caricature of the librarian, the passage nevertheless highlights the act of cataloguing as the core aim of the rationalizing work in the library; the result of this painstaking process is, of course, the catalogue. A means for listing and indexing the complete holdings of a library, the catalogue is the central nervous system of the library's organization. It serves as the primary interface to library books. In the past, the catalogue was actually an assembly of index cards or a

16 See Melvil Dewey, *A Classification and Subject Index for Cataloguing and Arranging the Books and Pamphlets of a Library* (Amherst, MA: 1876). "Decimal Classification Beginnings," Library Journal 45 (February 1920). Dewey biographer Wayne A. Wiegand called for a critical analysis of the DDC's approach to categorization based on the writings of Michel Foucault and Pierre Bourdieu, in Wiegand, "The 'Amherst Method': The Origins of the Dewey Decimal Classification Scheme," *Libraries & Culture 33*, no. 2 (Spring 1998): 175–94.

17 Resnais, *Toute la mémoire du monde*, 02:35.

18 Robert Musil, *The Man Without Qualities*, Vol. 1., trans. Sophie Wilkins (New York: Vintage Books, 1996), 503.

continuously expanding series of bound volumes; nowadays it is usually an online database that can be accessed remotely.

In its essential role as a list of items in a collection, the library catalogue bears some resemblance to the early exhibition catalogue, which originated as a simple list to carry as a reference while viewing the artworks in an exhibition. In fact, it was not until the mid-twentieth century that exhibition catalogues evolved into aesthetic and critical compendiums more ambitious in scope, size, and scholarship.[19] One important figure in this evolution was the Swedish art collector and curator Pontus Hultén (1924–2006), who first directed the Moderna Museet in Stockholm, and then moved on to establish and develop the Centre Pompidou in Paris in the 1970s and early 1980s. Influenced by Marcel Duchamp's writing and the radicality of his *La Boîte Verte* (1931), in the 1950s Hultén began to understand exhibition catalogues as "art experiments" that ought to correspond to their respective museum exhibitions but relay them beyond the institution's walls. Exemplary of the curator-editor, he was often described as such: "Hultén is a passionate reader and curator, who creatively processes his knowledge for himself and others in exhibitions and libraries. He uses literature and libraries in their most fundamental role: by liberating the immaterial, spiritual energy stored in them and transforming it into something new and idiosyncratic."[20] A profuse reading practice is thus leveraged as a means to reinvent the mode and display of the re-read collection.

Regarding its aim to be a comprehensive index, the library catalogue also shares its ambition with the encyclopaedia. In the second half of the eighteenth century, Denis Diderot edited what is considered the first modern encyclopaedia, the visual dictionary *Encyclopédie, ou Dictionnaire raisonné des sciences, des arts et des métiers*. Like our contemporary *Wikipedia*, it was written by way of collective effort, and like the aforementioned Library of Alexandria, it is an example of a utopian project to collect and represent all of human knowledge. The absurdity of any such endeavor is at the center of Borges's seminal story, "The Library of Babel" (1941). For Borges, it is above all the library's

19 See Pnina Wentz, "Writing about Art Exhibition Catalogues: A Literature Review," in *Exploring Science in Museums*, ed. Susan Pearce (London: The Athlone Press, 1996), 172–77.

20 See Lutz Jahre, "Zur Geschichte des Ausstellungskataloges am Beispiel der Publikationen von Pontus Hulten," in *Das Gedruckte Museum von Pontus Hulten*, ed. Lutz Jahre (Ostfildern: Cantz, 1996), 31. All translations in the text are the author's own unless otherwise indicated.

monstrous catalogue that expresses a sense of perversion. For, by containing all of its errors and their corrections, the catalogue's role is that of a palimpsest inevitably turning sense into nonsense. Borges thus accentuates the relationship between order and entropy, portraying the library as a nightmare and the apotheosis of paradoxical irrationality.

Lessons from Fungi

TOBY KIERS

I WANT YOU TO IMAGINE A MARKET ECONOMY THAT'S 400 MILLION years old, one that's so ubiquitous that it operates in almost every ecosystem of the world, so huge that it can connect millions of traders simultaneously, and so persistent that it survived mass extinctions. It's here, right now, under our feet. You just can't see it. And unlike human economies that rely on cognition to make decisions, traders in this market, they beg, borrow, steal, cheat, all in the absence of thought. So hidden from our eyes, plant roots are colonized by a fungus called arbuscule mycorrhizae. Now the fungus forms these complex networks underground of fine filaments thinner than even threads of cotton. So follow one of these fungi, and it connects multiple plants simultaneously. You can think of it as an underground subway system, where each root is a station, where resources are loaded and unloaded. And it's also very dense, so roughly the length of many meters, even a kilometer, in a single gram of dirt. So that's the length of 10 football fields in just a thimbleful of soil. And it's everywhere. So if you passed over a tree, a shrub, a vine, even a tiny weed, you passed over a mycorrhizal network. Roughly 80 percent of all plant species are associated with these mycorrhizal fungi.

So what does a root covered in fungi have to do with our global economy? And why as an evolutionary biologist have I spent the last 10 years of my life learning economic jargon? Well, the first thing you need to understand is that trade deals made by plant and fungal partners are surprisingly similar to those made by us, but perhaps even more strategic. You see, plant and fungal partners, they're not exchanging stocks and bonds, they're exchanging essential resources, and for the fungus, that's sugars and fats. It gets all of its carbon directly from the plant partner. So much carbon, so every year, roughly five billion tons of carbon from plants go into this network underground. For the root, what they need is phosphorus and nitrogen, so by exchanging their carbon they get access to all of the nutrients collected by that fungal network. So to make the trade, the fungus penetrates into the root cell of the host and forms a tiny structure called an arbuscule, which is Latin for "little tree." Now, you can think of this as the physical stock exchange of the trade market. The roots and fungi form complex underground networks to exchange essential resources. Our aim is to understand how organisms (without brains) evolve different trading strategies. How does a fungus sense local nutrient conditions, and make complex calculations about when and where to trade? How is this information integrated across the network? We develop tools to visually monitor where and when trade takes place across plant-fungal networks.

They Carry Us With Them

The Great Tree Migration

CHELSEA STEINAUER-SCUDDER

WHEN WE THINK OF MIGRATION, WHAT OFTEN COMES TO MIND IS the seasonal movement of animals from one region to another: a repeated, patterned journey in which creatures are drawn in one direction toward a food supply or resource, and in the other direction toward breeding grounds.

Thousands of species of migratory creatures—at least four thousand species of birds alone—embark on epic journeys across and around the world every year as they are pulled into flowing patterns of movement that correspond to the sun's steady pull on the Earth. Birds, insects, mammals, and fish follow felt sensory signals in currents of air and water, changes in season, the planet's magnetic field, the position of the sun and stars, subtle changes in temperature. Earth's ecological systems, in this way, are woven together by intricate and far-reaching threads of movement.

What about our rooted companions? The northeastern spruce-fir forests that the Bicknell's thrush journeys to every spring, or the stands of jack pine where the eastern bluebird builds its nests? We often admire trees for their steady rootedness, their resiliency in the face of change; for the gift of shade and companionship that a single long-lived tree might offer us and then our children and our grandchildren, even our great-grandchildren. But trees—or, more appropriately, forests—are perhaps not so rooted, so reliably *placed*, as we might think.

Right now, around the world, trees are on the move.

Some scientists prefer the phrase "shifts in range" to "migration" when it comes to forests—ecosystems defined by long-lived, woody beings that cannot pull up their roots from beneath the forest floor and walk or swim or fly when conditions around them indicate it is time to do so. But trees do move, they simply do it through successive generations.

Trees reproduce primarily through seed dispersal, relying upon animals, winds, and waters to carry their offspring to fertile soils where they might anchor into the ground and germinate. A mature tree will send seeds in all directions. In a stable environment, where conditions are much the same as when the parent tree began its life, a forest might continue to regenerate in roughly the same location and the same configuration of species, year after year, decade after decade.

But what if a new generation of seeds is cast into the wind during a period of drought? What if winters are no longer as cold as they once were? What if a certain pest can now survive in a forest where it once could not? Suddenly, seedlings might find themselves in a less friendly environment that they are not genetically well adapted to. Perhaps the only ones that will survive are those that happen to be carried, say, northward, or to a slightly higher elevation. As the climate changes in and around forests, seeds might succeed in places where they did not before or fail where they once succeeded.

If this pattern continues, the forest will begin a slow journey in a new direction.

Thus, although they do not move in a to-and-fro pattern annually in the way of the humpback whale, "migration" still seems an apt word to describe the movements of trees, even if such patterns of movement may take several—or many—human generations to reveal themselves as patterns. Certainly, trees do not migrate seasonally in the way we normally think of seasons, but there are many things trees do that don't fit easily into our normal human way of thinking—at least from our point of view, which tends to have a breadth of focus corresponding to our roughly eighty-year life span.

For example, if we here in the northeastern United States were to zoom out from our understanding of seasons as annual patterns, and step instead into a deeper time, we might begin to see "seasons" in a different way. From this vantage point, a season may be seen as more akin to, say, an era of glaciation.

Let's step back to about 14,600 years ago, near the end of the Pleistocene, that phenomenal age of mile-high ice, when glaciers ebbed and flowed over the land. We might notice that as the Laurentide Ice Sheet begins its slow retreat as temperatures warm, spruce trees are flowing up from the south: we watch as pointed evergreens with splays of emerald needles work their way across present-day Maine and southern Québec, spreading farther into Canada, settling along the rocky slopes and poorly drained soils that were recently carved from the ice. Fast-forward 3,000 years to the beginning of the Holocene. The climate is warmer and drier; the ice sheet is vanishing further; the range of the spruce is now shrinking as the trees are pushed farther northward and replaced by pine to the south. Then, in the mid-Holocene, roughly 6,000 years later, there is a period of drought. Much of the eastern hemlock disappears as the lack of water leaves the trees stressed and vulnerable to the infestation of a pest that overtakes the population. It takes 2,000 years for the hemlock to return. During this time spruce move southward again, settling into roughly the configuration that we find them in today.

From this long view of time, the movement of trees might appear to be as fluid and flowing as that of an arctic tern. For millions of years, the world's forests have been migrating in this way, drawn and pulled in one direction or another by the eras and eons of climate that our Earth has undergone in its long life. And they have done so quite successfully: Through the more than dozen glaciations that occurred during the Quaternary period—and the corresponding dramatic shifts in climate and temperature—just one species of tree is believed to have gone extinct in North America. The rest were able to keep up, largely through long-distance seed dispersal.

Migration, thus, is not new to forests. But the twenty-first-century climate crisis has greatly diminished the ability of trees to move *effectively*. Changes in climate and landscape are happening so quickly and introducing so many new and unexpected factors—onslaughts of pests, invasive plants, fungal disease, built environments that dissect and isolate ecosystems—that forests often cannot move fast enough to account for changing environmental factors.

The Earth now has an atmospheric CO_2 concentration of 419 parts per million, the highest the planet has seen in three to five million years. In 2019, NASA stated that eighteen of the nineteen warmest years on record had occurred since 2001. Around the world, scores of species of trees are moving north, or west, or upslope. Some species are losing ground, others are gaining it. In the eastern United States, eighty-six species of trees are currently on the move. Pines, spruce, and firs are generally heading north; oaks and maples are heading west. Here in Maine, seven of the ten most common species of tree are predicted to have moderate to severe reductions in suitable habitat within a century.

What do these changes to our forests mean? What are the trees taking with them and what is arriving in their wake? What is the relationship between the trees' migration and the ecological systems and human communities that they are leaving behind? What does the movement of these beings reflect back to us in the present and foreshadow for the future?

How do we bear witness? How do we bid farewell?

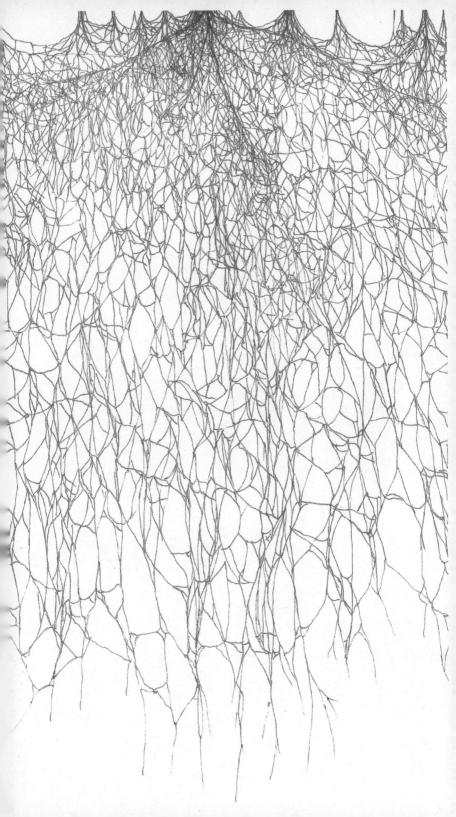

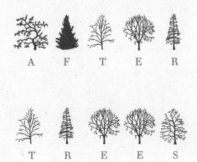

AFTER

TREES

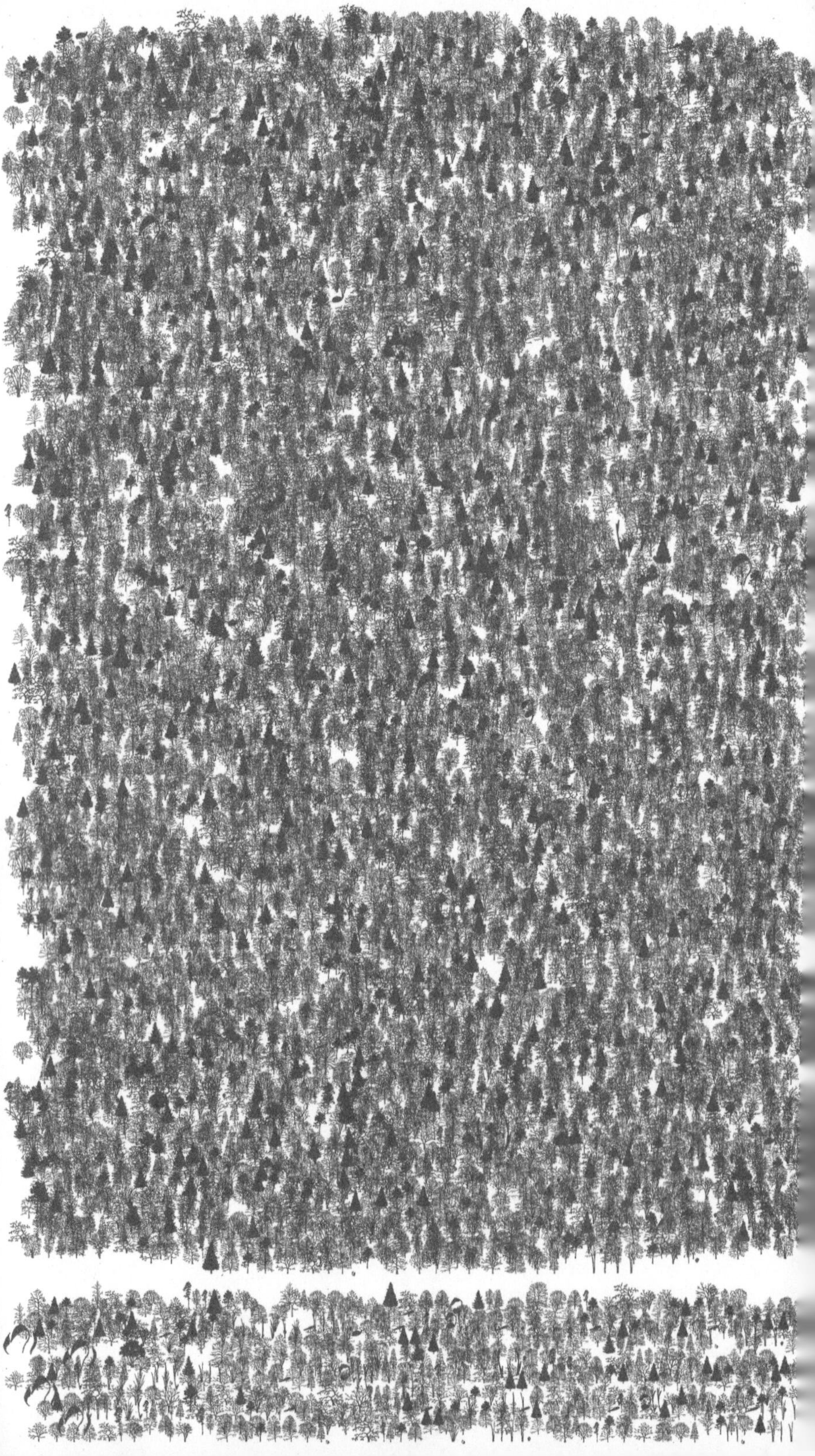

Afterword

Another World is Possible

KATIE HOLTEN

THIS BOOK IS A LOVE LETTER TO OUR VANISHING WORLD, WRITTEN with Trees.

I've always felt like a plant-person, moss and lichen covered; the land a part of me and me of it. The Irish landscape I grew up in is riddled with stone walls and stories, seventy thousand placenames and countless fairy trees. Irish placenames are derived from hidden histories or trees that used to grow there, ghost forests. Dair means 'Oak' and is found in many placenames around Ireland. Townlands contain Cill, Irish for 'cell' or 'church,' demonstrating how intimately entwined our very cells-selves are with the Catholic church! In the first experiment in colonization, our language was beaten out of us. We had to learn in secret "hedge schools."

Ireland's medieval Ogham, sometimes called a 'tree alphabet,' used trees for letters. The characters were called feda, 'trees,' or nin, 'forking branches,' due to their shapes. This ancient writing was read from the ground up—each character sprouting from a central line, like branches on a tree. Journeying from the heartwood of ancient Ogham to today's emojis, Aengus Woods introduces us to the strangeness of an alphabet of trees.

Written on bark, it is no coincidence that some of the first forms of writing used trees. Our capacity to produce language is innate, like a tree's ability to produce leaves. Buds burst with potential stories. Words are alive, emerging from and evolving with culture. What if we plant living time capsules with secret messages written to our future selves? Why not make our words *matter* by planting them? We could seed secret messages of resistance, plant blooming poems and cultivate landscapes of renewal.

I created a Tree Alphabet—a new ABC—by taking each of the 26 letters of the Latin alphabet and creating a corresponding tree drawing. These new 'characters' were converted into a font: a typeface that I call Trees. This font, the first of several, lets us type with Trees, translating our letters into trees, words into woods and stories into forests. I used the font to make the book

About Trees, which was published as a limited-edition artists' book by Broken Dimanche Press in 2015. I'm thrilled to have an opportunity to remake *About Trees* as *The Language of Trees*. At the heart of these books is the Tree Alphabet, a living alphabet that can be planted, allowing us to seed stories, watch them sprout and grow.

The Language of Trees is an archive of human knowledge filtered through many branches of thought. I hope the book takes readers on a journey—from prehistoric cave paintings to creation myths, from Tree Clocks in Mongolia and forest fragments in the Amazon to Emerson's language of fossil poetry, from Eduardo Kohn's anthropology beyond the human to Robin Wall Kimmerer's call for a new grammar of animacy—unearthing a grove of beautiful stories along the way.

We have much to learn from trees. Kimmerer and other scientists like Suzanne Simard and Toby Kiers study tree communities, inspiring ways for us to learn from—and live with—the natural world. They show how trees talk to each other using mycorrhizal fungi, an underground hyphal network. This natural language exists beyond our understanding of communication because trees 'speak' in frequencies that humans can't perceive. We can hear leaves rustle, branches creak and squeak in the wind, but trees make more sounds that are inaudible to the human ear but discernable by other beings. For example, trees undergoing stress form tiny bubbles inside their trunks creating ultrasonic vibrations.[21] Trees can also be transformed into instruments of joy, like Yo-Yo Ma's cello made from spruce and maple.[22]

Artists, writers, activists, musicians, engineers, philosophers, farmers, educators—people everywhere, and throughout time—have loved and learned from trees. Historians, linguists, and mathematicians use tree forms to understand the world. A simple mathematical game of trees shows us that there is a number—TREE(3)—that is so large no human can comprehend it and physics can't describe it.[23]

A few years before I was born, Christopher Stone, a Professor of Law at the University of Southern California, had an epiphany while speaking with

---

21 Gabe Popkin, Trees Call for Help—And Now Scientists Can Understand: Team identifies the sounds made by drought-stressed trees. *National Geographic*, April 16, 2013. https://www.nationalgeographic.com/science/article/130415-trees-drought-water-science-global-warming-sounds, last accessed September 11, 2022.

22 See David Haskell's recent books for more on the songs of trees.

23 Jay Bennett, Wrap your head around the enormity of the number TREE(3). *Popular Mechanics*, October 20, 2017. https://www.popularmechanics.com/science/math/a28725/number-tree3/, last accessed September 17, 2022.

his students—what if trees, like people, had rights? "I am quite seriously proposing that we give legal rights to forests, oceans, rivers and other so-called 'natural objects' in the environment," he wrote.

Today the movement to recognize these Rights of Nature is inspiring people around the world, with indigenous communities leading the way. Almost all successful Rights of Nature cases—so far—protect bodies of water. Why not trees? Paul Powlesland, founder of Law for Nature, told me, "I'm not aware of a draft Rights of Trees in general as they seem more difficult to conceptualize than rivers."[24] I believe we will soon see Rights for Forests and Trees.

The Climate Emergency demands that we learn the languages of trees and speak on their behalf. Learning other languages creates empathy, compelling us to reconsider our relationships with other beings. If trees have memories, respond to stress, and communicate, what can they tell us? And will we listen? Listening, speaking, reading and writing are how humans communicate and make sense of the world. The alphabet is how we organize information and knowledge; our networked world depends on it. Trees, the font, lets us renew our relationships with language, landscape, perception, time, memory and reading itself by slowing the reader down to decipher words in the woods.

Translation is perhaps the most intimate form of reading. When we translate our words into glyphs, such as trees, it forces us to re-read everything. The Tree Alphabet forces us to revisit the past, re-present the present, and reimagine the future by translating or re-writing what we think we already know.

And so letter by letter, tree by tree, we can reforest our stories, communities and our imaginations, reimagine public spaces, reconsider 'monuments' and restore biodiversity while rewilding language. We can also ingest the alphabet, seeding our stories in plant DNA, encoding messages at the molecular level.[25] History shows us that we become the stories we tell ourselves and our children. What stories do we want to leave behind? What do we want our ancestors to remember us for?

This book gathers many voices, both human and nonhuman, offering ways to learn from, through and with trees. Activists, health care workers, guardians

---

24 Paul Powlesland to the author in a direct message on Twitter, April 6, 2022.

25 Anne Trafton, A programming language for living cells, MIT News, March 31, 2016, https://news.mit.edu/2016/programming-language-living-cells-bacteria-0331, last accessed September 11, 2022.

and warriors like Winona LaDuke, Nemo Andy Guiquita, Kinari Webb and Valerie Segrest articulate the urgency of this moment by sharing their indigenous knowledge acquired through many generations. I am grateful for Tree People.

People and trees have always been entwined. When we protect plants, we protect ourselves. Today we are teetering on the edge of extinction along with most of life on Earth. The Amazon is on the verge of tipping from life-sustaining rainforest to savannah. Our civilization is sleepwalking into apocalypse. But when I'm shouting in the streets at climate protests I am surrounded by thoughtful, kind, powerful, joyful, determined people fighting to protect people, plants, water, trees and truth by working to create a better world. We need to nurture their messages of hope.

The alphabet is magic, a way to love the world intimately. With these 26 little letters we can create any word in the universe. Letters of the alphabet are like seeds planted on a blank page. I offer the Tree Alphabet as a gift for those who want to fall in love with the world by rewilding their words.

Learning the language of trees can help us think like the multicellular organisms that we are, inspiring new ways to live and work together. Trees can help us rewrite the broken stories that we have been telling ourselves. Today, in this time of planetary emergency, we need to reread origin stories and rediscover other ways of living in harmony with our kin. Beautiful re-imaginings are happening everywhere—people are Rewilding, Reforesting, Restoring and creating Radical Hope.

I offer *The Language of Trees* as a celebration of trees and our entangled relationship with them. I hope this book inspires us to consider how our human nature might re-merge with the state of nature. The book is also a call to action. An ecological civilization based on Rights of Nature is a survival imperative. Please join me in declaring emergency and advocating for the Rights of Nature, the Rights of Trees, Forests, Peatlands, Rivers, and Planet Earth.

Dear Reader, I invite you to download the free Trees font. Translate your words—your tweets, thoughts, and twigs of reason—into Trees. The act of compos(t)ing love letters to our future selves might just be what makes our future selves possible.

When I feel overwhelmed by what we've caused—climate change, pandemics, poverty, biodiversity loss, migration, war, ecocide—I find solace in the beauty of the living world, especially in trees. Trees are truthful. They fill my heart with joy. Their simplicity and quiet beauty—alone on a city sidewalk or together in a forest—slows down time. Tree Time occurs in ever widening circles, like tree rings. If humans embraced Tree Time we would understand that time is not linear. Past and future are as real as now, meaning our actions today will resonate with as yet unfurled leaves on our family tree.

Shortly before she died in August 2020, aged 99, the extraordinary artist Luchita Hurtado told Andrea Bowers, "Trees breathe out. We breathe in." Another world is possible. Together—with trees—we must breathe her into being.

Katie Holten
Chilmark, September 2022

Bibliography

Ackerman, Diane. *The Human Age: The World Shaped By Us*. New York: Norton, 2014.

Adams, Max. *The Wisdom of Trees: A Miscellany*. London: Head of Zeus, 2018.

—. *Trees of Life*. New York: Apollo, 2020.

Allen, Jessica L. & James C. Lendemer. *Urban Lichens: A Field Guide for Northeastern North America*. New Haven: Yale University Press, 2021.

Anderson, M. Kat. *Tending the Wild: Native American Knowledge and the Management of California's Natural Resources*. Berkeley: University of California Press, 2005.

Artaud, Antonin. *Antonin Artaud: Selected Writings*. Edited by Susan Sontag and translated by Helen Weaver. New York: Farrar, Straus and Giroux, 1976.

Atwood, Margaret. *Scribbler Moon*. Oslo: Future Library, forthcoming in 2114.

—. *The Year of the Flood*. New York: Doubleday, 2009.

Augé, Marc. Translated by John Howe. *Non-Places: Introduction to an Anthology of Supermodernity*. London: Verso, 1995.

Bachelard, Gaston. *The Poetics of Space*. Boston: Beacon Press Books, 1994.

Bai, Durga, Bhajju Shyam, and Ramsingh Urveti. *The Night Life of Trees*. Chennai: Tara Books, 2006.

Ballard, J.G. *Concrete Island*. New York: Vintage, 1994.

—. *The Complete Short Stories*. London: Harper Perennial, 2006.

—. *The Drowned World*. London: Berkley Books, 1962.

Barad, Karen. *Meeting the Universe Halfway: Quantum Physics and the Entanglement of Matter and Meaning*. Durham, NC: Duke University Press, 2007.

Barrow, John D. *The Artful Universe*. Oxford: Oxford University Press, 1995.

Battles, Matthew. *Tree*. New York: Bloomsbury Academic, 2017.

Baudelaire, Charles. Translated by Louise Varèse. *Paris Spleen*. New York: W. W. Norton, 1970.

Baum, Frank L. *The Wizard of Oz*. London: Penguin, 1995.

Beatty, Laura. *Pollard*. New York: Vintage, 2009.

Beckett, Samuel. *The Complete Dramatic Works of Samuel Beckett*. London: Faber & Faber, 2006.

Beer, Amy-Jane. *A Tree a Day: 365 of the World's Most Majestic Trees*. San Francisco: Chronicle Books, 2022.

Bejan, Adrian and Peder Zane. *Design in Nature: How the Constructal Law Governs Evolution in Biology, Physics, Technology, and Social Organizations*. New York: Doubleday, 2012.

Bell, Michael and Sze Tsung Leong. *Slow Space*. New York: Monacelli Press, 1998.

Benjamin, Walter. *The Arcades Project*. Cambridge, MA: Harvard University Press, 1999.

Bennett, Claire-Louise. *Pond*. London: Fitzcarraldo Editions, 2015.

Bennett, Jane. *Vibrant Matter: A Political Ecology of Things*. Durham, NC: Duke University Press, 2010.

Beresford-Kroeger, Diana. *Arboretum America: A Philosophy of the Forest*. Ann Arbor, MI: University of Michigan Press, 2003.

—. *The Global Forest: Forty Ways Trees Can Save Us*. New York: Viking, 2010.

—. *To Speak for the Trees: My Life's Journey from Ancient Celtic Wisdom to a Healing Vision of the Forest*. Toronto: Random House, 2019.

Berman, Marshall. *All That Is Solid Melts Into Air: Experience of Modernity*. London: Gardners Books, 1983.

Berry, Wendell. *The Peace of Wild Things*. New York: Penguin, 2018.

—. *The Unsettling of America: Culture and Agriculture*. Berkeley: University of California Press, 1996.

Bickford-Smith, Coralie. *The Song of the Tree*. New York: Penguin, 2021.

Bilott, Rob. EXPOSURE: *Poisoned Water, Corporate Greed, and One Lawyer's Twenty-Year Battle Against Dupont*. New York: Atria, 2019.

Blyton, Enid. *The Enchanted Wood*. London: Newnes, 1939.

—. *The Magic Faraway Tree*. London: Newnes, 1943.

—. *Up the Faraway Tree*. London: Newnes, 1951.

Bolaño, Roberto. *The Savage Detectives*. London: Picador, 2008.

—. *The Unknown University*. Cambridge, MA: New Directions, 2013.

Bonnett, Alastair. *Unruly Places: Lost Spaces, Secret Cities, and Other Inscrutable Geographies*. Boston: MA: Houghton Mifflinpol, 2014.

Bonneuil, Christophe and Jean-Baptiste Fressoz. Translated by David Fernbach. *The Shock of the Anthropocene: The Earth, History and Us*. New York: Verso, 2016.

Borges, Jorge Luis. *Fictions*. London: Calder Publications, 1975.

—. *Labyrinths*. London: Penguin Books, 1989.

Bourgon, Lyndsie. *Tree Thieves: Crime and Survival in the Woods*. New York: Little Brown, 2022.

Brand, Stewart. *The Whole Earth Catalog*. Menlo Park, CA: Portola Institute, 1968-1972.

Bridle, James. *Ways of Being: Beyond Human Intelligence*. London: Allen Lane, 2022.

Brockman, John., ed. *What Should We Be Worried About?* New York: Harper Collins, 2014.

Brown, Jane. *The Pursuit of Paradise: A Social History of Gardens and Gardening*. London: Harper Collins, 2000.

Brown, Peter G. & Peter Timmerman, eds. *Ecological Economics for the Anthropocene: An Emerging Paradigm*. New York: Columbia University Press, 2015.

Buckle, Lynn. *What Willow Says*. Dublin: époque press, 2021.

Byrne, David. *Arboretum*. Edinburgh, Canongate, 2019.

Cabanes, Valérie. *Rights for Planet Earth*. New Delhi: Natraj Publishers, 2017.

Caillois, Roger. *The Writing of Stones*. Charlottesville: University Press of Virginia, 1985.

Calvino, Italo. *Invisible Cities*. London: Vintage, 1997.

Campbell, Susan. *A History of Kitchen Gardening*. London: Frances Lincoln, 2006.

Camus, Albert. *The Plague*. London: Penguin Books, 1989.

Canclini, Nestor Garcia. *Art Beyond Itself: Anthropology for a Society Without a Story Line*. Durham, NC: Duke University Press, 2014.

Cannavò, Peter and Joseph Lane. *Engaging Nature: Environmentalism and the Political Theory Canon*. Cambridge, MA: MIT Press, 2014.

Carroll, Lewis. *Alice in Wonderland*. New York: W. W. Norton, 1992.

Carson, Rachel. *Silent Spring*. Originally serialized in the *New Yorker*, 1962.

Casey, Edward S. *Earth-Mapping: Artists Reshaping Landscape*. Minneapolis: University of Minnesota Press, 2005.

—. *Getting Back into Place: Toward a Renewed Understanding of the Place-World*. Bloomington, IN: Indiana University Press, 1993.

de Certeau, Michel. *The Practice of Everyday Life*. Berkeley, CA: University of California Press, 1984.

Challenger, Melanie. *On Extinction: How We Became Estranged from Nature*. London: Granta, 2011.

Childs, Craig. *Apocalyptic Planet: A Field Guide to the Future of the Earth*. New York: Vintage, 2013.

Chin, Ava. *Eating Wildly: Foraging for Life, Love and the Perfect Meal*. New York: Simon & Schuster, 2014.

Chomsky, Noam. *Optimism Over Despair: On Capitalism, Empire, and Social Change*. Chicago, IL: Haymarket Books, 2017.

Christensen, Inger. Translated by Susanna Nied. *Alphabet*. Cambridge, MA: New Directions, 2001.

—. *The Condition of Secrecy*. Translated by Susanna Nied. Cambridge, MA: New Directions, 2019.

Claeys, Gregory. *Utopianism for a Dying Planet: Life After Consumerism*. Princeton: Princeton University Press, 2022.

Coccia, Emanuele. Translated by Dylan J. Montanari. *The Life of Plants: A Metaphysics of Mixture*. Cambridge, MA: Polity, 2018.

Cocteau, Jean. *Round The World Again in Eighty Days*. London: Tauris Parke Paperback, 2000.

Cohen, Jeffrey Jerome. *Stone: An Ecology of the Inhuman*. Minneapolis: University of Minnesota Press, 2015.

Collins, Matt & Roo Lewis. *Forest: A Journey Through Wild and Magnificent Landscapes*. San Francisco: Chronicle Books, 2020.

Cook, Diane. *The New Wilderness*. London: One World, 2020.

Cosgrove, Denis, ed. *Social Formation and Symbolic Landscapes*. London: Croom Helm, 1984.

Coverley, Merlin. *Psychogeography*. Harpenden: Pocket Essentials, 2010.

Cox, Stan. *The Green New Deal and Beyond: Ending the Climate Emergency While We Still Can*. San Francisco: City Lights, 2020.

—. *The Path to a Livable Future: A New Politics to Fight Climate Change, Racism, and the Next Pandemic*. San Francisco: City Lights, 2021.

Culture Declares Emergency, ed. *Letters to the Earth*. London: HarperCollins, 2021.

Crang, Mike and Nigel Thrift, eds. *Thinking Space*. Milton Park, Abingdon, Oxon: Routledge, 2000.

Crary, Jonathan. *Suspensions of Perception: Attention, Spectacle, and Modern Culture*. Cambridge, MA: MIT Press, 1999.

Cronon, William. *Changes in the Land: Indians, Colonists, and the Ecology of New England*. New York: Hill and Wang, 2003.

Critchley, Simon. *Memory Theater*. London: Fitzcarraldo Editions, 2014.

Curtis, Wayne. *The Last Great Walk: The True Story of a 1909 Walk from New York to San Francisco and Why It Matters Today*. Emmaus, PA: Rodale, 2014.

Dabiri Emma. *What White People Can Do Next: From Allyship to Coalition*. London: Penguin, 2021.

Daily, Gretchen Cara and Katherine Ellison. *The Economy of Nature: The Quest to Make Conservation Profitable*. Washington D.C.: Island Press, 2003.

Daltun, Eoghan. *An Irish Atlantic Rainforest: A Personal Journey into the Magic of Rewilding*. Dublin: Hachette, 2022.

Daly, Herman E. *Beyond Growth: The Economics of Sustainable Development*. Boston: Beacon Press, 1997.

Daly, Herman E. Co-written with Joshua Farley. *Ecological Economics: Principles and Applications*. Washington D.C.: Island Press, 2003.

Daly, Herman E. and Kenneth Townsend, eds. *Valuing the Earth: Economics, Ecology, Ethics*. Cambridge, MA: MIT Press, 1993.

Dante. *The Divine Comedy: Inferno, Purgatorio, Paradiso*. London: Penguin Classics, 2013.

Davies, Jeremy. *The Birth of the Anthropocene*. Oakland: University of California Press, 2016.

Dawson, Ashley. *Extinction: A Radical History*. New York: OR Books, 2016.

Deakin, Roger. *Wildwood: A Journey Through Trees*. London: Hamish Hamilton, 2007.

Dean, Tacita and Hans Ulrich Obrist. *The Conversation Series*. Berlin: Buchhandlung Walther König, 2012.

Debord, Guy. Translated by Donald Nicholson-Smith. *The Society of the Spectacle*. New York: Zone Books, 1994.

Defoe, Daniel. *Robinson Crusoe*. London: Penguin, 1965.

De Landa, Manuel. *A Thousand Years of Nonlinear History*. London: Zone Books, 1997.

—. *War in the Age of Intelligent Machines*. London: Zone Books, 1991.

Deleuze, Gilles and Félix Guattari. *A Thousand Plateaus: Capitalism and Schizophrenia*. London: Athlone, 1988.

—. *Nomadology: The War Machine*. Los Angeles: Semiotext(e), 1986.

Demuth, Bathsheba. *Floating Coast: An Environmental History of the Bering Strait*. New York: W. W. Norton & Company, 2019.

Descola, Philippe. *The Ecology of Others*. Translated by Geneviève Godbout & Benjamin P. Luley. Chicago: Prickly Paradigm Press, 2013.

Deutsche, Rosalyn. *Evictions: Art and Spatial Politics*. Cambridge, MA: MIT Press, 1998.

Diaz, Natalie. *Postcolonial Love Poem*. Minneapolis: Graywolf Press, 2020.

Dick, Philip K. *Do Androids Dream of Electric Sheep?* New York: Doubleday, 1968.

Dillon, Brian. *Ruins: Documents of Contemporary Art*. London: Whitechapel, 2011.

—. *Sanctuary*. Berlin: Sternberg Press, 2009.

—. *Suppose a Sentence*. New York: New York Review Books, 2020.

Doheny-Farina, Stephen. *The Wired Neighbourhood*. Newhaven: Yale University Press, 1996.

Doherty, Gareth & Mohsen Mostafavi. *Ecological Urbanism*. Cambridge, MA: Harvard University Press, 2010.

Drori, Jonathon. *Around the World in 80 Trees*. New York: Laurence King Publishing, 2018.

Drucker, Johanna. *Inventing the Alphabet: The Origins of Letters from Antiquity to the Present*. Chicago: University of Chicago Press, 2022.

Dungy, Camille T. ed. *Black Nature: Four Centuries of African American Nature Poetry*. Athens, GA: University of Georgia Press, 2009.

—. *Trophic Cascade*. Middletown, CT: Wesleyan University Press, 2017.

Dunnett, Nigel and Noel Kingsbury. *Planting Green Roofs and Living Walls*. Portland, OR: Timber Press, 2004.

Dunnett, Nigel. Co-written with Andy Clayden. *Rain Gardens: Managing Water Sustainably in the Garden and Designed Landscapes*. Portland, OR: Timber Press, 2007.

Eco, Umberto. *Travels in Hyperreality*. London: Picador, 1987.

Ehrenreich, Ben. *Desert Notebooks: A Road Map for the End of Time*. Berkeley, CA: Counterpoint, 2020.

Elkin, Lauren. *Flâneuse: Women Walk the City in Paris, New York, Tokyo, Venice and London.* New York: Penguin, 2016.

Ellison, Rev Robert Lee "Skip". *Ogham: The Secret Language of the Druids.* Shorewood, IL: ADF Publishing, 2008.

Elliot, T.S. *The Wasteland.* New York: Harcourt Publications, 1967.

Ellsworth, Elizabeth and Jamie Kruse, eds. *Making the Geologic Now: Responses to Material Conditions of Contemporary Life.* Santa Barbara, CA: Punctum Books, 2012.

Epstein, Mark. *The Trauma of Everyday Life.* London: Penguin, 2013.

Faber, Michel. *The Book of Strange New Things.* Edinburgh: Canongate, 2014.

Fauconnier, Gilles, Eve Sweetser and Eileen Smith Sweet, eds. *Spaces, Worlds and Grammar: Cognitive Theory of Language and Culture.* Chicago: University of Chicago Press, 1996.

Findlay, John M. *Magic Lands: Western Cityscapes and American Culture after 1940.* Berkeley: University of California Press, 1992.

Finkelpearl, Tom. *What We Made: Conversations on Art and Social Cooperation.* Durham, NC: Duke University Press, 2013.

Fisher-Wirth, Ann and Laura-Gray Street. *The Ecopoetry Anthology.* San Antonio: Trinity University Press, 2013.

Fishman, Robert. *Bourgeois Utopias: The Rise and Fall of Suburbia.* New York: Basic Books, 1987.

Fleck, Richard F. *Henry Thoreau and John Muir Among the Native Americans.* Hamden, CT: Shoestring Press, 1985.

Flyn, Cal. *Islands of Abandonment: Nature Rebounding in the Post-Human Landscape.* London: HarperCollins, 2022.

Fogarty, Pádraic. *Whittled Away: Ireland's Vanishing Nature.* Dublin: Collins Press, 2017.

Foster, Charles. *Being a Beast: Adventures Across the Species Divide.* New York: Metropolitan Books, 2016.

Fowles, John. *The Tree.* New York: Ecco, 2010.

Fox, William L. *Aereality: On the World from Above.* Berkeley, CA: Counterpoint, 2009.

Frazer, Sir James George. *The Golden Bough.* Oxford: Oxford University Press, 2009.

Freeman, John. *Dictionary of the Undoing.* New York: MCD x FSG Originals, 2019.

—. *Wind, Trees.* Port Townsend, WA: Copper Canyon Press, 2022.

Fremeaux, Isabelle and Jay Jordan. *We Are 'Nature' Defending Itself: Entangling, Art, Activism and Autonomous Zones.* London: Pluto Press, 2021.

Gagliano, Monica, John C. Ryan and Patrícia Vieira, eds. *The Language of Plants: Science, Philosophy, Literature.* Minneapolis, University of Minnesota Press, 2017.

—. *The Mind of Plants: Narratives of Vegetal Intelligence.* Santa Fe: Synergetic Press, 2021.

Gamwell, Lynn. *Mathematics and Art: A Cultural History.* Princeton: Princeton University Press, 2015.

Gander, Forrest. *Core Samples from the World.* Cambridge, MA: New Directions, 2011.

—. *Twice Alive.* Cambridge, MA: New Directions, 2021.

Gander, Forrest & John Kinsella. *Redstart: An Ecological Poetics.* Iowa City: University of Iowa Press, 2012.

Gay, Ross. *The Book of Delights: Essays.* Chapel Hill: Algonquin, 2019.

Garreau, Joel. *Edge City: Life on the New Frontier.* New York: Doubleday, 1991.

Ghosh, Amitav. *The Great Derangement: Climate Change and the Unthinkable.* Chicago: University of Chicago Press, 2016.

—. *The Nutmeg's Curse: Parables for a Planet in Crisis.* Chicago: University of Chicago Press, 2021.

Gilio-Whitaker, Dina. *As Long as Grass Grows: The Indigenous Fight for Environmental Justice, from Colonization to Standing Rock.* Boston: Beacon Press, 2019.

Giono, Jean. *The Man Who Planted Trees.* Hartford, VT: Chelsea Green Publishing, 1985.

Gleick, James. *Chaos: Making a New Science.* New York: Penguin Books, 1988.

—. *Faster: The Acceleration of Just About Everything.* New York: Vintage, 2000.

—. *The Information: A History, a Theory, a Flood.* New York: Pantheon, 2011.

—. *Time Travel: A History.* New York: Pantheon, 2016.

—. *What Just Happened: A Chronicle from the Information Frontier.* New York: Vintage, 2003.

Goodell, Jeff. *How to Cool the Planet: Geoengineering and the Audacious Quest to Fix Earth's Climate.* Boston: Mariner Books, 2011.

Gordon, Robert J. *The Rise and Fall of American Growth: The U.S. Standard of Living Since the Civil War.* Princeton: Princeton University Press, 2016.

Goulson, David. *Silent Earth: Averting the Insect Apocalypse.* London: Random House, 2021.

Graeber, David and David Wengrow. *The Dawn of Everything: A New History of Humanity.* New York: Farrar, Straus and Giroux, 2021.

Grande, John K. *Art Nature Dialogues: Interviews with Environmental Artists.* New York: SUNY Press, 2004.

Greene, Graham. *Journey Without Maps.* London: Penguin, 1991.

Griffin-Pierce, Trudy. *Earth is My Mother, Sky is My Father: Space, Time and Astronomy in Navajo Sandpainting.* Santa Fe: University of New Mexico, 1995.

Griffiths, Jay. *Why Rebel.* London: Penguin Random House, 2021.

Grinde, Donald A., and Bruce E. Johansen. *Ecocide of Native America: Environmental Destruction of Indian Lands and Peoples.* Santa Fe, NM: Clear Lights Publishing, 1995.

Gros, Frederic. Translated by John Howe. *A Philosophy of Walking.* New York: Verso, 2014.

Grossman, Zoltán. *Unlikely Alliances: Native Nations and White Communities Join to Defend Rural Lands.* Seattle: University of Washington Press, 2017.

Grusin, Richard, ed. *The Nonhuman Turn.* Minneapolis: University of Minnesota Press, 2015.

Habermas, Jürgen. *The Structural Transformation of the Public Sphere.* Cambridge, MA: MIT Press, 1991.

Hadfield, Chris. *You Are Here: Around the World in 92 Minutes.* Canada: Random House, 2014.

Haeg, Fritz. *Edible Estates: Attack on the Front Lawn.* New York: Metropolis Books, 2008.

Hamilton, Clive. *Defiant Earth: The Fate of Humans in the Anthropocene.* Cambridge, MA: Polity, 2017.

Hanks, William F. *Referential Practice: Language and Lived Space Among the Maya.* Chicago: University of Chicago Press, 1990.

Harjo, Joy, ed, *When the Light of the World Was Subdued, Our Songs Came Through: A Norton Anthology of Native Nations Poetry.* New York: W. W. Norton & Company, 2020.

Harjo, Joy. *How We Became Human: New and Selected Poems 1975-2001.* New York: W. W. Norton & Company, 2004.

—. *Poet Warrior: A Memoir.* New York: W. W. Norton & Company, 2021.

Harman, Graham. *The Prince of Networks: Bruno Latuour and Metaphysics.* Melbourne: re.press, 2009.

Harrari, Yuval Noah. *Homo Deus: A Brief History of Tomorrow*. London: Harvill Secker, 2016.

—. *Sapiens: A Brief History of Humankind*. New York: Vintage, 2015.

Harraway, Donna J. *Simians, Cyborgs and Women: The Re-intention of Nature*. London: Free Association, 1991.

Harrison, Robert Pogue. *Forests: The Shadow of Civilization*. Chicago: University of Chicago Press, 1992.

Harvey, David. *The Urban Experience*. Oxford: Basil Blackwell, 1989.

Haskell, David George. *Sounds Wild and Broken: Sonic Marvels, Evolution's Creativity and the Crisis of Sensory Extinction*. New York: Viking, 2022.

—. *The Forest Unseen: A Year's Watch in Nature*. New York: Penguin Books, 2013.

—. *The Songs of Trees: Stories from Nature's Great Connectors*. New York: Penguin Books, 2018.

Hathaway, Michael J. *What a Mushroom Lives for: Matsutake and the Worlds They Make*. Princeton: Princeton University Press, 2022.

Heaney, Seamus. *North*. London: Faber & Faber. 1975.

—. *Seeing Things*. London: Faber & Faber. 1991.

Heim, Michael. *The Metaphysics of Virtual Reality*. Oxford, New York, 1993.

Hickel, Jason. *Less is More: How Degrowth Will Save the World*. London: Penguin Random House, 2021.

Hidalgo, César. *Why Information Grows: The Evolution of Order, from Atoms to Economics*. New York: Basic Books, 2015.

Higgins, Richard. *Thoreau and the Language of Trees*. Berkely, University of California Press, 2017.

Higgs, Kerryn. *Collision Course: Endless Growth on a Finite Planet*. Cambridge, MA: MIT Press, 2014.

Hildyard, Daisy. *Emergency*. London: Fitzcarraldo Editions, 2022.

Hillier, Bill. *Space is the Machine: A Configurational Theory of Architecture*. Cambridge, MA: Cambridge University Press, 1996.

Hillman, Mayer. Co-written with Tina Fawcett and Sudhir Chella Rajan. *How We Can Save the Planet: Preventing Global Climate Catastrophe*. New York: St. Martin's Press, 2008.

Hirsch, Eric and Michael O'Hanlon, eds. *The Anthropology of Landscape: Perspectives on Place and Space*. Oxford: Clarendon Press, 1995.

Hitchcock, Susan Tyler. *Into the Forest: The Secret Language of Trees*. Washington D.C.: National Geographic, 2022.

Hobhouse, Henry. *Seeds of Change: Six Plants That Transformed Makind*. Berkeley, CA: Counterpoint, 2005.

Hohenegger, Beatrice. *Liquid Jade: The Story of Tea from East to West*. New York: St. Martin's Press, 2006.

Holmes, Hannah. *The Secret Life of Dust: From the Cosmos to the Kitchen Counter, the Big Consequences of Little Things*. New York: John Wiley & Sons, 2001.

Holten, Katie. *About Trees*. Berlin: Broken Dimanche Press, 2015.

Holthaus, Eric. *The Future Earth: A Radical Vision for What's Possible in the Age of Warming*. New York: HarperCollins, 2020.

Homer et al. Translated by Richmond Lattimore. *The Iliad*. London: Penguin Books 1987.

Homer et al. Translated by E.V. Rieu and D.C.H. Rieu. *The Odyssey*. London: Penguin Books, 1991.

Hugo, Nancy R. *Seeing Trees: Discover the Extraordinary Secrets of Everyday Trees.* Portland, OR: Timber Press, 2011.

Hunter, Robert J. *Simple Things Won't Save the Earth.* Austin: University of Texas Press, 1997.

Huxley, Aldous. *Brave New World.* London: Flamingo, 1994.

—. *The Doors of Perception & Heaven and Hell.* New York: Harper and Row, 1954.

Iyer, Pico. *The Art of Stillness: Adventures in Going Nowhere.* New York: Simon & Schuster, 2014.

Jackson, Wes. *Consulting the Genius of the Place: An Ecological Approach to a New Agriculture.* Berkely, CA: Counterpoint, 2010.

Jacobs, Jane M. *Edge of Empire, Postcolonialism and the City.* London: Routledge, 1996.

Jahren, Hope. *Lab Girl.* New York: Vintage, 2017.

—. *The Story of More: How We Got to Climate Change and Where to Go from Here.* New York: Vintage, 2020.

Jameson, Frederic. *Postmodernism, or, the Cultural Logic of Late Capitalism.* Durham, NC: Duke University Press, 1990.

Jamieson, Dale and Bonnie Nadzam, *Love in the Anthropocene.* New York: OR Books, 2015.

Jamieson, Dale. *Ethics and the Environment.* Cambridge University Press, 2008.

—. *Reason in a Dark Time: Why the Struggle Against Climate Change Failed—and What it Means for Our Future.* Oxford: Oxford University Press, 2014.

Jeffery, Josie. *Seed Bombs: Going Wild with Flowers.* London: Ivy Press, 2011.

Jellicoe, Geoffrey and Susan Jellicoe. *The Landscape of Man: Shaping the Environment From Prehistory to the Present Day.* London, Thames & Hudson, 1995.

Johnson, Ayana Elizabeth and Katherine K. Wilkinson. *All We Can Save: Truth, Courage, and Solutions for the Climate Crisis.* London: One World, 2020.

Joyce, James. *Ulysses.* London: Penguin Classics, 1992.

—. *The Dubliners.* London: Penguin Books, 1996.

Kafka, Franz. *Amerika.* London: Minerva, 1992.

—. *The Complete Short Stories.* New York: Vintage Books, 1992.

—. *"Metamorphosis" and Other Stories.* London: Minerva, 1992.

Kastner, Jeffrey. *Land and Environmental Art.* New York: Phaidon, 2010.

Kaufman, L.A., *Direct Action: Protest and the Reinvention of American Radicalism.* New York: Verso, 2017.

Kay, Emma. *Worldview.* London: Book Works, 1999.

Keith, Michael and Steve Pile. *Place and the Politics of Identity.* Abingdon, Oxford: Routledge, 1993.

Kern, Stephen. *The Culture of Time and Space, 1880–1918.* Cambridge: Harvard University Press, 1986.

Khan-Cullors, Patrisse. *When They Call You a Terrorist: A Black Lives Matter Memoir.* New York: St. Martin's Press, 2018.

Kimmerer, Robin Wall. *Braiding Sweetgrass: Indigenous Wisdom, Scientific Knowledge, and the Teachings of Plants.* Minneapolis: Milkweed Editions, 2013.

—. *Gathering Moss: A Natural and Cultural History of Mosses.* Corvallis: Oregon State University Press, 2003.

King, Anthony D., ed. *Re-presenting the City: Ethnicity, Capital and Culture in the 21st Century Metropolis.* New York: New York University Press, 1996.

Kingsolver, Barbara. *Flight Behavior.* New York: Harper, 2013.

—. *Unsheltered*. New York: Harper, 2018.

Kinsella, Thomas and Sean O'Tuama. *An Duanaire: An Irish Anthology: 1600-1900, Poems of the Dispossessed*. Dublin: Dolmen Press, 1981.

Kleeman, Alexandra. *Something New Under the Sun*. New York: Hogarth, 2021.

Klein, Naomi. *On Fire: The (Burning) Case for a Green New Deal*. New York: Simon & Schuster, 2019.

—. *This Changes Everything: Capitalism vs. The Climate*. New York: Simon & Schuster, 2014.

Klingan, Katrin and Ashkan Sepahvand. *Textures of the Anthropocene: Grain Vapor Ray*. Cambridge, MA: MIT Press, 2015.

Kofman, Eleonore and Elizabeth Lebas, eds. *Henri Lefebvre: Writings on Cities*. Oxford: Blackwell, 1996.

Kohn, Eduardo. *How Forests Think: Toward an Anthropology Beyond the Human*. Berkely: University of California Press, 2012.

Kolbert, Elizabeth. *Field Notes from a Catastrophe: Man, Nature and Climate Change*. New York: Bloomsbury, 2006.

—. *The Sixth Extinction: An Unnatural History*. New York: Henry Holt & Company, 2014.

—. *Under a White Sky: The Nature of the Future*. New York: Crown, 2021.

Kostof, Spiro. *The City Shaped: Urban Patterns and Meanings through History*. London: Thames and Hudson, 1991.

Kresic, Neven. *Water in Karst: Management, Vulnerability, and Restoration*. New York: McGraw-Hill, 2012.

Krznaric, Roman. *The Good Ancestor: A Radical Prescription for Long-Term Thinking*. New York: The Experiment, 2020.

Kummer, Corby. *The Joy of Coffee*. Boston: Houghton Mifflin, 1995.

Kwon, Miwon. *One Place After Another: Site-Specific Art and Locational Identity*. Cambridge, MA: MIT Press, 2004.

LaDuke, Winona. *All Our Relations: Native Struggles for Land*. Chicago: Haymarket Books, 2016.

—. *Recovering the Sacred: The Power of Naming and Claiming*. Cambridge, MA: South End Press, 2005.

—. *The Winona LaDuke Chronicles: Stories from the Front Lines in the Battle for Environmental Justice*. Halifax: Fernwood Publishing, 2017.

—. *To Be a Water Protector: The Rise of the Wiindigoo Slayers*. Halifax: Fernwood Publishing, 2020.

Lambin, Eric. *An Ecology of Happiness*. Chicago: University of Chicago Press, 2012.

Lane, Robin Fox. *Thoughtful Gardening: Great Plants, Great Gardens, Great Gardeners*. New York: Particular Books, 2010.

Lanham, Drew J. *The Home Place: Memoirs of a Colored Man's Love Affair with Nature*. Minneapolis: Milkweed Edtions, 2017.

Lash, Scott and John Urry. *Economies of Signs and Space*. London: Sage, 1994.

Latour, Bruno, ed. *Reset Modernity!* Cambridge, MA: MIT Press, 2016.

Latour, Bruno. *After Lockdown: A Metamorphosis*. Cambridge, MA: Polity, 2021.

—. *An Inquiry into Modes of Existence: An Anthropology of the Moderns*. Cambridge, MA: Harvard University Press, 2013.

—. *Down to Earth: Politics in the New Climate Regime*. Cambridge, MA: Polity, 2018.

—. *Politics of Nature: How to Bring the Sciences into Democracy*. Cambridge, MA: Harvard University Press, 2004.

Le Guin, Ursula K. *Dreams Must Explain Themselves: The Selected Non-Fiction of Ursula K. Le Guin.* London: Gollancz, 2018.

—. *The Word for World is Forest.* New York: Berkley/Putnam, 1976.

Le Guin, Ursula K. and Brian Attebery, ed. *Ursula K. Le Guin: Always Coming Home: Author's Expanded Edition.* Washington D.C.: Library of America, 2019.

Lee, Jessica. J. *Two Trees Make a Forest: In Search of My Family's Past Among Taiwan's Mountains and Coasts.* New York: Catapult, 2020.

Lefebvre, Henri. *Introduction to Modernity.* London: Verso, 1995.

—. Translated by Donald Nicholson-Smith. *The Production of Space.* Oxford: Blackwell, 1991.

LeGates, Richard T. and Frederic Stout, eds. *The City Reader.* London: Routledge, 1996.

Lent, Jeremy. *The Web of Meaning: Integrating Science and Traditional Wisdom to Find Our Place in the Universe.* Gabriola Island, BC: New Society Publishers, 2021.

Leonardi, Cesare & Franca Stagi. *The Architecture of Trees.* Princeton: Princeton Architectural Press, 2019.

Lewis, C.S. *The Lion, The Witch and The Wardrobe.* London: Harper Collins, 1994.

Lima, Manuel. *The Book of Trees: Visualizing Branches of Knowledge.* Princeton: Princeton Architectural Press, 2014.

Limón, Ada. *The Hurting Kind.* Minneapolis: Milkweed Editions, 2022.

Lippard, Lucy. *Overlay: Contemporary Art and the Art of Prehistory.* New York: The New Press, 1995.

—. *The Lure of the Local: Senses of Place in A Multicentered Society.* New York: The New Press, 2007.

—. *Undermining: A Wild Ride Through Land Use, Politics, and Art in the Changing West.* New York: The New Press, 2014.

Liptrot, Amy. *The Outrun.* London: Canongate, 2018.

Logan, William Bryant. *Air: The Restless Shaper of the World.* New York: W. W. Norton & Company, 2012.

—. *Dirt: The Ecstatic Skin of the Earth.* New York: W. W. Norton & Company, 2007.

—. *Oak: The Frame of Civilization.* New York: W. W. Norton & Company, 2006.

—. *Sprout Lands: Tending the Endless Gift of Trees.* New York: W. W. Norton & Company, 2019.

Lopez, Barry, ed. *The Future of Nature: Writing on a Human Ecology from Orion Magazine.* Minneapolis: Milkweed Editions, 2007.

Lopez, Barry. *Arctic Dreams.* New York: Vintage, 2001.

—. *Embrace Fearlessly the Burning World.* New York: Random House, 2022.

Lovelock, James. *A Rough Ride to the Future.* London: Allen Lane, 2014.

—. *Gaia: A New Look at Life on Earth.* Oxford: Oxford University Press, 1979.

—. *Gaia: The practical science of planetary medicine.* London: Gaia Books, 1991.

Lucretius. *De Rerum Natura: The Nature of Things: A Poetic Translation.* Translated by David R. Slavitt. Berkely: University of California Press, 2008.

Luoma, Jon R. *The Hidden Forest: The Biography of an Ecosystem.* Corvallis: Oregon State University Press, 2006.

Lynn Haupt, Lyanda. *Rooted: Life at the Crossroads of Science, Nature, and Spirit.* New York: Little, Brown Spark, 2021.

MacCannell, Dean. *The Tourist: A New Theory of the Leisure Class.* Berkeley: University of California Press, 1999.

Macfarlane, Robert, Stanley Donwood and Dan Richards. *Holloway.* London: Penguin, 2013.

Macfarlane, Robert and Jackie Morris. *The Lost Words: A Spell Book*. London: Hamish Hamilton, 2017.

Macfarlane, Robert & Stanley Donwood. *Ness*. London: Penguin, 2019.

Macfarlane, Robert. *Is a River Alive?* London: Hamish Hamilton, forthcoming in 2025.

—. *Landmarks*. London: Penguin, 2015.

—. *Mountains of the Mind*. London: Penguin, 2003.

—. *The Gifts of Reading*. London: Penguin, 2017.

—. *The Old Ways: A Journey on Foot*. London: Penguin, 2012.

—. *The Wild Places*. London: Penguin, 2008.

—. *Underland: A Deep Time Journey*. London: Penguin, 2019.

Massey, Doreen. *Space, Place and Gender*. Minneapolis: University of Minnesota Press, 1994.

Macy, Joanna. *A Wild Love for the World*. Boulder: Shambhala, 2020.

Macy, Joanna and Chris Johnstone. *Active Hope: How to Face the Mess We're in with Unexpected Resilience & Creative Power*. Novato: New World Library, 2022.

Magan, Manchán. *Thirty-Two Words for Field: Lost Words of the Irish Landscape*. Dublin: Gill Books, 2020.

Maitland, Sara. *A Book of Silence*. London: Granta, 2008.

Malm, Andreas. *How to Blow Up a Pipeline: Learning to Fight in a World on Fire*. London: Verso, 2021.

Maloof, Joan. *Among the Ancients: Adventures in the Eastern Old-Growth Forests*. Washington D.C.: Ruka Press, 2011.

—. *Nature's Temples: The Complex World of Old-Growth Forests*. Portland, OR: Timber Press, 2016.

—. *Teaching the Trees: Lessons from the Forest*. Athens, GA: University of Georiga Press, 2010.

—. *The Living Forest: A Visual Journey into the Heart of the Woods*. Portland, OR: Timber Press, 2017.

—. *Treepedia: A Brief Compendium of Arboreal Lore*. Princeton: Princeton University Press, 2021.

Manaugh, Geoff and Nicola Twilley. *Until Proven Safe*. New York: MCD, 2021.

Mancuso, Stefano. *The Nation of Plants*. London: Other Press, 2021.

Manguel, Alberto. *A Reader on Reading*. New Haven: Yale University Press, 2011.

—. *Packing My Library: An Elegy and Ten Digressions*. New Haven: Yale University Press, 2018.

—. *The Library at Night*. New Haven: Yale University Press, 2009.

—. *With Borges*. London: Telegram Books, 2006.

Mann, Michael E. *The New Climate War: The Fight to Take Back Our Planet*. New York: PublicAffairs, 2021.

Marder, Michael. *The Philosopher's Plant: An Intellectual Herbarium*. New York: Columbia University Press, 2014.

Maroukis, Thomas C. *Peyote Road: Religious Freedom and the Native American Church*. Norma, OK: University of Oklahoma Press, 2012.

Marquez, Gabriel Garcia. *One Hundred Years of Solitude*. New York: Harper Perennial, 1993.

Marris, Emma. *Rambunctious Garden: Saving Nature in a Post-Wild World*. New York: Bloomsbury, 2011.

Marshall, Peter. *Nature's Webb: Rethinking our Place on Earth*. London: Routledge, 1996.

Mattelart, Armand. *The Invention of Communication*. Minneapolis: University of Minnesota Press, 1996.

McCarthy, Cormac. *The Road*. New York: Vintage Books, 2006.

McCarthy, Tom. *Remainder*. New York: Vintage Books, 2007.

McDonough, William and Michael Braungart. *Cradle to Cradle: Remaking the Way we Make Things*. New York: North Point Press, 2002.

McEwan, Ian. *The Comfort of Strangers*. London: Picador, 1982.

—. *The Cement Garden*. London: Picador, 1993.

McEwen, Christian and Mark Statman, eds. *Alphabet of the Trees: A Guide to Nature Writing*. New York: Teachers & Writers Collaborative, 2000.

McGregor, James H.S. *Back to the Garden: Nature and the Mediterranean World from Prehistory to the Present*. New Haven: Yale University Press, 2015.

McGuire, Bill. *Hothouse Earth: An Inhabitant's Guide*. London: Icon Books, 2022.

McKay, George. *Radical Gardening: Politics, Idealism and Rebellion in the Garden*. Frances Lincoln, 2011.

McKay, Robin, ed. *#ACCELERATE: The Accelerationist Reader*. Cambridge, MA: Urbanomic, 2014.

McKibben, Bill, ed. *The Global Warming Reader*. New York: OR Books, 2011.

McKibben, Bill. *Deep Economy: The Wealth of Communities and the Durable Future*. New York: St. Martin's Press, 2008.

—. *Eaarth: Making a Life on a Tough New Planet*. New York: St. Martin's Press, 2011.

—. *Oil and Honey: The Education of an Unlikely Activist*. New York: St Martin's Press, 2014.

—. *The End of Nature*. New York: Random House, 1989.

McMurtry, Larry. *Roads*. New York: Simon & Schuster, 2000.

McPhee, John. *The Control of Nature*. New York: Farrar, Straus and Giroux, 1989.

—. *Annals of the Former World*. New York: Farrar, Straus and Giroux, 1998.

Meehan, Aidan. *Celtic Designs: Maze Patterns*. London: Thames and Hudson, 1993.

Middleton, Beth Rose. *Trust in the Land: New Directions in Tribal Conservation*. Tucson: University of Arizona Press, 2011.

Miéville, China. *The City & The City*. New York: Del Rey, 2009.

Miller, Daegan. *This Radical Land: A Natural History of American Dissent*. Chicago: University of Chicago Press, 2018.

Miller, Daniel. *A Theory of Shopping*. Ithaca, NY: Cornell University Press, 1998.

Miller, Stuart and Sharon Seitz, eds. *The Other Islands of New York City: A History and Guide*. Taftsville, VT: Countryman Press, 2001.

Millstone, Erik. *The Atlas of Food: Who Eats What, Where, and Why*. New York: Routledge, 2008.

Minshull, Duncan. *While Wandering: A Walking Companion*. London: Vintage UK, 2014.

Mitchell, W.J.T., ed. *Landscape and Power*. Chicago: University of Chicago Press, 1994.

Mitchell, William J. *City of Bits: Space, Place and the Infobahn*. Cambridge, MA: MIT Press, 1995.

Mitchell, William J., Charles Moore, and William Turnbull. *The Poetics of Gardens*. Cambridge, MA: MIT Press, 1988.

Mitchell, Timothy. *Carbon Democracy: Political Power in the Age of Oil*. New York: Verso Books, 2011.

Moggach, Tom. *The Urban Kitchen Gardener: Growing and Cooking in the City*. London: Kyle Books, 2012.

Monbiot, George. *Feral: Rewidling the Land, the Sea, and Human Life*. Chicago: University of Chicago Press, 2014.

—. *Regenesis: Feeding the World Without Devouring the Planet*. London: Penguin Random House, 2022.

Montgomery, Beronda L. *Lessons from Plants*. Cambridge, MA: Harvard University Press, 2021.

Moor, Robert. *On Trails: An Exploration*. New York: Simon & Schuster, 2017.

Moore, Kathleen Dean. *Earth's Wild Music: Celebrating and Defending the Songs of the Natural World*. Berkeley, CA: Counterpoint Press, 2021.

More, Thomas. *Utopia*. London: Penguin Books, 1965.

Morton, Timothy. *Dark Ecology: For a Logic of Future Coexistence*. New York: Columbia University Press, 2016)

—. *Humankind: Solidarity with Non-Human People*. New York: Verso, 2017.

—. *Ecology Without Nature: Rethinking Environmental Aesthetics*. Cambridge, MA: Harvard University Press, 2007.

—. *Hyperobjects: Philosophy and Ecology after the End of the World*. Minneapolis: University of Minnesota Press, 2013.

—. *The Ecological Thought*. Cambridge, MA: Harvard University Press, 2010.

Mukherjee, Siddhartha, ed. *The Best American Science and Nature Writing 2013*. Boston: Houghton Mifflin, 2013.

Mukherjee, Siddhartha. *The Emperor of All Maladies: A Biography of Cancer*. New York: Scribner, 2010.

—. *The Gene: An Intimate History*. New York: Scribner, 2016.

—. *The Song of the Cell: : An Exploration of Medicine and the New Human*. New York: Scribner: 2022.

Myles, Eileen, ed. *Pathetic Literature*. New York: Grove Atlantic, 2022.

Myles, Eileen. *evolution*. New York: Grove Atlantic, 2018.

—. *The Importance of Being Iceland*. Cambridge, MA: Semiotext(e), 2009.

Nadkarni, Nalini. *Between Earth and Sky: Our Intimate Connection to Trees*. Berkeley, CA: University of California Press, 2009.

Natarajan, Priyamvada. *Mapping the Heavens: The Radical Scientific Ideas that Reveal the Cosmos*. New Haven: Yale University Press, 2016.

Nelson, Melissa K., ed. *Original Instructions: Indigenous Teachings for a Sustainable Future*. Rochester, VT: Bear and Company, 2008.

Newitz, Annalee. *Scatter, Adapt, and Remember: How Humans Will Survive a Mass Extinction*. New York: Doubleday, 2013.

Nezhukumatathil, Aimee. *World of Wonders: In Praise of Fireflies, Whale Sharks, and Other Astonishments*. Minneapolis: Milkweed Editions, 2020.

Ní Dochartaigh, Kerri. *Thin Places: A Natural History of Healing and Home*. London: Canongate Books, 2021.

Nisbet, James. *Ecologies, Environments, and Energy Systems in Art of the 1960s and 1970s*. Cambridge, MA: MIT Press, 2014.

Nixon, Rob. *Slow Violence and the Environmentalism of the Poor*. Cambridge, MA: Harvard University Press, 2013.

Norgaard, Kari Marie. *Living in Denial: Climate Change, Emotions, and Everyday Life*. Cambridge, MA: MIT Press, 2011.

O'Brien, Flann. *The Third Policeman*. London: MacGibbon and Kee, 1967.

O'Connell, Mark. *Notes from an Apocalypse: A Personal Journey to the End of the World and Back.* London: Granta, 2020.

—. *To Be a Machine: Adventures Among Cyborgs, Utopians, Hackers and the Futurists Solving the Modest Problem of Death.* London: Granta, 2017.

Odell, Jenny. *How to Do Nothing: Resisting the Attention Economy.* New York: Melville House, 2019.

Offill, Jenny. *Weather.* New York: Penguin Random House, 2020.

Orwell, George. *Nineteen Eighty-Four.* London: Penguin, 1954.

—. *Animal Farm: A Fable in Two Acts.* London: Samuel French, 1964.

Ovid, *Metamorphosis.* Oxford: Oxford Paperbacks, 1998.

Page, Michael and Robert Ingpen. *Encyclopedia of Things That Never Were: Creatures, Places and People.* London: Penguin, 1998.

Paine, Thomas. *The Rights of Man.* London: Dover, 1999.

Pakenham, Thomas. *Meetings with Remarkable Trees.* New York: Random House, 1998.

Parikka, Jussi. *A Geology of Media.* Minneapolis: University of Minnesota Press, 2015.

Parkes, Don and Nigel Thrift, eds. *Times, Spaces, and Places: A Chronogeographic Perspective.* New York: John Wiley & Sons, 1980.

Pavord, Anna. *The Curious Gardener: A Gardening Year.* New York: Bloomsbury, 2010.

Pearce, Fred. *Climate and Man: From the Ice Ages to the Global Greenhouse.* 1989.

—. *A Trillion Trees: Restoring Our Forests by Trusting in Nature.* Vancouver: Greystone Books, 2022.

Pendell, Dale. *Pharmako/Gnosis: Plant Teachers and the Poison Path.* Berkeley: North Atlantic Books, 2010.

Perec, Georges. *Life: A User's Manual.* Boston: David R. Godine, 1987.

Phillips, Carl. *Then the War: And Selected Poems, 2007-2020.* New York: Farrar, Straus and Giroux, 2022.

Pile, Steve. *The Body and the City: Psychoanalysis, Space and Subjectivity.* London: Routledge, 1996.

Pinkson, Tom Soloway. *The Shamanic Wisdom of the Huichol: Medicine Teachings for Modern Times.* Rochester, VT: Destiny Books, 2010.

Pirsig, Robert. *Zen and the Art of Motorcycle Maintenance: An Inquiry into Values.* New York: Morrow, 1974.

Pollan, Michael. *A Place of My Own: The Architecture of Daydreams.* New York: Penguin, 1997.

—. *The Botany of Desire: A Plant's-Eye View of the World.* New York: Bloomsbury, 2002.

—. *This is Your Mind on Plants.* New York: Penguin Press, 2021.

Pollock, Griselda. *Vision and Difference: Femininity, Feminism, and the Histories of Art.* London: Routledge, 1988.

Powers, Richard. *Bewilderment.* New York: W. W. Norton & Company, 2021.

—. *The Overstory.* New York: W. W. Norton & Company, 2018.

Preston, Richard. *The Wild Trees: A Story of Passion and Daring.* New York: Random House, 2008.

Prigogine, Ilya, Isabelle Stengers and Alvin Toffler. *Order Out of Chaos: Man's New Dialogue with Nature.* New York: Bantam Books, 1984.

Princen, Thomas. *Treading Softly: Paths to Ecological Order.* Cambridge, MA: MIT Press, 2010.

Proulx, Annie. *Barkskins.* New York: Simon & Schuster, 2016.

Pugh, Simon. *Reading Landscape: Country – City – Capital.* Manchester: Manchester University Press, 1990.

Quammen, David. *Spillover: Animal Infections and the Next Human Pandemic.* New York: W. W. Norton & Company, 2012.

—. *The Tangled Tree: A Radical New History of Life.* New York: Simon & Schuster, 2018.

Raban, Jonathan. *Soft City.* London: The Harvill Press, 1998.

Raffles, Hugh. *The Book of Unconformities: Speculations on Lost Time.* New York: Pantheon, 2020.

Rakowitz, Michael. *Circumventions.* Paris: Onestar Press, 2004.

Rawlence, Ben. *The Treeline: The Last Forest and the Future of Life on Earth.* New York: St. Martin's Press, 2022.

Reader, John. *Cities.* New York: Atlantic Monthly Press, 2004.

Reid, John W. and Thomas E. Lovejoy. *Ever Green: Saving Big Forests to Save the Planet.* New York: W. W. Norton & Company, 2022.

Rendell, Ruth. *Art and Architecture: A Place Between.* New York: Tauris, 2006.

Rewers, Ewa. *Language and Space: The Post-Structuralist Turn in the Philosophy of Culture.* Bern: Peter Lang Publishing, 1999.

Reynolds, Mary. *We Are the ARK: Returning Our Gardens to Their True Nature Through Acts of Restorative Kindness.* Portland, OR: Timber Press, 2022.

Reynolds, Richard. *On Guerilla Gardening: A Handbook of Gardening Without Boundaries.* New York: Bloomsbury, 2008.

Rich, Adrienne. *Collected Poems: 1950-2012.* New York: W. W. Norton & Company, 2016.

Rich, Nathaniel. *Losing Earth: A Recent History.* New York: MCD X FSG, 2019.

—. *Second Nature: Scenes from a World Remade.* New York: MCD X FSG, 2021.

Rimas, Andrew and Evan D. G. Fraser. *Empires of Food: Feast, Famine and the Rise and Fall of Civilizations.* Berkeley, CA: Counterpoint Press, 2012.

Robinson, Andrew. *The Story of Writing: Alphabets, Hieroglyphs & Pictograms.* London: Thames & Hudson, 2007.

Robinson, Kim Stanley. *The Ministry for the Future.* London: Orbit, 2020.

Robinson, Tim. *Listening to the Wind.* Minneapolis: Milkweed Editions, 2019.

—. *Stones of Aran: Labyrinth.* New York: NYRB Classics, 2009.

—. *Stones of Aran: Pilgrimage.* London: Penguin, 1986.

Roelstraete, Dieter. *Richard Long: A Line Made by Walking.* Afterall Books, 2010.

Rosenberg, Daniel and Anthony Grafton. *Cartographies of Time.* Princeton: Princeton Architectural Press, 2010.

Roussel, Raymond. *Locus Solus.* Paris: Editions Flamarion, 1998.

Laurie, Erynn Rowan. *Ogam: Weaving Word Wisdom.* Stafford: Megalithica Books, 2007.

Roy, Arundhati. *The God of Small Things.* London: Random House, 2008.

Roy, Sumana. *How I Became a Tree,* New Haven: Yale University Press, 2021.

—. *V. I. P.: Very Important Plant.* Swindon: Shearsman Books, 2022.

Sacks, Oliver. *Gratitude.* New York: Knopf, 2015.

—. *Oaxaca Journal.* New York: Vintage, 2012.

—. *The Island of the Colorblind.*

Saint-Exupéry, Antoine de. *Le Petit Prince.* London: Heinemann, 1958.

Saladino, Dan. *Eating to Extinction: The World's Rarest Foods and Why We Need to Save Them.* New York: Farrar, Straus and Giroux, 2022.

Sanderon, Eric W. *Mannahatta: A Natural History of New York City.* New York: Abrams, 2009.

—. *Terra Nova: The New World After Oil, Cars, and Suburbs.* New York: Abrams, 2013.

Saramago, José. *The Cave.* London: Vintage, 2003.

Saunders, Gary. *My Life with Trees*. Kentville, Nova Scotia: Gaspereau Press, 2015.

Saunders, William S., ed. *Nature, Landscape, and Building for Sustainability*. Minneapolis: University of Minnesota Press, 2008.

Savoy, Lauret. *Trace: Memory, History, Race, and the American Landscape*. Berkeley: Counterpoint Press, 2015.

Scarry, Elaine. *On Beauty and Being Just*. Princeton: Princeton University Press, 2001.

—. *Thinking in an Emergency*. New York: W. W. Norton & Company, 2012.

Schama, Simon. *Landscape and Memory*. London: Fontana Press, 1995.

Scranton, Roy. *Learning to Die in the Anthropocene: Reflections on the End of a Civilization*. San Francisco: City Lights, 2015.

Sebald, W.G. *The Rings of Saturn*. London: Harvill Press, 1998.

Seiter, David. *Spontaneous Urban Plants: Weeds in NYC*. New York: Archer, 2016.

Sennett, Richard. *The Conscience of the Eye: The Design and Social Life of Cities*. New York: W. W. Norton & Company, 1992.

—. *The Fall of Public Man*. London: Faber and Faber, 1993.

—. *The Uses of Disorder: Personal Identity and City Life*. New York: W. W. Norton & Company, 1992.

Dr. Seuss, *The Lorax*. New York: Random House, 1971.

Shafak, Elif. *The Island of Missing Trees*. New York: Penguin Viking, 2021.

Shaviro, Steven. *The Universe of Things : On Speculative Realism*. Minneapolis: University of Minnesota Press, 2014.

Sheldrake, Merlin. *Entangled Life: How Fungi Make Our Worlds, Change Our Minds & Shape Our Futures*. London: Random House, 2020.

Sherman, Sean. *The Sioux Chef's Indigenous Kitchen*. Minneapolis: University of Minnesota Press, 2017.

Short, Damien. *Redefining Genocide: Settler Colonialism, Social Death, and Ecocide*. London: Zed Books, 2016.

Silbey, Jessica. *Against Progress: Intellectual Property and Fundamental Values in the Internet Age*. Stanford: Stanford University Press, 2022.

Silverstein, Shel. *The Giving Tree*. New York: Harper & Row, 1964.

Simard, Suzanne. *Finding the Mother Tree: Discovering the Wisdom of the Forest*. New York: Knopf, 2021.

Simmel, Georg. *On Individuality and Social Forms*. Chicago: University of Chicago Press, 1971.

Simpson, Leanne Betasamosake. *Noopiming: The Cure for White Ladies*. Minneapolis: University of Minnesota Press, 2021.

Sloterdijk, Peter. *Spheres Trilogy: Bubbles, Globes, Foam*. Cambridge, MA: MIT Press, 2011, 2014, 2016.

Smit, Tim. *The Lost Gardens of Heligan*. London: Orion, 1997.

Smith, P.D. *City: A Guidebook for the Urban Age*. New York: Bloomsbury, 2012.

Smith, Patti. *Just Kids*. New York: Ecco, 2010.

Smith, Tracy K. and John Freeman, eds. *There's a Revolution Outside My Love*. New York: Vintage, 2021.

Smith, Zadie. *Changing My Mind: Occasional Essays*. New York: Penguin, 2010.

—. *Feel Free*. New York: Penguin, 2018.

—. *On Beauty*. New York: Penguin, 2006.

—. *White Teeth*. New York: Vintage, 2001.

Soja, Edward W. *Postmetropolis: Critical Studies of Cities and Regions*. Oxford: Blackwell, 2000.

Solà, Irene. *When I Sing, Mountains Dance*. Minneapolis, Graywolf Press, 2022.

Solnit, Rebecca and Rebecca Snedeker. *Unfathomable City: A New Orleans Atlas*. Berkeley, CA: University of California Press, 2013.

Solnit, Rebecca. *A Book of Migrations: Some Passages in Ireland*. New York: Verso, 1997.

—. *A Field Guide to Getting Lost*. New York: Penguin, 2005.

—. *Encyclopedia of Trouble and Spaciousness*. San Antonio: Trinity University Press, 2014.

—. *Infinite City: A San Francisco Atlas*. Berkeley, CA: University of California Press, 2010.

—. *Orwell's Roses*. New York: Viking, 2021.

—. *Storming the Gates of Paradise*. Berkeley, CA: University of California Press, 2007.

—. *Wanderlust: A History of Walking*. New York: Penguin Books, 2001.

Speer, James H. *Fundamentals of Tree Ring Research*. Tucson: University of Arizona Press, 2012.

Springer, Anna-Sophie and Etienne Turpin. *Fantasies of the Library*. Berlin: K. Verlag & Haus der Kulturen der Welt, 2015.

St. George, Zach. *The Journeys of Trees: A Story about Forests, People, and the Future*. New York: W. W. Norton & Company, 2020.

Mandel, Emily St. John. *Station Eleven*. New York: Knopf, 2014.

Stamets, Paul, *Mycellium Running: How Mushrooms Can Help Save the World*. Berkeley, CA: Ten Speed Press, 2005.

Standage, Tom. *An Edible History of Humanity*. Atlantic Books, 2010.

Stafford, Fiona. *The Long, Long Life of Trees*. New Haven: Yale University Press, 2016.

Steel, Carolyn. *Hungry City: How Food Shapes Our Lives*. New York: Vintage, 2009.

Stengers, Isabelle. *In Catastrophic Times: Resisting the Coming Barbarism*. London: Open Humanities Press, 2015.

Steyerl, Hito. *Duty Free Art: Art in the Age of Planetary Civil War*. New York: Verso, 2017.

Stilgoe, John R. *What is Landscape?* Cambridge, MA: MIT Press, 2015.

Stone, Christopher D., *Should Trees Have Standing: Towards Legal Rights for Natural Objects*. Burlington, VT: William Kaufmann Inc., 1974.

Sullivan, Robert. *The Meadowlands: Wilderness Adventures at the Edge of a City*. New York: Anchor, 1999.

—. *The Thoreau You Don't Know: What the Prophet of Environmentalism Really Meant*. Harper Collins, 2009.

Sussman, Rachel. *The Oldest Living Things in the World*. Chicago: University of Chicago Press, 2014.

Suzuki, David and Wayne Grady. *Tree: A Life Story*. Vancouver: Greystone Books, 2004.

Swift, Jonathan. *Gulliver's Travels*. London: Penguin, 1994.

Switek, Brian. *Written in Stone: Evolution, the Fossil Record, and Our Place in Nature*. New York: Bellevue Literary Press, 2010.

Taylor, Astra. *Democracy May Not Exist, But We'll Miss it When it's Gone*. New York: Metropolitan Books, 2019.

Thomas, Leah. *The Intersectional Environmentalist: How to Dismantle Systems of Oppression to Protect People + Planet*. New York: Voracious, 2022.

Thunberg, Greta. *No One is Too Small to Make a Difference*. London: Penguin, 2019.

Thunberg, Greta, Svante Thunberg, Beata Ernman, and Malena Ernman. *Our House is on Fire: Scenes of a Family and a Planet in Crisis*. London: Penguin, 2020.

Tippett, Krista. *Becoming Wise: An Inquiry into the Mystery and Art of Living*. New York: Penguin Press, 2016

Tokarczuk, Olga. *Flights*. Translated by Jennifer Croft. London: Riverhead Books, 2019.

—. *The Books of Jacob.* Translated by Jennifer Croft. London: Riverhead Books, 2021.

Tree, Isabella. *Wilding: The Return of Nature to a British Farm.* London: Picador, 2018.

Triple Canopy, ed. *Speculations ("The future is…..")* New York: Triple Canopy, 2015.

Tsing, Anna Lowenhaupt. *The Mushroom at the End of the World: On the Possibility of Life in Capitalist Ruins.* Princeton: Princeton University Press, 2015.

Tsing, Anna, Anne Swanson, Elaine Gan, and Nils Bubandt, eds. *Arts of Living on a Damaged Planet: Ghosts and Monsters of the Anthropocene.* Minneapolis: University of Minnesota Press, 2017.

Twain, Mark. *Following the Equator.* New York: Dover Publications, 1990.

VanderMeer, Jeff. *Ambergris.* New York: MCD X FSG, 2020.

—. *Borne.* New York: MCD X FSG, 2017.

—. *The Southern Reach Trilogy.* New York: FSG Original, 2014.

Van Horn, Gavin, Robin Wall Kimmerer and John Hausdoerffer, eds. *Kinship: Belonging in a World of Relations.* Chicago: Center for Humans & Nature, 2021.

Vaughan-Lee, Emmanuel, ed. *Emergence Magazine: Volumes 1-4.* Inverness, CA: 2019-2023.

Vaughan-Lee, Llewellyn. *Spiritual Ecology: The Cry of the Earth.* Point Reyes, CA: The Golden Sufi Center, 2016.

Verne, Jules. *20,000 Leagues Under the Sea.* London: Penguin, 1994.

—. *Around the World in Eighty Days.* London: Penguin, 1994.

—. *Journey to the Centre of the Earth.* London: Penguin, 1994.

Vidler, Anthony. *The Architectural Uncanny: Essays in the Modern Unhomely.* Cambridge, MA: MIT Press, 1992.

Vince, Gaia. *Adventures in the Anthropocene: A Journey to the Heart of the Planet We Made.* London: Chatto & Windus, 2014.

—. *Nomad Century: How to Survive the Climate Upheaval.* London: Penguin, 2022.

—. *Transcendence: How Humans Evolved Through Fire, Language, Beauty and Time.* London: Penguin, 2020.

Viney, Michael. *A Year's Turning.* Newtownards, Northern Ireland: Blackstaff Press, 1997.

Virilio, Paul. *Speed and Politics.* Los Angeles: Semiotext(e), 1986.

Vogel, Steven. *The Life of a Leaf.* Chicago: University of Chicago Press, 2012.

Wallace-Wells, David. *The Uninhabitable Earth: Life After Warming.* London: Penguin UK, 2019.

Wallerstein, Immanuel. *Historical Capitalism with Capitalist Civilization.* New York: Verso, 1983.

Walmsley, Anthony. *Made Landscapes: From Prehistory to the Present.* Falcon Press, Philadelphia, 1975.

Wapner, Paul. *Living Through the End of Nature: The Future of American Environmentalism,* Cambridge: MIT Press, 2010.

Wark, McKenzie. *Molecular Red: Theory for the Anthropocene.* New York: Verso Books, 2015.

Webb, Kinari. *Guardians of the Trees: A Journey of Hope Through Healing the Planet.* New York: Flatiron Books, 2022.

Weintraub, Linda. *To Life! Eco Art in Pursuit of a Sustainable Planet.* Berkeley: University of California Press, 2012.

Weisman, Alan. *The World Without Us.* New York: St. Martin's Press, 2007.

Weiss, Allen S. *Mirrors of Infinity: The French Formal Garden and 17th Century Metaphysics.* Princeton: Princeton Architectural Press, 1995.

—. *Unnatural Horizons: Paradox and Contradiction in Landscape Architecture.* Princeton: Princeton Architectural Press, 1998.

Wells, Lisa. *Believers: Making a Life at the End of the World*. New York: Farrar, Straus & Giroux, 2021.

Welter, Volker M. *Biopolis: Patrick Geddes and the City of Life*. Cambridge, MA: MIT Press, 2002.

Wertheim, Margaret. *The Pearly Gates of Cyberspace: A History of Space from Dante to the Internet*. New York: W. W. Norton & Company, 1999.

Wildcat, Daniel. *Red Alert!: Saving the Planet with Indigenous Knowledge*. Golden, CO: Fulcrum, 2009.

Williams, Raymond. *The Country and the City*. London: Chatto & Windus, 1973.

Williams, Terry Tempest. *Erosion: Essays of Undoing*. New York: Sarah Crichton Books, 2019.

—. *Finding Beauty in a Broken World*. New York: Knopf, 2009.

—. *The Hour of Land: A Personal Topography of America's National Parks*. New York: Sarah Crichton Books, 2016.

—. *When Women Were Birds: Fifty-Four Variations on Voice*. New York: Macmillan, 2013.

Wilson, Edward O. *Half Earth: Our Planet's Fight for Life*. New York: Liveright, 2016.

Wilson, Elizabeth. *The Sphinx in the City: Urban Life, the Control of Disorder, and Women*. Berkeley: University of California Press, 1992.

—. *The Contradictions of Culture: Cities, Culture and Women*. London: Sage Publications, 2001.

Woodhouse, Keith Makoto. *The Ecocentrists: A History of Radical Environmentalism*. New York: Columbia University Press, 2018.

Wood, Paul. *London is a Forest*. London: Quadrille Publishing, 2019.

Woodworth, Paddy. *Our Once and Future Planet: Restoring the World in the Climate Change Century*. Chicago: University of Chicago Press, 2013.

Woolf, Virginia. *A Room of One's Own*. London: Penguin Classics, 2002.

Worton, Holly. *If Trees Could Talk: Life Lessons from the Wisdom of the Woods*. Tribal Publishing, 2019.

Wright, C.D. *Casting Deep Shade: An Amble*. Port Townsend, WA: Copper Canyon Press, 2019.

Yong, Ed. *An Immense World: How Animal Senses Reveal the Hidden Realms Around Us*. New York: Random House, 2022.

—. *I Contain Multitudes: The Microbes Within Us and a Grander View of Life*. New York: Ecco, 2018.

Zittel, Andrea. *Lay of My Land*. New York: Prestel, 2011.

Zittel, Andrea and Trevor Smith, eds. *Andrea Zittel: Critical Space*. New York: Prestel Publishing, 2005.

Zukin, Sharon. *Landscapes of Power: From Detroit to Disney World*. Berkeley: University of California Press, 1991.

Sources

Image credits: pp. ix, xiv, 21, 83, 93, 119, 123, 139, 143, 147, 183, 209, 230-231, 249, 304: All artworks by Katie Holten. p. ix: *Seeds (Tree Alphabet, germinating)*, ink on paper, 2022. p. 21: *Love Letters (OM, said to be the original vibration of the universe, with roots that trace back to the origin of the world. When chanted, OM vibrates at the frequency of 432Hz—the same vibrational frequency found in all things throughout nature)*, ink on paper, 2021. p. 83: *A Trillion Tiny Trees (For Amy)*, ink on paper, 2022. p. 93: *Trees are Sexy*, ink on paper, 2022. p. 119: *Leaves (Tree Alphabet, punctuation)*, ink on paper, 2022. p. 123: *Forest*, ink on paper, 2019, originally published by *Emergence Magazine*, 2020. p. 139: *Catalpa leaf (For Aimee)*, ink on paper, 2022. p. 143: *Shadow (Fern)*, oak gall ink on paper, 2018, originally published in *Our Plant Community: A Salmon Creek Farm Collaborative Field Guide*, 2020. p. 147: *Twigs for an Irish Tree Alphabet (After Ulysses)*, ink on paper, 2018. p. 183: *The World's First Trees (Fossilized slices of Cladoxylopsida, a 374-million-year-old tree, reveal a hollow core surrounded by numerous bundles of xylem (the larger black spots), with soft tissue between. The smaller black dots are roots.)*, pencil and ink on paper, 2022. p. 209: *Shadow (Juniper)*, cyanotype (inverted), 2018. pp. 230-231: Below: *Irish Tree Alphabet (Ogham A-Z)*, above: *Ogham Haiku (Today Birds Sing Clouds Float Trees Root)*, ink on paper, 2020. p. 249: *Forest (Roots)*, ink on paper, 2019. p. 304: *Seeds (Irish Tree Alphabet, punctuation)*, ink on paper, 2020.

Katie Holten's *Tree Alphabet* drawing was commissioned for the exhibition About Trees at the Zentrum Paul Klee, Bern, Switzerland, October 17, 2015–January 24, 2016.

Katie Holten's *Trees Typeface*, 2015. A free font created by the artist for her book *About Trees*, published by Broken Dimanche Press in 2015. Everyone is invited to download the font and write in Trees. Katieholten.com/books#/abouttrees

Image Credits: pp. xvi, 16, 40, 70, 94, 124, 158, 188, 204, 250: A selection of leaf silhouettes in the following order: Quince, Plum, Walnut, Grape, Apple, Morello, Hazlenut, Fig, Gooseberry, Mulberry. From Åse Eg Jørgensen's 2014 Kompendium 19: Blad 2 / Leaf 2.

Winona LaDuke's text "The Ojibwe New Year" was originally published on her blog Winonaladuke.com on April 16, 2022. Reprinted here courtesy of the author.

"He who plants a tree / Plants a hope" are the first two lines from Lucy Larcom's undated poem "Plant a Tree."

Tacita Dean's essay "Michael Hamburger" was first published in *Tacita Dean: Seven Books Grey*, MUMOK/Steidl, 2011. Reprinted here courtesy of the artist.

"I am the seed of the free. I intend to bear great fruit." Sojourner Truth.

Pedro Reyes's text "Palas por Pistolas" first appeared on the artist's website, Pedroreyes.net/palasporpistolas.php. Reprinted here courtesy of the artist.

Lucy O'Hagan's "Acorn Bread Recipe" was first shared at the Wild Awake hearth. Wildawake.ie. Reprinted here courtesy of the author.

Rachael Hawkwind used her "Oak Gall Ink Recipe" to create the oak gall ink used in the making of drawings for *Our Plant Community: A Salmon Creek Farm Collaborative Field Guide*, created by Alex Arzt and Fritz Haeg, printed by A Magic Mountain, 2020. Reprinted here courtesy of the artist.

Robert Macfarlane's text "Branches, Leaves, Roots and Trunks" is extracted from his 2015 book *Landmarks*, published by Hamish Hamilton and reprinted here with permission.

Brian J. Enquist's essay "Tree Theory, Biogeography and Branching" was written in March 2015 for Katie Holten's book *About Trees*. Reproduced here courtesy of the author.

Andrea Bowers's essay "Cultivating the Courage to Sin" was originally published as the press release for her solo exhibition of the same title at Capitain Petzel, Berlin, Germany, September 19–November 9, 2013. Reprinted here courtesy of the artist.

Zadie Smith's text "The Wrong Trees" is a sentence extracted from the first page of her 2012 book *NW*, published by Penguin. Reprinted here courtesy of the author.

James Gleick's essay "Fractal Vision" was first published in *The New York Times Magazine* on December 21, 2010. Reprinted here courtesy of the author.

Ada Limón, "It's the Season I Often Mistake" from *The Hurting Kind*. Copyright © 2022 by Ada Limón. Reprinted with the permission of the author and The Permissions Company, LLC on behalf of Milkweed Editions, Milkweed.org.

César A. Hidalgo's text is extracted from his book *Why Information Grows: The Evolution of Order, from Atoms to Economics*, published by Penguin, 2015. Reprinted here courtesy of the author.

Futurefarmers text "Tree University" first appeared on the Artforum.com website as "500 Words: Amy Franceschini" on December 10, 2014. Reprinted here courtesy of the artists.

Jorge Luis Borges's text is extracted from the short story "Funes, the Memorious" in his 1962 book *Ficciones*, translated by Anthony Kerrigan and published by Grove Press. Kerrigan was the first to translate "Funes el memorioso" into English. His translation appeared in the second issue of the short-lived *Avon Book of Modern Writing* in 1954. Reproduced here by permission of Grove/Atlantic, Inc.

Plato's text "Under a Plane Tree" is extracted from *Phaedrus*, c. 360 B.C.E. From a five-volume edition of *The Dialogues of Plato* translated by Benjamin Jowett. Provided by The Internet Classics Archive. Available online, Classics.mit.edu/Plato/phaedrus.html.

Radiohead's "Fake Plastic Trees": words and music by Thomas Yorke, Edward O'Brien, Colin Greenwood, Jonathan Greenwood and Philip Selway. © 1994 Warner/Chappell Music Ltd. All Rights in the U.S. and Canada Administered by WB MUSIC CORP. All Rights Reserved. Reprinted here by permission.

Extracted from "The Painter and the Planetarian: **Luchita Hurtado**: In conversation with Andrea Bowers about history, nature, and art as a form of shouting" which appeared in *URSULA*, Issue 2, Spring 2019. © The Estate of Luchita Hurtado. Courtesy the Estate of Luchita Hurtado and Hauser & Wirth.

Thomas Princen's essay "The Elm Stand" is extracted from his 2010 book *Treading Softly: Paths to Ecological Order*, published by MIT Press. Reprinted here courtesy of the author.

Irene Kopelman's text "The Exact Opposite of Distance" is extracted from *The Exact Opposite of Distance: Notes on Representation Volume 5*, from her series of books edited by ROMA publications. Reprinted here courtesy of the artist.

Kerri ní Dochartaigh's words are extracted from a conversation with BJ Hegedus for American Booksellers Association's "Indies Introduce" series, March 30, 2022. Reproduced courtesy of the author.

Valerie Segrest's text "Medicine of the Tree People" first appeared in *YES! Magazine*, Summer 2022 issue. Reprinted here by kind permission of the author and *YES! Magazine*.

Åse Eg Jørgensen's contribution is from her 2014 booklet *Kompendium 19*, published by Forlaget Space Poetry. The Kompendium series are smallscale artist books, printed on A4 paper, folded to A5 and sewn by hand. The series includes titles such as *Learning Icelandic, Flint, First There is a Mountain...* and *Blad/Leaf*.

Ada Lovelace's text "Sketch of the Analytical Engine" is extracted from *Scientific Memoirs* by Luigi Federico Menabrea in the "Bibliothèque Universelle de Genève," 1843 (Vol. 3, page 696). Translated, with notes, by Ada King, Countess of Lovelace. This document is the definitive exposition of Charles Babbage's Analytical Engine, which described many aspects of computer architecture and programming more than a hundred years before they were "discovered" in the twentieth century.

Author's Note: Ada Lovelace's text is translated here into binary code and typeset in the Trees Typeface. A bit (short for binary digit) is the smallest unit of data in a computer and has a value of either 0 or 1. Because 8 bits equals 1 byte, the text is sorted into groups of 8. The designer Oliver Spieker explains it this way: "To summarize: we have made trees into drawings into a typeface on a computer which operates with 0s and 1s and then we have turned a text into what a computer on a basic level operates with when it operates with text and then turned this output into the font that came out of drawings that were based on trees."

"*An Droighneán Donn*" arranged by **Susan McKeown**, from her album *Blackthorn*. World Village, 2005. Susan learned the song from the singing of Sara and Rita Keane, whose version appears on their album *At the Setting of the Sun*, and added a verse from a version collected from a Mrs. Murphy in South Armagh by Luke Donnellan, which appears in Pádraigín Ní Uallacháin's *A Hidden Ulster*, Four Courts Press, 2003. Reprinted here courtesy of the artist.

A version of **Nicola Twilley**'s essay "The Tree with the Apple Tattoo" was originally published on *Edible Geography*, Ediblegeography.com on February 12, 2013. Reprinted here courtesy of the author.

Amy Harmon's text "Millenniums of Intervention" is extracted from her article "A Race to Save the Orange by Altering its DNA," first published in *The New York Times* on July 27, 2013. Reprinted here courtesy of the author.

Jonathon Miller Weisberger's text "Cacao: The World Tree and Her Planetary Mission" is extracted from his essay in *The Mind of Plants: Narratives of Vegetal Intelligence*, published by Synergetic Press. Reprinted here by kind permission of the author and Synergetic Press.

Roz Naylor's essay "Tree of Life" was written in June 2015 for *About Trees*. The essay makes use of the following sources: *The evolving sphere of food security* (2014), Naylor, R. L. (ed.); *Solar-powered drip irrigation enhances food security in the Sudano-Sahel* (2010), Burney, J., Woltering, L., Burke, M., Naylor, R., & Pasternak, D., PNAS, 107(5), 1848-1853 and Trees for Life International, Treesforlife.org. Reproduced here courtesy of the author.

Jessica J. Lee, excerpts from *Two Trees Make a Forest: In Search of My Family's Past Among Taiwan's Mountains and Coasts*. Copyright © 2020 by Jessica J. Lee. Reprinted with permission of the author and Little Brown Book Group Limited. Reproduced with permission of the Licensor through PLSclear.

Ursula K. Le Guin's text "The Word for World is Forest" is the title of her 1976 science fiction novel, published by Putnam Publishing Group. © Ursula K. Le Guin Literary Trust.

Eduardo Kohn's text is extracted from his 2013 book *How Forests Think: Toward an Anthropology beyond the Human*, published by University of California Press. Reprinted here courtesy of the author.

Gaia Vince's text "Forests" is extracted from her 2014 book *Adventures in the Anthropocene: A Journey to the Heart of the Planet We Made*, published by Chatto & Windus. Reprinted here courtesy of the author.

E. J. McAdams's word "Bewilderness" was a source word for *Trees are Alphabets*, an improvisational writing project with branches, installed at The Bronx Museum of the Arts in September 2015. Reprinted here courtesy of the author.

Elizabeth Kolbert's text "Islands on Dry Land" is extracted from her 2014 book *The Sixth Extinction: An Unnatural History*, published by Bloomsbury Publishing Plc. Reprinted here by kind permission of the author and Bloomsbury Publishing Plc. © Elizabeth Kolbert, 2014.

Maya Lin's essay "Ghost Forest" is extracted from the exhibition catalog that accompanied her public art work at Madison Square Park, New York and was on view from May 10 through November 14, 2021. Reprinted with permission of the artist and Madison Square Park Conservancy, New York.

Forrest Gander's poem 'Forest' was originally commissioned for and published in *Emergence Magazine* as part of a collaborative multi-media project with Katie Holten. Reproduced here courtesy of the poet and *Emergence Magazine*.

Katie Holten's drawing *Forest* was originally commissioned for and published in *Emergence Magazine* as part of a collaborative multi-media project with Forrest Gander. Reproduced here courtesy of the artist and *Emergence Magazine*.

Tanaya Winder's poem *Being* was published in *Poetry,* March 2021. Reproduced here by kind permission of the author.

Aengus Woods's essay "Of Trees..." was specially commissioned for Katie Holten's book *About Trees*. The essay makes use of the following sources: *Confessions* (397–400) by St. Augustine; *Dialectic Of Enlightenment: Philosophical Fragments* (1944) Max Horkheimer & Theodor W. Adorno; *The Secret Languages of Ireland* (1937) by R.A.S. Macalister; *Moby Dick; Or, The Whale* (1851) by Herman Melville; *Philosophical Investigations* (1953) by Ludwig Wittgenstein; Wikipedia entries for Auraicept na n-Éces, Bríatharogam, Emoji, Hobo, Kennings, Ogham and Ogham Tract as well as "Let's Talk Art: How a Guggenheim Gallery Guide Cracked On Kawara's Code" by Ben Slyngstad, from the blog of the Guggenheim Museum. Reprinted here by kind permission of the author.

Anna-Sophie Springer's text "Legere and βιβλιοθήκη: The Library as Idea and Space" is an excerpted section (pp. 15-29) from her essay "Melancholies of the Paginated Mind: The Library as Curatorial Space" in the 2015 book *Fantasies of the Library*, edited by Anna-Sophie Springer and Etienne Turpin. *Fantasies of the Library* was the first volume in the *intercalations: paginated exhibition* series co-published by K. Verlag & HKW, 2015. Reprinted here courtesy of the author.

Toby Kiers's essay "Lessons From Fungi" is extracted from her TED Talk and work to Protect the Underground with SPUN. Together with GlobalFungi, Global Soil Mycobiome Consortium, the Crowther Lab, researchers, and local communities across the globe, SPUN is building the largest database of fungal network diversity ever assembled. This will allow us to identify high priority underground ecosystems by quantifying biodiversity hot-spots and endemic fungal species. Spun.earth. Reprinted here by permission of the author.

Chelsea Steinauer-Scudder's essay "They Carry Us With Them: The Great Tree Migration" first appeared on *Emergence Magazine*'s website. Reprinted here by kind permission of the author and *Emergence Magazine*.

Katie Holten's *Bibliography* is an ongoing project started in 2000. It was recently updated to accompany the monthly *Sunday Salons: Art and Activism in the Anthropocene* series that she hosts with Dillon Cohen in their home in New York City.

Contributors

JORGE LUIS BORGES (1899-1986) was an Argentine poet, essayist, and short-story writer whose works have become classics of twentieth century world literature.

Los Angeles based artist **ANDREA BOWERS**'s work explores the intersection between activism and art. Her main focus is the necessity of nonviolent protest and civil disobedience in the lives of women. Her intricate photorealist drawings and videos pay homage to a multitude of movements particularly feminism, climate justice, and immigrant rights.

INGER CHRISTENSEN (1935-2009) was one of Europe's leading contemporary experimentalists. Her works include poetry, fiction, drama, and essays. Her ingeniously crafted poetry and prose have been variously labeled as naturalist, experimental, formalist, and structuralist; essentially, her work defies labels. Her work has been translated into over thirty languages. Her entire poetic oeuvre, plus selected prose, is published in the U.S. by New Directions.

WILLIAM CORWIN is a sculptor and journalist from New York. He has exhibited at The Clocktower, LaMama and Geary galleries in New York, as well as galleries in London, Hamburg, Beijing and Taipei. He has written regularly for the *Brooklyn Rail*, *Artpapers*, *Bomb*, *Artcritical*, *Raintaxi*, and *Canvas*, and formerly for *Frieze*.

NICOLE DAVI is a professor at William Paterson University and a scientist at the Tree Ring Laboratory at Columbia University's Lamont-Doherty Earth Observatory. She develops and interprets high-resolution tree-ring records in order to further our understanding of past natural and recent anthropogenic climate change over the past 2000 years.

TACITA DEAN lives and works in Berlin and Los Angeles. Solo exhibitions include The Paul J. Getty Museum, LA (2022); MUDAM, Luxembourg (2022); La Fondazione, Rome (2021), Royal Opera House, London (2021),

Kunstmuseum Basel (2021); The National Gallery and The National Portrait Gallery, London (2018); Museo Tamayo, Mexico City (2016); and the Turbine Hall, Tate Modern, London (2011).

CAMILLE T. DUNGY is the author of the essay collection *Guidebook to Relative Strangers: Journeys into Race, Motherhood, and History*, and four collections of poetry, most recently *Trophic Cascade*. She has edited three anthologies, including *Black Nature: Four Centuries of African American Nature Poetry*. Her honors include the 2021 Academy of American Poets Fellowship, a Guggenheim Fellowship, an American Book Award, and fellowships from the NEA in both prose and poetry. She is a University Distinguished Professor at Colorado State University. Camilledungy.com

BRIAN J. ENQUIST is a plant ecologist and an external professor at The Santa Fe Institute. He researches how physical constraints at the level of the individual influence larger scale ecological and evolutionary patterns.

This symbol represents extinction. The circle signifies the planet, while the hourglass inside serves as a warning that time is rapidly running out for many species. The world is currently undergoing a mass extinction event, and this symbol is intended to help raise awareness of the urgent need for change.

AMY FRANCESCHINI is an artist who uses various media to encourage formats of exchange and production. An overarching theme in her work is a perceived conflict between humans and nature.

FUTUREFARMERS is a group of diverse practitioners aligned through an interest in making work that is relevant to the time and place surrounding them. Founded in 1995, the design studio serves as a platform to support art projects, an artist in residence program, and their research interests.

CHARLES GAINES is an American artist whose work interrogates the discourse relating aesthetics and politics. Taking the form of drawings, photographic series, and video installations, the work consistently invokes the use of systems as a generative part of the artist's practice.

FORREST GANDER, born in the Mojave Desert, lives in California. A translator/writer with degrees in geology and literature, he received the Pulitzer Prize, Best Translated Book Award, and fellowships from the Library of Congress, Guggenheim, and US Artists Foundations. His book *Twice Alive* focuses on human and ecological intimacies.

ROSS GAY is the author of four books of poetry: *Against Which*; *Bringing the Shovel Down*; *Be Holding*; and *Catalog of Unabashed Gratitude*, winner of the 2015 National Book Critics Circle Award. His first collection of essays, *The Book of Delights*, is a *New York Times* bestseller. His new collection of essays, *Inciting Joy*, was released by Algonquin in October of 2022. Rossgay.net

AMITAV GHOSH grew up in India, Bangladesh and Sri Lanka. He is the author of many books including *The Circle of Reason*, *The Shadow Lines*, *The Hungry Tide*, *The Ibis Trilogy*, *The Great Derangement: Climate Change and the Unthinkable*, *Gun Island* and *The Nutmeg's Curse*.

JAMES GLEICK is the author of several books charting the development of science and technology, beginning with *Chaos: Making a New Science* and including most recently *Time Travel: A History*.

NEMO ANDY GUIQUITA is a Waorani Indigenous leader and Women and Health Coordinator for the Confederation of Indigenous Nationalities of the Ecuadorian Amazon, or CONFENIAE. She is currently working on women's issues and on intercultural health issues such as ancestral medicine. CONFENIAE is a regional indigenous organization that represents about 1,500 communities, belonging to the Amazonian nationalities, Kichwa, Shuar, Achuar, Waorani, Sapara, Andwa, Shiwiar, Cofan, Siona, Siekopai and Kijus. Amazonia80x2025.earth

FRITZ HAEG's work has included edible gardens, public dances, educational environments, animal architecture, domestic gatherings, temporary encampments, publications, and occasionally buildings for people. He is currently restoring Salmon Creek Farm, a commune founded in 1971 in Mendocino, California.

AMY HARMON is a Pulitzer Prize-winning reporter for *The New York Times* who covers the social impact of science and technology. She has been a Guggenheim Fellow and a visiting scholar at the Arthur J. Carter Journalism Institute at New York University. She received the Science in Society award from the National Association of Science Writers for her article excerpted here.

RACHAEL HAWKWIND is a craftsperson, builder, and adventurer who enjoys working with sustainable materials and interacting with nature. She is a long-time contributor to Fritz Haeg's Salmon Creek Farm project.

CÉSAR A. HIDALGO directs the Center for Collective Learning at the Artificial and Natural Intelligence Institute (ANITI) at the University of Toulouse. Prior to joining ANITI, he led the Collective Learning group at MIT. Hidalgo is the author of dozens of peer-reviewed papers and three books. His latest book is *How Humans Judge Machines* (MIT Press, 2021).

KATIE HOLTEN is an artist and activist whose work explores the tangled relationships between humans and the natural world. She has created a Tree Museum, Tree Alphabets, a Stone Alphabet, and a Wildflower Alphabet to share the joy she finds in her love of the more-than-human world.

Born in Maiquetía, Venezuela, in 1920, **LUCHITA HURTADO** dedicated over eighty years of her extensive oeuvre to the investigation of universality and transcendence. Developing her artistic vocabulary through a coalescence of abstraction, mysticism, corporality and landscape, the breadth of her experimentation with unconventional techniques, materials, and styles speak to the multicultural and experiential contexts that shaped her life and career.

NATALIE JEREMIJENKO is an artist, engineer and inventor with a speciality in environmental and urban issues.

ÅSE EG JØRGENSEN is a Danish artist and graphic designer based in Copenhagen. For more than 40 years she has been co-editor on *Pist Protta* (Danish art periodical). She often works collaboratively and is part of an artist-run exhibition space (LOKALE) in Copenhagen. Her practice spans all kinds of printed matter.

TOBY KIERS investigates how cooperation between species evolves and persists. Kiers co-founded the Society for the Protection of Underground Networks (SPUN) in 2021 with the aim of mapping, conserving and harnessing mycorrhizal networks that regulate the Earth's climate and ecosystems. She is currently a Research Chair and Professor of Evolutionary Biology at the Vrije Universiteit in Amsterdam.

ROBIN WALL KIMMERER is a mother, scientist, decorated professor, and enrolled member of the Citizen Potawatomi Nation. She is the author of *Braiding Sweetgrass: Indigenous Wisdom, Scientific Knowledge and the Teaching of Plants* and *Gathering Moss: A Natural and Cultural History of Mosses*. Kimmerer lives in Syracuse, New York, where she is a SUNY Distinguished Teaching Professor of Environmental Biology, and the founder and director of the Center for Native Peoples and the Environment.

EDUARDO KOHN is interested in the exploration and capacitation of sylvan thinking in all its valences. He is the author of *How Forests Think: Toward an Anthropology Beyond the Human* (University of California Press, 2013), which won the 2014 Gregory Bateson Book Prize. He teaches anthropology at McGill University.

ELIZABETH KOLBERT is the author of *Field Notes from a Catastrophe: Man, Nature, and Climate Change*, *The Sixth Extinction*, for which she won the Pulitzer Prize, and *Under a White Sky: The Nature of the Future*. She is a staff writer for *The New Yorker*. Kolbert lives in Williamstown, Massachusetts, with her husband and children.

IRENE KOPELMAN is a visual artist working on the notion of difference and sameness in nature. Her strategy for exploring this topic requires collaborating with natural scientists and includes drawing as a key factor for understanding natural forms. Currently she lives and works in Amsterdam.

WINONA LADUKE is a Harvard-educated economist, environmental activist, author, hemp farmer, grandmother, and a two-time former Green Party vice presidential candidate with Ralph Nader. She is also the executive director of the nonprofit, Indigenous-led environmental justice organization,

Honor the Earth. She is the author of seven books, including her latest, *To Be a Water Protector: Rise of the Wiindigoo Slayers* (Fernwood Press/Columbia University, 2020).

LUCY LARCOM (1824-1893) was an American poet, abolitionist, and teacher. Larcom's poetry was first included in the anthology *Female Poets of America* (1849), and her collections of poetry include *Similitudes, from the Ocean and Prairie* (1853) and *Poems* (1868). Larcom's most enduring work is her autobiography, *A New England Girlhood, Outlined from Memory* (1889).

URSULA K. LE GUIN (1929-2018) was a celebrated author of more than 60 works of fiction, poetry, children's books and essays. The breadth of imagination and caliber of her writing garnered many distinctions, including Hugos, Nebulas, and the National Book Foundation Medal for Distinguished Contribution to American Letters.

JESSICA J. LEE is a British-Canadian-Taiwanese author and environmental historian. She is the author of two books of nature writing: *Turning* (2017) and *Two Trees Make a Forest* (2019). Jessica is the founding editor of *The Willowherb Review* and teaches creative writing at the University of Cambridge.

ADA LIMÓN is the 24th Poet Laureate of the United States. She is the author of six books of poetry, including *The Carrying*, which won the National Book Critics Circle Award for Poetry. Her new book of poetry, *The Hurting Kind*, is out now from Milkweed Editions.

MAYA LIN is known for large-scale environmental artworks, architectural works and memorial designs. In *Boundaries* (2006), she writes: "I see myself existing between boundaries, a place where opposites meet; science and art, art and architecture, East and West. My work originates from a simple desire to make people aware of their surroundings." A committed environmentalist, Lin is at work on a website, her final memorial, *What is Missing?*, raising awareness about habitat loss and biodiversity.

ADA LOVELACE, born August Ada Bryon (1815-1852), was the daughter of poet Lord Byron and mathematician Lady Byron. An English analyst, metaphysician, and founder of scientific computing, she is known for her work on Charles Babbage's early mechanical general-purpose computer, the Analytical Engine.

ROBERT MACFARLANE is the author of many books exploring landscape, memory, movement and language, most recently *Underland: A Deep Time Journey* (2019). He is currently working on his next book, *Is a River Alive?* He is a Fellow of Emmanuel College, Cambridge.

E.J. MCADAMS is a poet, artist, and collaborator who lives in Harlem. He explores language and mark-making in the urban environment using procedures and improvisation with found and natural materials.

Grammy award-winning and BBC award-nominated singer-songwriter **SUSAN MCKEOWN**, from Dublin, is also the founder and director of Cuala Foundation.

ROZ NAYLOR is the Director of the Center on Food Security and the Environment and a Professor of Earth Systems Science at Stanford University.

AIMEE NEZHUKUMATATHIL is the author of the collection of nature essays *World of Wonders: In Praise of Fireflies, Whale Sharks, & Other Astonishments* (Milkweed Editions, 2020). She is also the author of four books of poetry, most recently, *Oceanic*. She is professor of English and creative writing in the University of Mississippi's MFA program.

KERRI NÍ DOCHARTAIGH is a mother and writer from the north-west of Ireland, now living in Clare with her family. She writes about nature, literature and place for the *Guardian*, the *Irish Times*, the BBC and others. Her first book, *Thin Places*, was published in 2021. Her second book, *Cacophony of Bone*, was published in May 2023.

SUSANNA NIED is an American writer and translator. Her translations have appeared in publications such as *Granta* and *Tin House*, and in several anthologies. For her work with Inger Christensen's poetry, she has received the Landon Translation Prize of the Academy of American Poets, the American-Scandinavian Association/PEN Translation Prize, and the John Frederick Nims Memorial Prize of *Poetry Magazine*.

LUCY O'HAGAN is passionate about supporting people to re-establish their connection with themselves, their communities and to nature, of which we are a part. She is particularly interested in rewilding and rekindling the knowledge and skills we once knew so intimately, which connect us to our place in the world.

Scottish artist **KATIE PATERSON**'s conceptual projects make use of sophisticated technologies and specialist expertise to stage intimate, poetic and philosophical engagements between people and their natural environment. Since graduating from the Slade School of Fine Art in 2007 she has gone on to exhibit internationally.

CARL PHILLIPS is the author of *Then the War, Wild Is the Wind, Reconnaissance, Riding Westward, and The Rest of Love.* He is the recipient of numerous honors, including the Lambda Literary Award, the Pushcart Prize, the Academy of American Poets Prize, and fellowships from the Guggenheim Foundation and the Library of Congress.

PLATO (c. 427–347 BC) was a Greek philosopher, student of Socrates, teacher of Aristotle, and founder of the Academy. He is the author of philosophical works of unparalleled influence in Western thought. His works contain discussions in aesthetics, political philosophy, theology, cosmology, epistemology, and the philosophy of language.

RICHARD POWERS is the author of thirteen novels, including *Bewilderment, The Overstory* and *Orfeo*, and the recipient of a MacArthur Fellowship, the Pulitzer Prize, and the National Book Award. He lives in the foothills of the Great Smoky Mountains.

THOMAS PRINCEN is the author of *The Logic of Sufficiency* (2005), *Treading Softly: Paths to Ecological Order* (2010) and lead editor of *Ending the Fossil Fuel Era* (2015) and *Confronting Consumption* (2002), all published by MIT Press. He teaches social and ecological sustainability at the University of Michigan.

RADIOHEAD are an English alternative rock band from Oxfordshire, UK which formed in 1985. Their albums include *Pablo Honey* (1993), *The Bends*

(1995), *OK Computer* (1997), *Kid A* (2000), *Amnesiac* (2001), *Hail to the Thief* (2003), *In Rainbows* (2007), *The King of Limbs* (2011), *A Moon Shaped Pool* (2015) and *Kid A Mnesia* (2021).

COLIN RENFREW is a British archaeologist, paleolinguist, and peer, noted for his work on radiocarbon dating, the prehistory of languages, archaeogenetics, and the protection of antiquities. Now retired, he was Senior Fellow of the McDonald Institute for Archaeological Research at the University Cambridge.

PEDRO REYES is an artist and architect whose work addresses the interplay of physical and social space. His work explores interpersonal relationships as well as political and economical participation. For his work on disarmament, Reyes was granted the Luxembourg Peace Prize in 2021. He lives and works in Mexico City.

MARY REYNOLDS is a reformed internationally acclaimed landscape designer. The youngest woman in history to win a gold medal for garden design at the RHS Chelsea Flower Show in 2002, she has since given that all up to be part of the solution to the crisis we are all living through, the climate and biodiversity collapse. She is founder of the global movement *We Are the ARK*.

SUMANA ROY is the author of *How I Became a Tree*, a work of nonfiction, *Missing: A Novel*, *My Mother's Lover and Other Stories*, and two poetry collections, *Out of Syllabus* and *V. I. P.: Very Important Plant*.

VALERIE SEGREST is an enrolled member of the Muckleshoot Indian Tribe and cofounder of Tahoma Peak Solutions. She is a nutrition educator who specializes in local and traditional foods. She recently served as the Native American Agriculture Fund's Regional Director for Native Food and Knowledge Systems.

SUZANNE SIMARD is a professor of forest ecology at the University of British Columbia and author of the book *Finding the Mother Tree*. She is a pioneer on the frontier of plant communication and is known for her work on how trees interact and communicate using below-ground fungal networks, which has led to the recognition that forests have hub trees, or Mother Trees, which are large, highly connected trees that play an important role in the flow of information and resources in a forest.

ZADIE SMITH is the author of the novels *White Teeth*, *The Autograph Man*, *On Beauty*, *NW*, and *Swing Time*; a short story collection, *Grand Union;* and three collections of essays, *Changing My Mind*, *Feel Free*, and *Intimations*. Smith writes regularly for *The New Yorker* and *The New York Review of Books*. She is a Fellow of the Royal Society of Literature and a Member of the American Academy of Arts and Letters.

ANNA-SOPHIE SPRINGER is a writer, editor, curator, and codirector of K. Verlag, an independent Berlin-based press exploring the book as a site for exhibition making. Her practice merges curatorial, editorial, and artistic interests in order to produce new geographical, physical, and cognitive proximities, often in relation to historical archives.

CHELSEA STEINAUER-SCUDDER is a writer based in northern New England. As a staff writer and editor for *Emergence Magazine*, she explores the human relationship to place. Her work has been featured in *The Common*, *Crannóg Magazine*, *Inhabiting the Anthropocene*, and the *EcoTheo Review*. She is currently writing her first book.

ROBERT SULLIVAN is the author of numerous books, including *The Meadowlands*, *Rats*, and *My American Revolution*. A contributing editor at *A Public Space*, he lives in Philadelphia.

RACHEL SUSSMAN is a Brooklyn-based artist. She is a TED speaker, Guggenheim, NYFA, and MacDowell Fellow, and member of Al Gore's Climate Reality Leadership Corps. Her book, *The Oldest Living Things in the World*, is a *New York Times* bestseller.

SOJOURNER TRUTH, born Isabella Baumfree; c. 1797, was an American abolitionist and women's rights activist. Truth was born into slavery in Swartekill, New York, but escaped with her infant daughter to freedom in 1826. She gave herself the name Sojourner Truth in 1843. Her best-known speech was delivered extemporaneously, in 1851, at the Ohio Women's Rights Convention in Akron, Ohio. The speech became widely known during the Civil War by the title "Ain't I a Woman?"

NICOLA TWILLEY is co-host of the award-winning *Gastropod* podcast and a frequent contributor to *The New Yorker*. Her first book, *Until Proven Safe: The History and Future of Quarantine,* was co-authored with Geoff Manaugh and published by MCD, a division of Farrar, Straus & Giroux, in July 2021. She is currently writing a book on the topic of refrigeration for Penguin Press.

GAIA VINCE is a journalist specializing in science and the environment. She was the news editor of *Nature* and online editor of *New Scientist*. Her work has appeared in *The Guardian*, the *Times*, and *Scientific American*. She blogs at WanderingGaia.com and tweets at @Wandering-Gaia. She is the author of *Adventures in the Anthropocene, Transcendence* and *Nomad Century*.

KINARI WEBB is the founder of Health In Harmony, an international nonprofit dedicated to reversing global heating and understanding that rainforests are essential for the survival of humanity, and a cofounder of Alam Sehat Lestari (ASRI). Dr. Webb splits her time between Indonesia, international site assessments, and the San Francisco Bay Area. *Guardians of the Trees* is her debut.

Ethnobotanist **JONATHON MILLER WEISBERGER** has spent three decades studying rainforest plant medicine traditions in Ecuador and Costa Rica. His book *Rainforest Medicine: Preserving Indigenous Science and Biodiversity in the Upper Amazon* was published in 2013. He is the steward at Ocean Forest Ecolodge Retreat on the Osa Peninsula of Costa Rica. Oceanforest.org

Poet, writer, and educator **TANAYA WINDER** is an enrolled member of the Duckwater Shoshone Tribe. Her collections of poetry include *Words Like Love* (2015) and *Why Storms are Named After People and Bullets Remain Nameless* (2017). Winder blends storytelling, music, and poetry to teach about different expressions of love, healing, and "heartwork." Tanayawinder.com

AENGUS WOODS is a philosopher, critic and curator based in Ireland. He is the author (with Clive Murphy) of *DIWIF: Demonic Interventions With IKEA Furniture*, (New York: Printed Matter Inc, 2014). His writings have appeared in the *Irish Times*, *Dublin Review of Books*, *The Millions* and *NPR*.

ANDREA ZITTEL has used the arena of her day-to-day life to develop and test prototypes for living structures and situations. A-Z West was founded in Joshua Tree in 2000. She is also co-organizer of High Desert Test Sites, a non-profit that supports experimental art projects in the Joshua Tree region.

Acknowledgements

TREES, thank you! You breathe out, so we can breathe in. Thank you to all those who plant, tend and nurture trees.

This book has been germinating for decades, so there are too many people, organizations and communities who have helped me along the way to name them all here. I hope that you'll know yourself how grateful I am and that you will smile even if you don't see your name mentioned here.

The Language of Trees would not be possible without the generosity of all the contributors. Thank you all. I am immensely grateful to everyone for sharing their work with me here and to those who helped make it happen. Thank you to Simon Prosser for his support over the years and for assistance with Robert Macfarlane and Zadie Smith's contributions. Thank you also to Georgia Garrett at RCW literary agency for assistance with Zadie Smith's words. Thank you to Jessica Bullock as well as Veronica Brusilovski and Klara Rossby at The Wylie Agency and Hannah Vose at the University of Chicago Press for assistance with Amitav Ghosh's contribution. Thank you to Alexandra Sugarman at The Robbins Office and Claire Weatherhead at Bloomsbury for assistance with Elizabeth Kolbert's contribution. Thank you to Vaughan Ashlie Fielder at The Field Office for graciously helping with Ada Limón and Ross Gay's contributions. Thank you to Victoria Fox at FSG for assistance with contributions from Carl Phillips and Kinari Webb. Thank you to Suzanna Tamminen at Wesleyan University Press for assistance with Camille T. Dungy's poem; Frederick Courtright at The Permissions Company for assistance with Jessica J. Lee's contribution; Rebecca O'Malley at Hachette Book Group USA for help with Mary Reynolds's text; Christopher Wait from New Directions and Dr. Suzanne Fairless-Aitken from Bloodaxe Books for assistance with Inger Christensen's words translated by Susanna Nied; Patrícia Vieira and Deborah Parris Snyder from Synergetic Press for help with Jonathon Miller Weisberger's essay. Thank you to *Orion Magazine* for helping with Robin Wall Kimmerer's contribution. Thank you to Luz Massot at LABOR for translation assistance in my correspondence with Nemo Andy Guiquita.

Thank you to Theo Le Guin for generously granting permission to translate Ursula K. Le Guin's words into Trees, and for letting me know where she found inspiration for her descriptions of certain imaginary landscapes. I hope this book will bring me to Portland so I can walk in her steps in Forest Park.

Thank you to Carl Phillips for not only graciously sharing his essay *Among the Trees*, but also letting me share his forest at the Laumeier Sculpture Park in St. Louis. Thank you, Carl! I am grateful to Dana Turkovic at Laumeier for inviting me to create a new work for the exhibition *Forest Through the Trees*.

I am enormously grateful to Robert Macfarlane for sharing his words with me and for sharing my tree alphabets with his Twitter community. Thank you to James Gleick for sharing his words here, for standing me up in Venice and introducing me to *The Overstory* by Richard Powers. Thanks to Jim, I was one of the first to fall in love with it. Thank you to Richard for writing that astounding book, for your kind words about the Tree Alphabet and for nudging the American publishing industry towards sustainable paper.

Thank you to Forrest Gander and Ashwani Bhat for inviting me into their home and sharing those magical days in the Redwoods. Forrest, it was a privilege to talk trees and explore how we might learn from them and become more lichen-like. I hope that we can do it again.

I am honored to include the work of many wonderful artists here. I am grateful to each of them and to their studios and galleries for their assistance. Thank you all, including; Marine Pariente at Marian Goodman Gallery; Siobhan Maguire in Katie Paterson's studio; Tina in Tacita Dean's studio; Dakota Higgins in Charles Gaines's studio; Maya Lin's studio; Truth Murray-Cole at Madison Square Park; Randy Kennedy, Joseph Conder and Maisey Cox at Hauser & Wirth.

Enormous gratitude to Ida Bencke and John Holten at Broken Dimanche Press for their generosity in helping me create the original incarnation of this book: *About Trees*. Their visionary publishing house in Berlin provided a welcome home for an artist trying to create a crazily ambitious book with zero funding in six months. Their series *Parapoetics—a Literature beyond the Human* was the perfect home for *About Trees*. People still tell me how the book changed them. I am so very grateful to Beata Niedhart and Oliver Spieker at Form und Konzept (FUK) for their patience and warmth as they helped me figure out how exactly to write with Trees. Thank you to Katie Brown and Terry Berkowitz for their design assistance with creating the original Trees font.

Thank you to Peter Fischer and Brigitt Bürgi at the Zentrum Paul Klee in Bern, Switzerland for inviting me to participate in the group exhibition

About Trees in 2015. That was when I realized that my tree drawings could replace all the letters in the alphabet, creating a Tree Alphabet. The invitation from the ZPK arrived as I was starting a series of Sunday Salons exploring the possibilities for Art and Activism in the Anthropocene. I am grateful to those who shared their work at the Sunday Salons, including Roy Scranton, Amy Harmon, Smudge Studio, Dale Jamieson, David Haskell, Jennifer Jacquet, Holly Jean Buck, Oliver Kellhammer, Sasha Brown, Irene Kopelman, Sasha Engelmann, Jol Thomson, Sarah Resnick, Wendy Tronrud, Mary Annaïse Heglar, and all our guests.

I am extraordinarily grateful to Masie Cochran at Tin House in the USA for finding *About Trees* and having the heart to bring it back into the world in this new form. A special thank you to Sarah Rigby at Elliott & Thompson for passionately bringing *The Language of Trees* to print in Ireland and the UK. Thank you to Caro Clarke at Portobello Literary for helping to make that possible. Thank you to Pippa Crane for her help rewilding the trees and forests in this edition. Thank you to all the staff at Elliott & Thompson for helping to get this book into your hands.

I am grateful to Ross Gay for writing the introduction. His poem 'A Small Needful Fact' made me gasp when I first read it years ago. It still makes me gasp. I am honoured that Ross has generously shared his words here to introduce us to *The Language of Trees*.

Thank you to Stephen Sparks at Point Reyes Books for sparking fruitful conversations and connections between people and books. Their series, Thinking Like a Mountain, shares beautiful new books, including *How I Became a Tree* by Sumana Roy. Thank you to Sumana for sharing with me an early copy of *V.I.P. Very Important Plant*.

Thank you to Kerri ní Dochartaigh for sharing her words with me for this edition of the book. I'm thrilled that we could magically make that happen. Thanks also to Hillary Ellison and Helen O'Leary for talking about trees, colour, and book covers.

I wouldn't be able to make my work without the quiet time and space offered by a room of one's own. I am very grateful to all the residencies that hosted me over the years while this book was germinating, including Mac-Dowell, Cill Rialaig, Camargo Foundation, Oak Spring Garden Foundation, Leitrim Sculpture Center and the Irish Museum of Modern Art. Thank you also to family and friends who hosted me while I moved around following the trees, including Candy Holten, Shelly Holten and Nick Adkins, Susan

MacWilliam, Mariateresa Sartori, Chelsea Steinauer-Scudder, John Derryberry and Todd Standley. A special thank you to Ed Cohen and Victoria Shaw for the opportunity to work in their ever so beautifully quiet homes in Roxbury and Chilmark.

Thank you! Eileen Myles, Ava Chin, Jeff VanderMeer, John Freeman, Max Porter, Mundi Vondi, Sean Sherman, Mecca Bos, Leanne Betasamosake Simpson, Jennifer Croft, Ben Frost, Leslie at The Sojourner Truth Project, Nora Lawrence at Storm King Art Center, and Astrid Meek in Wangechi Mutu's studio.

Thank you for talking and thinking about trees with me over the years: Georgia Silvera Seamans, William Bryant Logan, Lindsay Campbell, Eric Sanderson, Bram Gunther, E.J. McAdams, Laura Hoffmann, Danica Novgorodoff, Dan Graham, Lothar Baumgarten, Brian O'Doherty, Richard Wentworth, Ellen Harvey, Eve Mosher, Daniel Smith, Sonja Dümpelmann and all the other tree people.

I am grateful for the Arts & Humanities Fellowship from New York City's Urban Field Station for providing me with the opportunity to create the New York City Tree Alphabet, an alphabetical planting palette. Thank you to Barbara Smith for helping me create the NYC Trees font. I do hope that one day we can plant people's messages around the city. Thank you to Emma Lucy O'Brien at VISUAL CARLOW for inviting me to create an Irish Tree Alphabet and somehow pulling it all together during all the early COVID-19 lockdowns in Spring 2020. Thank you to Colm O'Neill for helping me create the Irish Trees font and to Jessica Traynor for showing us *How to Write a Forest*.

Thank you to all the online communities that sprouted during the COVID lockdowns. I am grateful to all those who have invited me into their classrooms. Thank you to Devaki Bhaya for bringing me to Stanford University to party with trees. Thank you to Michael Hrebeniak for inviting me to create a curriculum for Forest Thinking for the New School of the Anthropocene. Thank you to Stephen O'Neill for inviting me to join LIT: Literature and Ireland's Trees. Thank you to Seoidin O'Sullivan for our Tree School.

Thank you to all the groups who have created safe spaces for me and others fighting to save the trees and life on Earth, including Rise and Resist, Save East River Park, Extinction Rebellion NYC, Extinction Rebellion Ireland, Writers Resist, PEN America, Declare Emergency, Revolution for Non-Violence, Friends of the Earth Northern Ireland, Irish Wildlife Trust, Save

Old Growth, Society of Fearless Grandmothers, Greta Thunberg, Alexandria Villaseñor, Flossie Donnelly, Avery the activist, and others. I am grateful for your humor, love, and courage.

Thank you to all the Rights of Nature advocates for generously leading the way, including James Orr, Lynda Sullivan, Declan Owens, Pádraic Fogarty, Mary McGuiggan and Valérie Cabanes.

Thank you to Friends of Ardee Bog for their love and commitment to our precious peatland.

Thank you to Christine Zehner for starting our Friday Meditation group in March 2020 and holding space for us every Friday since. I am grateful for all the highs and lows, and all our glorious words!

I am grateful to Emmanuel Vaughan-Lee, Seana Quinn and Hannah Merriman at *Emergence Magazine*, Martin Doyle at the *Irish Times*, and Amber Massie-Blomfield at Writers Rebel for inviting me to share my words while I was still trying to understand what the Tree Alphabets are and what the language of trees could be.

Thank you to Jessica Silbey for our conversations on intellectual property and talking me through what it could be to translate into Trees.

This book was a joy to make. It was also incredibly difficult to make. During the twelve months that I worked on it, I was suffering from undiagnosed long Covid, specifically dysautonomia. Like many people suffering from autonomic disorders, I visited a *lot* of doctors who told me there was nothing wrong with me. I am grateful to Dr David Putrino, Director of Rehabilitation Innovation, Department of Rehabilitation and Human Performance at Mount Sinai in New York City, for swiftly diagnosing me. Thank you to David and physical therapist Michael Krypos for helping me learn how to live with it. It was a lovely surprise that my CT scan shows clustered nodules with tree-in-bud. This book is going to print as the buds are appearing on the trees here in New York City and my own body contains tiny budding trees.

As ever, I am eternally grateful to Candy Holten for making it all possible. These years of travel bans and USCIS failure have left me in limbo, unable to get home to Ireland for longer than any other time in my life. I miss the soggy green dampness, the craic, and the lichen and moss-covered trees.

Dillon Cohen, thank you for everything.

I would like to dedicate this book to Aoife and Heidi Holten. Every day they astonish me with drawings and stories. I can't wait for the beautiful books and things that they will plant in the future.

First published in North America by Tin House, Portland, Oregon
© Katie Holten 2023

First published in the UK in 2023
by Elliott & Thompson
2 John Street WC1N 2ES
www.eandtbooks.com

ISBN: 978-1-78396-748-3

2 3 4 5 6 7 8 9

A catalogue record for this book is available from the British Library.

Interior design by Beth Steidle and Pippa Crane
Typeset in Essones, Garamond Premier Pro, and Trees

Printed by CPI Group (UK) Ltd, Croydon, CR0 4YY

The Forest Stewardship Council® is an international nongovernmental
organization that promotes environmentally appropriate, socially
beneficial and economically viable management of the world's forests.
To learn more, visit www.fsc.org

MIX
Paper | Supporting
responsible forestry
FSC® C013604